A Woman God Can Lead

Discovery House Publishers

Books, music, and videos that feed the soul with the Word of God

Box 3566 Grand Rapids, MI 49501

A Woman
God
Can Lead

Lessons from Women of the Bible
Help You Make Today's Choices

by Alice Mathews

For Randall
my beloved companion for nearly five decades;
For Kent,
our only son, now at home with God in heaven;
And for Susan, Karen, and Cheryl,
women of vision and integrity
who happen to be our delightful daughters

Discovery House Publishers is affiliated with
RBC Ministries, Grand Rapids, Michigan 49512.

Discovery House books are distributed to the trade exlusively
by Barbour Publishing, Inc., Uhrichsville, Ohio 44683.

Library of Congress Cataloging-in-Publication Data

Mathews, Alice, 1930–
[Woman God can use]
A woman God can lead : lessons from women of the Bible
help you make today's choices / by Alice Mathews.
p. cm.
Contents: A woman God can use—A woman Jesus can teach.
ISBN 1-57293-038-1

1. Women of the Bible. 2. Bible stories, English.
3. Women—Religious life. I. Mathews, Alice, 1930– Woman Jesus
can teach. II. Title.
BS575.M36 1998   220.9'2'082—dc21   98-7252
CIP

Printed in the United States of America

07 08 09
PP
9 10 8

Contents

Introduction
vii

Preface
xiii

Eve: How to See Long-term Consequences in Little Decisions
1

Leah: How to Live With a Man Who Doesn't Love You
17

Rahab: How to Choose for God in Your Culture
35

Deborah: How to Lead When Called by God to Do So
49

Ruth: How to See God in the Dailiness of Life
65

Hannah: How to Deal With Depression
81

Abigail: How to Live With a Difficult Husband
97

The Widow of Zarephath: How to Cope When Times Are Tough
115

Huldah and Miriam: How to Use Your Spiritual Gifts Wisely
131

Esther: How to Use Power to Benefit Others
147

The Proverbs 31 Woman: How to Keep Your Priorities Straight
163

Mary: How to Bring Christ to Your World
175

Jesus: How to Be a Disciple of the Master Teacher
189

Mary: How to Relate to the Family of Faith
197

The Woman at the Well: How to Face Your Self "As Is"
209

Mary and Martha: How to Live Successfully in Two Worlds
229

Martha and Mary: How to Nourish Hope in Times of Loss
241

The Canaanite Woman: How to Pursue Faith in Life's Crises
255

The Hemorrhaging Woman: How to Find Jesus in Your Pain
267

Two Widows: How to Give and Receive Graciously
279

A Sinful Woman: How to Cultivate an Attitude of Gratitude
293

The Woman Taken in Adultery: How to Respond to the God
of the Second Chance
305

Mary of Bethany: How to Make Jesus Your Priority
317

Mary Magdalene: How to Walk by Faith and Not by Sight
327

Introduction

Our world is entering a new century and a new millennium. As all the digits move from 1999 to 2000, prophets of doom paint scenarios of mass destruction while wide-eyed visionaries spin dreams of unimaginable advances. But for most of us, we're so caught up in the daily grind that we pay little attention to the hype and hoopla over the ending of one millennium and the beginning of another .

Yet we sense that as women, we live in what historians call a "paradigm shift"—a time when old beliefs and old attitudes are being forcibly challenged by new beliefs and new attitudes. We have to choose from options that women in other times and other places didn't have. To choose wisely, we must know which of these new beliefs and attitudes are firmly anchored in the Word of God, and which are merely products of our times and our traditions. In light of Scripture we may be called to reexamine our attitudes about women's roles, about marriage and family life, about education, about jobs, about personal growth. The shift has begun and it will continue. That makes this turn-of-the-millennium period both frightening and exhilarating.

It is frightening because many of us grew up firmly anchored in the old paradigm. We don't know what to make of the new attitudes and new opportunities before us. At the same time, we may feel a quiver of excitement because we know we have more options than women have ever had.

As we struggle to find our footing as Christian women in the shifting sand of today's expectations and opportunities, we may think that our times are unique. Not so. A hundred years ago women were going through a paradigm shift every bit as dramatic as the one we face today.

Victorian women lived within the paradigm historian Barbara Welter has called "the cult of true womanhood." Inside that paradigm women became the guardians of purity and gentility for the nation. This was new. Throughout much of Western history, women had been seen as dangerous beings—temptresses, witches, or earthbound creatures with no taste for godliness. But with the feminization of the churches after the American Revolution, women were elevated to high ground. They came to be considered morally superior to men and were given responsibility to promote godliness in their homes. The true woman was pious, pure, domestic, and submissive.

That paradigm was one of strictly enforced separate spheres. The English poet Tennyson put it this way:

Man for the field, the woman for the hearth;
Man for the sword, and for the needle she.
Man with the head, and woman with the heart;
Man to command, and woman to obey;
All else confusion.

A woman's sphere was the home. She could not venture into the public arena. During the nineteenth century women were not allowed to vote, could not enter most colleges and universities, and were barred from most professions. Women, the politicians said, were to use their purity, virtue, and morality to lift men up. They were to remain "above the political collusion of this world." That translated into no real citizenship, no right to own property, and no opportunity to vote. Scientists told women that their smaller brains could not survive the rigors of higher education and their reproductive capacity would be harmed by too much thinking. That was the paradigm in the nineteenth century.

But these women, within their separate sphere, took their moral superiority seriously. Godly evangelical women began Sunday schools for poor children to teach them to read. They established maternal associations to help Christian mothers learn how to nurture their children. Then came their efforts to wipe out prostitution and to enforce premarital chastity. From there woman began crusading against alcohol abuse and against slavery. When mission boards refused to appoint single women for missionary service, highly successful women's boards were created. And women began calling for the right to vote. In the process, the lines became blurred between the public sphere of men and the private sphere of women.

While many of these changes were carried out within the Victorian paradigm of the virtuous "true woman," women at the end of the nineteenth century found themselves caught in the cross-currents of new freedoms, new opportunities, new possibilities.

Today we stand on their shoulders. We take for granted their hard-won victories—the right to vote, to earn college degrees, to enter any profession, to own property. We forget—or we never knew—the agony many of these women experienced as they struggled to find God's will for their lives. They faced a paradigm shift every bit as drastic as the one that confronts us today. They heard many contradictory voices. They, too, had to turn to the Scriptures again and again to find the path of God for their lives.

But that period a hundred years ago was not the first time women had to learn to live within limitations or find ways to do God's will and widen their spheres. From the beginning of recorded time women have struggled with tough choices. They have wrestled with the restrictions that fenced them in. They have sometimes bowed, sometimes rebelled against the powerful who ruled them. They lived out their lives balancing their understanding of God's will for them against the demands others made upon them. Some lived lives of quiet desperation. Others found strength and comfort in their relationship to the living God.

Some made wise decisions. Others made destructive choices.

- *Eve* reached for a piece of fruit—just a piece of fruit—and brought upon herself and upon all her sisters since that time the devastating consequences of the Fall.
- *Miriam*—a prophetess through whom God spoke—chose to rebel against her brother's leadership and became leprous.
- *Esther* chose to risk her life for her captive people, and she saved a nation.
- *Rahab* chose to hide the Israelite spies and became an ancestress of the Messiah.
- *The widow of Zarephath* chose to share her last bit of bread with a starving prophet and was miraculously fed throughout a long famine.

- *Abigail* chose to go against her husband's wishes and saved an entire household. She also ended up marrying the king-designate.
- *Ruth* chose to stay with her mother-in-law, Naomi, in an alien land and found happiness there in the arms of a loving husband.

Choices. Life is full of them. We have to make them, but every choice we make brings risk. The Greek word we translate as *choice* is *hairesis.* It is also the word we translate as a *tenet* or a *heresy.* We cannot make our choices lightly because a choice can lead us into heresy. Like our Victorian sisters at the turn of the last century, we turn to the Word of God, the Bible, for help in making wise decisions. Our only sure anchor is the Scriptures, God's infallible Word. There we can learn by precept and by example.

In the pages that follow we will watch biblical women wrestle with problems that are sometimes different from our own, sometimes surprisingly similar to those we face. As we watch real women fail or triumph, we can find principles that will clarify the answers we seek.

One last word. When we talk abut the freedom to make choices, we discover there are two kinds of women. Some want freedom *to choose.* Others want freedom *from choice.* The Scriptures provide examples of both. In the Bible we find a wider scope for choice than many women realize is there. At the same time, we find biblical fences that keep our choices from becoming heresy. To choose wisely, we must know God's Word and apply it well. As we do that, we can become women of worth, wise women, women whom God can lead.

Preface

As a small child in a Detroit Sunday school class, I learned the stories of Jesus—how He walked on water and calmed the sea, how He healed the sick and raised the dead to life again, how He fed hungry people and drove crooked merchants from the temple. Before I could read well enough to find my place in a hymnbook, I had learned to sing

> Fairest Lord Jesus, Ruler of all nature,
> O Thou of God and man the Son:
> Thee will I cherish, Thee will I honor,
> Thou my soul's glory, joy and crown.

The first line made sense to me: Jesus was a tireless miracle-worker who had control over all nature. The second line I only dimly understood, but I was learning that the wonderful human being, Jesus, was also God. The last two lines formed a response to Jesus Christ that even I as a child could feel, though I wasn't clear about what "my soul's glory, joy and crown" meant.

Somewhere in the years that followed I lost sight of the Jesus of the Gospels. His place was taken by a more abstract Christ whose perfections removed Him from my daily grind. Most of the books I read and sermons I heard hovered in the Old Testament or the Epistles. If they swooped over the Gospels, it was only for a quick tour of the twin peaks of the Incarnation and the Substitutionary Atonement of Christ. Everything in between dropped from view. The Jesus of the Gospels was theologized into a neat doctrine sandwiched between God the Father and the Holy Spirit. Though I prayed in Jesus' name daily and took non-Christians on evangelistic tours of Jesus' work of redemption in His death on the cross, I didn't find the person of Jesus particularly relevant to my life.

In 1974 I began a three-year weekly journey through the gospel according to John with a group of collegians in Vienna, Austria. The first part of chapter 1 concerned the Jesus I had studied most: the eternal Word through Whom all things were made. Teaching this put me on comfortably familiar ground. This was the stuff of most of my studies. But as we moved into Jesus' earthly life and ministry, I felt less and less at ease with the Jesus I met in John's gospel. I wanted the collegians in my class to worship this Jesus and give their lives to Him. But He said and did strange things. He sounded rude to His mother. It looked as if He couldn't care less whether the religious leaders liked Him or not. The "gentle Jesus, meek and mild" almost seemed to enjoy riling people and needlessly flaunting conventions.

As a Bible teacher I felt caught between my commitment to honor the integrity of the Scriptures and my desire to cover up the puzzling things in Jesus' life that might offend the new Christians and non-Christians in my class. In the process I had to struggle with my unacknowledged feelings about the kind of person I thought Jesus ought to have been. In the pages of John's gospel I met a Man who didn't behave in the way I thought the disembodied, spiritualized Christ of the Epistles would behave.

That began what has become for me a continuing fascination with Immanuel, God in the flesh, the Jesus who walked the dusty roads and mountain paths of Israel. When I began work three years ago on this series of studies, first for a class and later for publication, I found myself deeply moved by the words and actions of the God-Man recorded for us by Matthew, Mark, Luke, and John. At times as I have worked on these chapters, I've been overcome by powerful emotions of sadness, of anger, of love, of joy. I've met again and fallen in love with the Savior of the world, who happens to be the Savior of individual women and men. I found a Man filled with compassion for women caught on the barbed wire of life. I've held my breath as He defied convention and took enormous risks to offer hope, new life, or a second chance to women despised and ground down into dust under the feet of thoughtless religious leaders. In the process, I've experienced in a fresh way Peter's descriptive words:

> Though you have not seen him, you love him; and even though you do not see him now, you believe in him and are filled with an inexpressible and glorious joy, for you are receiving the goal of your faith, the salvation of your souls. (1 Peter 1:8–9)

If I could have any wish for those who read this book, it would be that Jesus Christ will step off these pages into your life and grip you with His marvelous, risk-taking love so that you will want nothing more than to follow Him and learn from Him all the days of your life.

Eve: How to See Long-term Consequences in Little Decisions

What are the toughest decisions you have to make? Cafeterias rank high among my more difficult decisions. I *hate* standing in that line, unsure what is ten feet down the display case that I'll miss if I decide to take the food in front of me. I go to great lengths to avoid having to eat in a cafeteria.

My hang-up with cafeteria decisions doesn't make a lot of sense. The food generally isn't that expensive—or that good. So who cares if I could have made a better decision? There's always tomorrow!

Maybe you have a tougher time deciding on that new pair of shoes or the menu for Saturday night's dinner party. Whatever it is that we hate about decisions, the fact is that we all have to make them and make them and make them. In a study a few years ago at the University of Minnesota, Dr. Erich Klinger found that all of us make anywhere from three hundred to seventeen hundred decisions every day of our lives.

We decide *whether* to get up in the morning. Then we decide *when* to get up—early, late, somewhere in between. Then we decide *how* to get up—both literally and figuratively on the right or the wrong side of the bed. Thereafter we *really* get into decision-making—what to wear, what to put on first, whether to brush our teeth or brush our hair first, what to eat for breakfast, whether or not to wash the dishes, and on and on. A lot of those decisions don't rank high as earth-shaking choices. Often they add up, however, to a good or bad start for our days.

Think about the most important decisions you've made in your lifetime. What were they? For some of you, choosing your marriage partner is probably near or at the top of the list. Whatever you want to say or leave unsaid about your marriage, you've probably made few other decisions that rank with that one in changing the direction of your life.

What other decisions have you made that seemed momentous to you at the time? You may have agonized over them. Your first date with Mr. Right! What should you wear? Should you shop for a new dress? Should you shoot your budget for the next six months on the "right" outfit for this important date?

Perhaps you're redecorating the living room and can't decide whether to order the white brocade couch or the mauve velvet one. Six months or six years later, you may not even remember some of these decisions because they turned out to be not particularly important at all.

Perhaps you've struggled with whether to marry at all—or to remarry after a bad marriage and a heart-ripping divorce. Or maybe you are married and can't decide whether to have children. These are major decisions.

Then there are the decisions we make that, six months or six years later, startle us by their importance when we look back on the results of those choices. You bought your present house for all the wrong reasons, but after moving there you discovered that your new neighborhood changed your life. Perhaps your neighbor is now your best friend. She may have brought you to a Bible study where you were introduced to Jesus Christ. You are now a different person.

Or perhaps you met your neighbor's husband and have been enmeshed in a secret affair that has changed everything for you—the dynamics in your own marriage, your relationship with your neighbor, and your own sense of inner integrity. The casual decisions sometimes turn out to be the most dramatic and life-changing of all.

Decisions. We make them. Then they turn around and make us. Sometimes they break us. Let me tell you about a woman who faced a decision. It was probably not a decision most of us would put in the life-changing category. It was a casual decision about a piece of fruit. The fruit looked delicious. It had a nutritious smell to it as well. Someone said it would make her wise.

What's the big deal? The next time you stand in the produce section of your supermarket and choose the right bunch of bananas or sort through the strawberries, think about this woman and the decision she made about some fruit.

The woman's name is Eve. Actually, we don't find that out until the end of the story. In the story as we read it in Genesis, the first book of the Bible, she is merely "the woman." She was the only woman. She didn't have to be called anything else to be singled out of the crowd. She stands at the head of the female half of the human race. We can learn a lot from the decisions she made.

A lot started with Eve! She's called "the mother of all living." She is also "the mother of all dying." Look at her in Genesis 1:26–28:

> Then God said, "Let us make man in our image, in our likeness, and let them rule over the fish of the sea and the birds of the air, over the

livestock, over all the earth, and over all the creatures that move along the ground."

So God created man in his own image, in the image of God he created him; male and female he created them. God blessed them and said to them, "Be fruitful and increase in number; fill the earth and subdue it. Rule over the fish of the sea and the birds of the air and over every living creature that moves on the ground."

As the climax to this splendid hymn of creation, God majestically crowned all that He had done with the creation of Man—humankind, male and female. Note that the first man and the first woman were created in the image of God.

It is on the basis of this image, this likeness, that Eve and Adam were given dominion over God's creation. It wasn't that the man and woman were stronger than the lions, tigers, and hippopotami around them. It was that they stood between God and His created world as His representatives. Imaging God in the world, they had a responsibility to care for everything God put under them.

In addition to ruling God's creation, Adam and Eve were also told to be fruitful and increase in number. Have kids. As God looked over all He had accomplished, He said, "This is very good!"

So far, so good. We've seen creation from a distance. Now as we move into Genesis 2, God takes us back for a slow-motion rerun of what happened in Genesis 1:27. We discover that God created the man and the woman in quite different ways and the differences are significant. Read Genesis 2:7: "The LORD God formed the man from the dust of the ground and breathed into his nostrils the breath of life, and the man became a living being."

Adam was created from the dust of the ground, just as his name—*Adamah* in Hebrew—states. If God were making him today, He might call him "Dusty."

If you've read through the next verses in Genesis 2, you've discovered that Adam had a wonderful life in Eden. In verse 8 we see him placed in a garden of God's design—surely something to see! In verse 9 we learn that he had an unlimited food supply that was both nutritious and esthetically pleasing. In the following verses we read about wonderful rivers for fishing or swimming and about mountains of fine gold and precious stones. In verse 15 we see that God gave him something to do that would keep him active and in good shape. So what was the problem? Read verse 18: "The LORD God said, 'It is not good for the man to be alone. I will make a helper suitable for him.'"

Adam's problem was that as long as he was alone, he was only half the story. He needed another person like himself to define him. God created him in His image. Adam could go fishing with a rhinoceros, but he could not discuss the next day's schedule with him. Adam could play catch with one of the newly-created cocker spaniels, but they could not admire the sunset together. Adam was created in God's image and the animals were not. The Triune God had built a need into Adam for fellowship with another creature who also bore this image. All that was feminine in the nature of God needed human imaging as well.

Eve was no afterthought. She was indispensable. In God's words in verse 18, Adam's being without Eve was "not good."

With that fact established, you'd think that God would get right on with the task of creating the woman. Not so. Read Genesis 2:19–20:

> Now the LORD God had formed out of the ground all the beasts of the field and all the birds of the air. He brought them to the man to see what he would name them; and whatever the man called each living creature, that was its name. So the man gave names to all the livestock, the birds of the air and all the beasts of the field. But for Adam no suitable helper was found.

God knew that the animal parade was a charade. In bringing the animals to Adam, He was setting up an object lesson. He wanted Adam to learn something. He wanted him to learn that he did not yet have any counterpart on earth. Adam had to discover his uniqueness as a human being. God was preparing Adam for the big moment when Eve would be brought to him. Adam had to understand that he and Eve would stand together in a circle of creation nothing else in the world could occupy. Created in God's image, only they could enjoy fellowship with one another and with their Creator.

Now that Adam was set up for it, God made His next move. Read Genesis 2:21–22:

> So the LORD God caused the man to fall into a deep sleep; and while he was sleeping, he took one of the man's ribs and closed up the place with flesh. Then the LORD God made a woman from the rib he had taken out of the man, and he brought her to the man.

"The man slept through the woman's creation," Nancy Tischler has observed, "and has been puzzled by woman ever since."

Have you ever wondered why God switched methods of creation when He had the other one down pat? Up to this point God had made living organisms from the ground. In verse 9 He made the trees grow out of the ground. In verse 7 He made man from the dust of the earth. In verse 19 He formed all of the animals and birds from the ground. You'd think, once He had a good method going, He'd stick with it. No. God introduced a new method, one that would remove all shadow of doubt that the man and the woman shared an essential identity.

Adam could never say, "Eve, you were formed of the same stuff as I, but so were the animals. Maybe you're more like them than you are like me." No, Adam and Eve were of the same essence. They were both created in the image of God. They both had dominion. They were both to share in populating the earth.

In Genesis 2:23 we read Adam's ecstatic recognition of this: "The man said, 'This is now bone of my bones and flesh of my flesh; she shall be called "woman," for she was taken out of man!' " He knew who she was. She was "womb/man," a part of his own being.

But who is this woman, Eve? She was a flawless woman in a flawless world with a flawless relationship to her Creator and to her husband. In her we see the complete woman. She was free to be human, and free to be all that any woman could wish. Eve shows us what humanity was born to be.

Eve also shows us what humanity chose to become. Continue the story in Genesis 3. There we find a serpent slithering up to Eve to start a conversation that ended in disaster. But before we overhear the two of them talking, we need to pick up one more detail from Genesis 2:16–17: "And the LORD God commanded the man, 'You are free to eat from any tree in the garden; but you must not eat from the tree of the knowledge of good and evil, for when you eat of it you will surely die.'"

In the midst of all the opulence of Eden stood a tree whose fruit God had told Adam and Eve they could not eat. Was God playing some kind of game with them? Was He tantalizing them, tempting them beyond their ability to withstand?

To understand that tree, we have to understand one more thing involved in our being created in the image of God. In the heart of the universe, the stars move predictably in their cycles. Springtime and harvest are fixed in the natural course of things. All nature is programmed to respond as God designed it to respond. Birds fly. Fish swim. Deer run.

But in the midst of all creation, a man and a woman stand who have been created with a difference. They can choose. They can choose to love God and obey Him. Or they can choose to turn their backs on God and go their own independent way. They are the one unprogrammed element in the universe.

God validated choice and He validated His image in us by giving us the power to choose. The tree was there so that Eve and Adam could voluntarily choose to keep themselves in fellowship with God.

All of our loves are bound up in choice. Without the power to choose, to say that we love has no meaning. We can demand obedience. We cannot demand love. The tree gave Eve and Adam the opportunity to love God meaningfully. The tree, through its very presence, was a visible reminder to the man and woman that they were creatures, dependent on their Creator.

With that in mind, return now to the conversation in Genesis 3:1–7:

> Now the serpent was more crafty than any of the wild animals the LORD God had made. He said to the woman, "Did God really say, 'You must not eat from any tree in the garden'?" The woman said to the serpent, "We may eat fruit from the trees in the garden, but God did say, 'You must not eat fruit from the tree that is in the middle of the garden, and you must not touch it, or you will die.' " "You will not surely die," the serpent said to the woman. "For God knows that when you eat of it your eyes will be opened, and you will be like God, knowing good and evil."
>
> When the woman saw that the fruit of the tree was good for food and pleasing to the eye, and also desirable for gaining wisdom, she took some and ate it. She also gave some to her husband, who was with her, and he ate it. Then the eyes of both of them were opened, and they realized they were naked; so they sewed fig leaves together and made coverings for themselves.

Choices. What was the choice Eve made? It was just a decision about a piece of fruit. Or was it? Behind our little decisions often lurk big decisions. For Eve it was really a decision to doubt the goodness of God. It was a way of saying that God had misrepresented Himself, that He really did not have their best interests at heart.

Eve chose to listen to Satan's lie. She chose to believe that God had lied because He did not want His creatures becoming like Himself. Her choice—and Adam's choice, as he took the fruit from her hand and ate it—demonstrates the paradox of being created in God's image: We are free to put our will above God's will. We are free to thumb our nose at our Creator. All around us are people—perhaps in our families and in our circle of friendships—who have decided that they can live without God and dispense with His Word and His will.

Out of that choice made by the first woman and the first man flow three consequences that you and I live with today. The first one we have already seen in Genesis 3:7. Their eyes were opened and they knew they were naked. The symbolism is clear: they realized what they had done. They felt guilt about disobeying God. In the following verses we see their confrontation with the One from whom they were now trying to hide:

> Then the man and his wife heard the sound of the LORD God as he was walking in the garden in the cool of the day, and they hid from the LORD God among the trees of the garden. But the LORD God called to the man, "Where are you?"
>
> He answered, "I heard you in the garden, and I was afraid because I was naked; so I hid."
>
> And he said, "Who told you that you were naked? Have you eaten from the tree that I commanded you not to eat from?"
>
> The man said, "The woman you put here with me—she gave me some fruit from the tree, and I ate it."

10

Eve

Then the LORD God said to the woman,
"What is this you have done?"
The woman said, "The serpent deceived me,
and I ate" (3:8–13).

Fellowship with God was destroyed. Adam and Eve
hid. The first alienation Adam and Eve experienced was
alienation from God, their Creator.

Not only the vertical relationship was broken. Note
Adam's response to God's question: he shifted the
blame to Eve. When God turned to question Eve, she
shifted the blame to the serpent.

Blame replaced trust and love. The human race was
now divided. Alienation lurks at the root of every
relationship. Psychologists and psychiatrists are kept
busy by an entire society trying to deal with the blame,
the guilt, the recriminations, and the alienation that
separate us from one another. We live in a world full of
problems growing out of this horizontal alienation.
Our divorce courts testify to that. Our organizations to
help the abused and the abusing witness to that.
Women face horrendous problems in and out of
marriage, in and out of the workplace, because blame
and guilt have replaced love and trust.

Disobedience to God broke the vertical relationship
between us and God. It also broke the horizontal
relationships between men and women, between
parents and children, between people bound up in
every kind of human relationship.

Third, it broke the harmonious relationship God
had created between nature and the first man and
woman. The woman would fulfill her destiny in
bearing children, but she would now do so with pain.

The man would continue as a gardener, but he would have to contend with cursed ground, ground that would produce thorns and thistles. Our relationship to God, our relationships to one another, and our relationship to the created world around us are all broken by an independent spirit.

Note that neither the woman nor the man was cursed. The serpent was cursed and the ground was cursed. To the woman and the man would come the natural consequences of living in a fallen world and dealing with hostile nature.

Note, too, that the prophecies God made concerning Eve and Adam were a way of turning the tables on their original condition. Eve, equal in Eden, would be ruled by her husband. Adam, taken from the ground and placed in dominion over the ground, would now be sweating in painful toil to make the ground produce food for his family. In the end he would return to the ground, "for dust you are and to dust you will return."

As we follow the man and woman out of the garden, we meet Eve only two more times. In chapter 4 we read that she gave birth to Cain, then Abel, and in verse 25 she gave birth to a son named Seth. All of her other children remained nameless, and her own death passed without mention. Weary year followed weary year for this woman. She bore two sons whose antagonism ended in murder and exile.

Yes, she gained what she had been promised, a knowledge of both good and evil. She knew toil, pain, loss, and death. Many women have lived lives of great tragedy. But no other woman has ever known the anguish Eve must have known as she moved from Eden to alienation—alienation from God, from her husband, and from a benevolent environment. To have known the good as she knew it must have made the evil that much more stark in its awfulness.

For Eve still reflected the image of God. It was a marred image, but it was the image of God, nevertheless. She was cut off from fellowship with the One she was designed to relate to. She knew the emptiness, the anguish of remembering what she was designed to be without the possibility of becoming all she was meant to be!

Within the tragic denouement of this story lay one tiny ray of hope for Eve. That tiny ray has become a life-changing beam of hope for us today. Buried in the curse on the serpent was God's word that He would "put enmity between you and the woman, and between your offspring and hers; he will crush your head, and you will strike his heel."

Even in the midst of meting out punishments and prophecies for the sin of Adam and Eve, God was concerned with reestablishing a relationship with those who bear His image. He warned Satan that his victory was not forever. The day would come when one would be born of the seed of the woman—an unusual statement when "seed" or semen always came from the man—who would crush the head of the serpent.

Here was the first word of promise, the first hint of a future deliverer from sin. The bad news contained good news. God had not written off His creatures. The play had not ended. The curtain had not yet gone down on the final act.

If you think back to high school or college English classes, you may remember reading plays by

Shakespeare and other writers. Some plays were called comedies. Others were labeled tragedies. For many of us a comedy is a funny play with lots of great one-liners. That isn't the way, however, that comedy differs from tragedy. Both tragedies and comedies follow the same basic plot.

In the first act the writer gets the woman up a tree. In the second act a bear stands at the base of the tree making growling sounds. In the third act—well, that's where we find out whether the play is a tragedy or a comedy. The difference lies in the ending. In a tragedy, the story unwinds without hope. Once it starts, wrong decisions lead to wrong endings. A comedy, on the other hand, also includes bad decisions by the players. But somehow the crises and the hurts turn around, and, in the end, everything works out for the best.

God doesn't write tragedies. Eve's story is tragic, not only for her, but for the whole human race. For you. For me. Once she made that decision about eating a piece of appealing fruit, she could not change the ending for herself, for Adam, for Cain and Abel, for Seth, or for any of her descendants.

But the Author could step into the story and change the ending. God could take all the bad decisions and the pain and sorrow and use them to make a happy ending. He gave the first hint of that in Genesis 3:15. He promised that a descendant of hers would defeat Satan and his power in the world.

You and I live not as Eve lived, waiting for the fulfillment of God's promise. You and I live with that promise fulfilled. Jesus Christ has come, and through Him you and I can have a relationship with God.

The apostle Paul knew that fact would make a difference in the lives of first-century Greeks living in Corinth. He wrote to them, "In Adam all die, so in Christ all will be made alive" (1 Corinthians 15:22).

In Christ I can be made alive. In Christ you can be made alive. In Him we can experience a vertical relationship with our Creator, a relationship Eve and Adam threw away in exchange for a shot at being like God. We can choose to have God write a happy ending to the drama of our lives. We can choose to have Him establish a relationship that is not broken by our independence and our bad choices. We can then watch Him bring healing to human relationships that weigh us down.

We can choose. If you have not already made that choice, now is a good time to choose a vertical relationship with God through Jesus Christ.

Eve is not the end of the story. She is the beginning. With her this book begins. The book will end with another woman, one who said "Yes" to God and brought our Savior into the world. Between Eve and Mary stretch thousands of years and thousands of women. This book looks at the ways some of these women met the tragedies life forced on them as flawed people in a fallen world. It is a story of alienation. It is a story of sin in the world. It is a story of women whose histories remind us that our struggles are not new. But it is also the story of hope. It is the story of choices—good ones, bad ones, sometimes choices people didn't think were especially important.

As you and I learn from other women, we can choose to be women whose eyes are turned Godward. We can choose wisely and live.

Questions for group discussion or personal reflection:

1. Describe some decision you made that seemed big at the time but had no long-term effect on your life.
2. Describe some decision you made that seemed small at the time but had a major effect on your life.
3. What do you think are the consequences of choosing to live life without taking God's will into consideration?
4. What does "grace" mean and how does it apply to us when we recognize that we have in some way "voted against God" in our decision making?

Leah: How to Live With a Man Who Doesn't Love You

In the musical, *The Sound of Music*, when Maria decides to teach the Von Trapp children to sing, she strums a few chords on her guitar and then sings,

Let's start at the very beginning,
A very good place to start.
When you read, you begin with A-B-C.
When you sing, you begin with do-re-mi.

When you talk about marriage, you go back to the very beginning where it all started in Genesis 2:18: "The LORD God said, 'It is not good for the man to be alone. I will make a helper suitable for him.' " And once that was done, the writer of Genesis tells us in verse 24, "For this reason a man will leave his father and mother and be united to his wife, and they will become one flesh."

You remember the story. Adam was alone, and God said that's not good. To make Adam fully conscious of his aloneness, God brought a complete animal parade to pass in front of the only human being on earth to remind him that he had no counterpart in the universe. Adam needed someone to share life with him. He was created to be in relationship. Alone, Adam was only half the story. So God created Eve and brought her to him. Then all the pieces were in place for a magnificent marriage.

17

With a flawless beginning, these two—the man and the woman—had an ideal situation. They were created in the image of God and were placed in a garden where they had challenging work without fatigue and stress.

You know what happened next. It had to do with a piece of fruit, a command from God, and a choice. Out of that choice flowed alienation. Alienation from God their Creator. Alienation from nature, which would now master them, exhaust them, and eventually absorb them back into itself. Alienation from one another as blame replaced trust and hierarchy replaced equality. And finally an internal alienation as each one became a walking civil war, torn between their hopes and fears, vacillating between their fundamental need for relationships and their resentment at having to pay the cost of those relationships. They were now flawed people living in a fallen world.

Death had invaded life. We live with that reality. Death invades the vitality of our relationships. Within each one of us is a deep longing for the perfect relationship. All our lives we crave that relationship so much that we are dissatisfied with anything less. Coming to terms with the fact that we are fallen people in a fallen world is tough business. We don't want to give up our dreams and to acknowledge that death has also invaded our relationships.

Within only six generations from Adam and Eve the perfect relationship between one man and one woman has given way to polygamy. In Genesis 4:19 we learn that Lamech married two women, Adah and Zillah. The one-flesh relationship—a oneness that is not only physical but also mental, emotional, and spiritual—is no longer possible for a man who acquires wives like he acquires cattle or sheep or gold.

Leah

When we turn to Genesis 29, we meet two women—Leah and her sister Rachel—who are rival co-wives locked in a polygamous relationship. Rachel, the younger one, is the apple of her husband's eye. Leah is not loved.

How do you live with a man who doesn't love you? Leah can help you evaluate your relationships more realistically.

We first meet Leah as a pawn in someone else's deception. Jacob had cheated his brother Esau out of his birthright and had fled from Canaan back to Paddan Aram, the land of his ancestors. He has come to the household of his Uncle Laban, his mother's brother. Laban has just invited him to stay with him and work for him. The two men discussed the wages Laban would pay Jacob, and our story picks up with Genesis 29:16–30:

> Now Laban had two daughters; the name of the older was Leah, and the name of the younger was Rachel. Leah had weak eyes, but Rachel was lovely in form, and beautiful. Jacob was in love with Rachel and said, "I'll work for you seven years in return for your younger daughter Rachel."
>
> Laban said, "It's better that I give her to you than to some other man. Stay here with me." So Jacob served seven years to get Rachel, but they seemed like only a few days to him because of his love for her.
>
> Then Jacob said to Laban, "Give me my wife. My time is completed, and I want to lie with her."
>
> So Laban brought together all the people of the place and gave a feast. But when evening came, he took his daughter Leah and gave her to

Jacob, and Jacob lay with her. And Laban gave his servant girl Zilpah to his daughter as her maidservant.

When morning came, there was Leah! So Jacob said to Laban, "What is this you have done to me? I served you for Rachel, didn't I? Why have you deceived me?"

Laban replied, "It is not our custom here to give the younger daughter in marriage before the older one. Finish this daughter's bridal week; then we will give you the younger one also in return for another seven years of work."

And Jacob did so. He finished the week with Leah, and then Laban gave him his daughter Rachel to be his wife. Laban gave his servant girl Bilhah to his daughter Rachel as her maidservant. Jacob lay with Rachel also, and he loved Rachel more than Leah. And he worked for Laban another seven years.

If you grew up attending Sunday school, you know this story well. Your first sympathy probably goes to Jacob. After all, a bargain is a bargain. He bargained for Rachel, not Leah. His crafty uncle pulled a fast one and stuck him with Leah.

Of course, Jacob himself had been pretty crafty. He had deceived his blind father, Isaac, and cheated his brother, Esau. So he wasn't exactly without blame himself. But we still feel sorry for Jacob. After seven years of labor, he went through all of the traditional feasting to celebrate his wedding to Rachel. He waited in the darkened tent for his bride to be delivered to him, saw only dimly the heavily veiled woman enter in the dark and assumed she was Rachel. What a shock the next morning to discover that plain-vanilla Leah had been substituted for the gorgeous Rachel!

Where do your sympathies lie? It is easy to get so caught up in feeling sorry for Jacob that we forget what it must have been like to be Leah that morning. Some commentators speculate that Leah had also been in love with Jacob during those seven years and that she was a willing accomplice to her father's scheme. Nothing in the text confirms that. Whether she went to Jacob's tent that night, heavily swathed in wedding veils, as a willing accomplice or as a dutiful daughter merely obeying her father, she could not have been thrilled the next morning when Jacob made a scene with his father-in-law, Laban.

If Leah had ever hoped for Jacob's love, if she had ever dared think that she could compete with her beautiful younger sister, all illusions were dashed when Jacob hit the tent roof about the deception. She was unloved, undesired, unsought. And one week later she was the displaced wife as Jacob took Rachel to himself.

I doubt that there are many, if any, women in America today who were married under the same circumstances as Leah. But deception of one sort or another has been part of many courtships. If you are married and you think back to your own wedding, did you get what you bargained for? Or did you feel cheated by your partner in some way? Life can seem bleak indeed when the most important relationship in our experience turns out to be marred at the outset by deception or disappointment. Alienation at work. We live in a sinful world and build relationships with sinful people. We bring our own sinfulness to those relationships. No wonder deception and disappointment creep in.

One of the loveliest words in this sad story of Leah the Unloved comes, however, in Genesis 29:31: "When the LORD saw that Leah was not loved, he opened her womb, but Rachel was barren. Leah became pregnant and gave birth to a son."

God was not blind to Leah's plight. He saw the ache in her heart. God did something about her situation. He enabled her to give Jacob a son. The sovereign God saw Leah's need and moved to meet it. And in the process He was working out His plan for Jacob and Jacob's descendants, even in the way He would send Jesus Christ, the Messiah and Redeemer, into the world.

Part of Leah's handicap was that she was no candidate for Miss Mesopotamia and she had a sister who was. Rachel was splendid to look at—beautiful face, wonderful figure. Besides that, when she first appears in Genesis 29:6–12, she dances off the page, full of vitality and energy. In short, she simply had it all. It is no surprise that Jacob flipped when he saw her. No wonder the Bible tells us that working for her for seven years "seemed like only a few days to him because of his love for her."

Then there's Leah. The only thing we know about her is that she had "weak eyes." Commentators and translators have had a field day with the Hebrew word here translated "weak." We don't really know what Leah's eyes were like. Some say they were sore. She may have been verging on blindness and Laban wanted to get rid of her quickly before that happened. The King James Version translates the word "tender." The Living Bible paraphrase tells us that she had "lovely eyes." All of these are possibilities. Perhaps Leah had only one good feature—her beautiful eyes. Or perhaps her eyes were so disfiguring that everything else faded into insignificance. The important thing is that whatever she looked like, she grew up in the shadow of a beautiful sister, and she came off at a strong disadvantage in the comparison.

Could God have created Leah as beautiful as Rachel? Certainly. So, if He really cared about her, why didn't He? It would have saved her great grief. Why did God wait until Leah was the unloved wife of Jacob to do something nice for her?

Isaiah the prophet reminds us that "as the heavens are higher than the earth, so are [God's] ways higher than your ways and [His] thoughts than your thoughts" (55:9). When we look more closely at Leah, we see that had God made her equally as beautiful as her sister Rachel, the chances are good that she would not have been pawned off on Jacob. If that had been the case, Jacob would never have had the particular sons through whom God worked for Israel and for a fallen world. God often works in our lives, not by giving us a perfect situation, but by showing His power and love in our very imperfect situations. He works for our *ultimate* good by allowing us to struggle in less than perfect relationships.

Leah was unloved. But God saw that and opened her womb. Not once, but at least seven times. Each time as Leah holds that tiny new life in her arms and names that child, we get a glimpse into her mind, into her heart, into her needs.

In Genesis 29:32, cradling her firstborn son, "She named him Reuben, for she said, 'It is because the LORD has seen my misery. Surely my husband will love me now.' "

Soon after, in Genesis 29:33, "She conceived again, and when she gave birth to a son she said, 'Because the LORD heard that I am not loved, he gave me this one, too.' So she named him Simeon."

As if two sons were not enough, we read in Genesis 29:34, "Again she conceived, and when she gave birth to a son she said, 'Now at last my husband will become attached to me, because I have borne him three sons.' So he was named Levi."

Three sons. Is that enough? Apparently not, for we read in Genesis 29:35, "She conceived again, and when she gave birth to a son she said, 'This time I will praise the LORD.' So she named him Judah. Then she stopped having children."

Four little boys all in a row. Can you see Leah outside her tent on a hot Mesopotamian summer day calling "Reuben! Simeon! Levi! Judah!"? Listen to the progression in Leah's understanding and her faith as you hear those names.

Reuben—"Behold, a son!" Leah recognized that God had seen her misery and had opened her womb and had given her a son. She interpreted that fact as God's way of enabling her to gain her husband's love. But did it work out that way? Apparently not. Nine months, ten months, twelve months later, Simeon was born.

Simeon—"hearing." Leah said, "The LORD has heard that I am not loved." She was still unloved. Reuben's birth had not caused Jacob to love her. He still had eyes only for Rachel. Now God had heard Leah's sighs. He had seen her tears. He had understood her deep desire for the love of Jacob and had given her a second son. Surely this time Jacob would love her. But did he?

Again Leah gave birth to a son and called him *Levi*—"joined." She explained his name. "Now at last my husband will become attached to me, because I have borne him three sons."

Hope springs eternal in the human breast. Leah hoped, first with Reuben, then with Simeon, and now with Levi, that each new little son would make a difference in the marriage, that somehow Jacob would begin to love her as he loved Rachel. She still hoped for equal if not first place in his heart. With the passage of time after the birth of each little boy, hope was deferred and then dashed to the ground. All of her efforts to win Jacob's love—with God's help—were fruitless. He still had eyes only for the beautiful but barren Rachel. Many wives go to extraordinary lengths to win or to keep the love of husbands who do not respond to them in love. Just as often, as with Leah, that hope springing eternal becomes hope deferred or hope dashed to the ground.

It is tough to live in a relationship without deep mutual committed love. Everything in us cries out for it. After all, that was God's original intent for marriage when He created the man and woman and brought them together in Eden.

Marriage in Eden was more than sex. It was a marriage of minds. It was a marriage of goals. It was a marriage of interests. It was a marriage of spirits. And it was a marriage of two bodies becoming one to symbolize all the oneness a man and a woman could experience in every other dimension of their lives together. It was a total unity that was possible only in Eden. In their perfection Adam and Eve could have that relationship.

As a flawed woman married to a flawed man, I cannot have that total and unblemished union with my husband. My needs get in the way of his needs. His wishes collide with mine. It is easy to become disillusioned about a relationship that cannot be perfect. So we try and we long and we wish for something better. In today's world, if we despair of achieving it with Mr. Wonderful #1, we may decide to try it with Mr. Wonderful #2 or Mr. Wonderful #3.

In a day when we are surrounded with media telling us that romantic love is the basis of strong marriages, it is hard to hang onto the fact that a magnificent marriage can be built on something other than love. In the disappointment of feeling less loved than you'd like, is it possible to find resources for happiness in a less than perfect marriage?

Look at Leah when her fourth son was born. She named him *Judah* which means "praising." She explained that name by saying, "This time I will praise the LORD." For the first time in naming her sons, Leah turned from expressing her yearning for Jacob's love to accepting and basking in God's love.

Leah's focus had shifted from what she lacked to what she had. True, nothing had changed with Jacob. He was still starry-eyed over Rachel. Leah could not change him. But she could change herself. She could change her focus. She could recognize the hand of God in her life, giving her significance.

The most important step toward joy in a loveless marriage is to change our focus from what we do *not* have to what we *do* have. Leah had four sons in a day when sons were everything. She woke up to the richness of her situation and said, "This time I will praise the LORD."

Leah

* * *

Genesis 30 opens with the spotlight now on Rachel:

> When Rachel saw that she was not bearing Jacob any children, she became jealous of her sister. So she said to Jacob, "Give me children or I'll die!"
>
> Jacob became angry with her and said, "Am I in the place of God, who has kept you from having children?"
>
> Then she said, "Here is Bilhah, my maidservant. Sleep with her so that she can bear children for me and that through her I too can build a family."

Then we see the race heat up. Bilhah had a son by Jacob who legally became Rachel's child. We know this because it was Rachel who named the little boy. She called him *Dan*, saying "God has vindicated me; he has listened to my plea and given me a son."

If it worked once, maybe it would work twice. So Rachel sent Bilhah to Jacob again. Again the servant became pregnant and bore a son. Again Rachel named the new baby, this time *Naphtali*. Do you know what *Naphtali* means and what Rachel had in mind when she chose that name? *Naphtali* means "wrestlings," and Rachel explained her choice by saying, "I have had a great struggle with my sister, and I have won!"

Had she? The score was actually four to two in Leah's favor. But nervous because her sister could close in on her, Leah jumped into the same game and gave her maidservant, Zilpah, to Jacob also. When Zilpah gave birth to a son, Leah called him *Gad*, meaning "fortune." Yes, her riches were increasing. The score was now five to two, still in Leah's favor.

It had worked twice for Rachel. Perhaps it would work twice for Leah. So once again she sent Zilpah to sleep with Jacob. Once again Zilpah became pregnant and bore a son. This time Leah named him *Asher* meaning "happy." She exclaimed, "How happy I am! The women will call me happy!"

What a switch! The loved and favored Rachel was desolate. The miserable, unloved Leah exclaimed, "How happy I am!" The tables were turned. The woman who "had it all" at the beginning was eaten up with jealousy and frustration. The substitute wife, who wanted so desperately to know her husband's love, now had learned to focus on what she had, not on what she lacked. She could say, "How happy I am!"

* * *

I would be happy if the story ended with Genesis 30:13. Leah sounded "victorious" over her loveless marriage. She praised God for what she had and didn't focus on what she lacked. It would be nice to think that she stayed that way for the rest of her life. But our battles seldom stay won. In the day-to-day rivalry of Rachel and Leah, a rivalry that lasted a lifetime, Leah's battle to live above her loveless marriage had to be fought again and again.

We gain insights into the relationship between the two sisters in the story that follows in Genesis 30:14–17:

Leah

During wheat harvest, Reuben went out into the fields and found some mandrake plants, which he brought to his mother Leah. Rachel said to Leah, "Please give me some of your son's mandrakes."

But she said to her, "Wasn't it enough that you took away my husband? Will you take my son's mandrakes too?"

"Very well," Rachel said, "[Jacob] can sleep with you tonight in return for your son's mandrakes."

So when Jacob came in from the fields that evening, Leah went out to meet him. "You must sleep with me tonight," she said. "I have hired you with my son's mandrakes." So he slept with her that night.

God listened to Leah, and she became pregnant and bore Jacob a fifth son.

This trivial incident demonstrates the daily tensions in Jacob's household. Little Reuben had found some mandrakes in the field. The mandrake is a plant that grows close to the ground, has dark crinkly leaves, and bears a yellow fruit the size of a plum and shaped like a tomato. What made it important was that it was called a love apple. People believed that mandrakes helped a woman become fertile.

Remember Rachel's exclamation to Jacob at the beginning of Genesis 30? "Give me children, or I'll die!" Now you can understand why, when she saw Reuben with love apples, she asked Leah to give some to her. But you can also understand Leah's answer. "Wasn't it enough that you took away my husband? Will you take my son's mandrakes too?"

The relationship between Leah and Rachel was still colored by rivalry and recrimination. No wonder that, years later, the marriage of two sisters to the same man was forbidden in the Mosaic Law (Leviticus 18:18). Rachel would do anything to get pregnant. Leah could not forget that Rachel held her husband's heart in her careless hands. So the bargaining began. In the end Rachel agreed to let Jacob sleep with Leah that night in exchange for the mandrakes.

Ironically, it was the woman without the mandrakes who became pregnant. The woman who believed in the magical qualities of those little yellow love apples remained barren.

When Leah's fifth son was born, she called him *Issachar,* meaning "reward." She explained his name by saying, "God has rewarded me for giving my maidservant to my husband." I'm not sure what she meant by that! Zilpah had given Jacob two sons. Because sons were so important in ancient families, did Leah mean that her willingness to give Zilpah to Jacob merited a special reward? It hadn't happened to Rachel. At any rate, she saw Issachar's birth as a reward from God.

In the text it appears that almost immediately Leah conceived again and bore Jacob a sixth son whom she named *Zebulun,* meaning "honor." Hear her explanation of that name: "God has presented me with a precious gift. This time my husband will treat me with honor, because I have borne him six sons."

Note the ways in which Leah's understanding of life had grown. After her first son was born, she said, "Surely my husband will love me now." After the third son came along, she said, "Now at last my husband will become attached to me." Now at the birth of her sixth son, she has scaled down her expectations. She said simply, "This time my husband will treat me with honor." She was becoming more realistic about what would or would not happen in her marriage.

Contentment in a loveless marriage will never come as long as we cling to the ideal of romantic love and lose sight of the good gifts of God we have already received. Leah focused on Zebulun as "a precious gift" from God.

Many years had passed since that morning when Jacob awakened and discovered that the bride in his tent was Leah and not Rachel. During all those years Rachel wanted a child more than anything else in the world. After long years of waiting—with the score standing at nine (including daughter Dinah) for Leah and only two for Rachel by her maidservant—Rachel's cry for a child was heard by God and she became pregnant. Son Joseph was born, and Rachel's first request was, "May the LORD add to me another son."

God heard her prayer but with consequences she probably did not anticipate. By this time Jacob had worked for Laban for twenty years. One scoundrel was being fleeced by another scoundrel. So Jacob made the decision to return to Canaan with his large family of two wives, two concubines, ten sons and one daughter.

As the family journeyed west, the unthinkable happened. Rachel, nearing the end of the journey and pregnant with her second son, died in childbirth. What she wanted more than anything else in the world became the cause of her final separation from the man who loved her. The woman with every reason to be happy died giving birth to a son she named *Ben-Oni*, "son of my sorrow."

It is easy to look at a woman with breath-stopping beauty and a marvelous figure and the undying love of her man, and think that she must be the happiest of all women. But hear Rachel's sorrow. Hear her complaint. Things are often not what they appear to be.

And what of Leah? God had sovereignly removed her rival from the family circle. Rachel was gone. Leah was now the Number One Wife. We do not know whether Jacob learned to love her any more than he had at the time of that first deception. We do not know how many more years they lived together. We know only that when Leah died, Jacob buried her in the ancestral burial ground, the cave of Machpelah, where Abraham and Sarah, Isaac and Rebekah were buried. He honored her in her death.

At the end of the book of Ruth, after Boaz had bested the nearer kinsman and had won Ruth as his bride, the elders of the city of Bethlehem prayed, "May the LORD make the woman who is coming into your home like Rachel and Leah, who together built up the house of Israel" (4:11).

Leah the unloved was Leah the foremother who helped build up the house of Israel. Of the twelve sons of Jacob who became the progenitors of the twelve tribes of Israel, six were born to Leah.

Out of Leah's personal sadness came rich blessing for Israel. It was Leah who gave birth to Judah, from whom came Israel's greatest king, David, and from whom came the Lion of the tribe of Judah, our Lord Jesus Christ.

Leah, the plain older sister of beautiful Rachel, lived in a very difficult situation and survived. Like her, we, too, are fallen people in a fallen world. We are people scarred by alienation from each other and from ourselves. Life seldom, if ever, comes to us in a way that is fully satisfying. Most of the time it comes with an edge of dissatisfaction—not quite enough love, not quite enough care, not quite enough honor, not quite enough esteem. Almost, perhaps, but never as much as we'd like.

Like Leah, we can focus on what we lack and be miserable. Or also like Leah, we can decide to focus on what we have and make up our minds that "this time we will praise the LORD."

How do you live with a husband who doesn't love you? You change your focus. In the process, you will not only end up exclaiming with Leah, "How happy I am!" but you will someday find that God has worked His miracle through your sadness, touching the world with blessing through you.

Questions for group discussion or personal reflection:

1. What do you think are the indispensable elements of a good marriage?
2. How important is love in a good marriage?
3. How do you know that love is present in a marriage?
4. What do you think a woman can do if she feels that her husband does not love her?

Rahab: How to Choose for God in Your Culture

Imagine that you're driving to the supermarket and you are approaching an intersection with a traffic light. When you are a hundred feet from the crossing, the light turns yellow. What decision are you likely to make in the next split second?

Will you hit the accelerator hard and roar through, possibly on the yellow but probably on the red? Or will you hit the brake and take no chances?

The decision you make in that split second will depend on a number of factors. For one, your schedule will have an impact on your decision. Are you running behind or do you have all morning free for grocery shopping?

Another thing affecting your decision is how you feel about obeying the law at all times. Some of us are compulsive about that. For others skating along the rim of the law is an invigorating challenge.

A third factor is the way you feel about getting a ticket, having to explain it to your family, or having to take the time to talk to a police officer.

Of course, your personality will affect the decision you make. If you're a Type A who can't stand waiting at red lights, you'll probably bear down on the accelerator and barrel through the intersection.

Once you've made that decision, you may have more decisions ahead. Assume that you've finished collecting your groceries and you're now checking out. The clerk gives you a ten-dollar bill in your change instead of the five you should receive. What decision will you make in the next split second? Will you call her attention to the mistake or will you pocket the ten without saying anything?

Once again, your decision in that split second will depend on a number of factors. You may remember the times you bought produce in that store and it turned out to be rotten inside: the lettuce was rusty, the cantaloupe was tasteless, or the apples were mushy. Or perhaps the last time you bought cottage cheese there, you had to toss it out because it had already turned sour. In that split second you may decide that you are merely reimbursing yourself for all the times the store has cheated you with bad merchandise.

What you believe about the store and what you believe about honesty and justice will determine what you do when you have to make a split-second decision about the wrong change in a check-out line.

This isn't a new problem. People have faced choices like these for thousands of years. Ever since Eve made a decision about a piece of fruit in that long-ago garden, people have had to make quick decisions in life. Those decisions are usually made on the basis of our beliefs about ourselves, about our society, and about the universe. Is there a God? If so, how does He impact what I choose to do? What do I believe about Him that influences the decisions I make every day?

When we turn to Joshua 2, we see a woman who made a split-second decision that changed her life from bottom to top. Her name was Rahab. She practiced the oldest profession on earth, prostitution. She had already made some major decisions about the worth of her body and the worth of her soul. In Joshua 2 we meet her as she faces another decision.

To understand that decision, however, we need to move back forty years and set the stage for Rahab's quick decision. God's people, the twelve tribes of Israel, were held as slaves in Egypt. Under the leadership of a remarkable family trio—Moses, Aaron, and Miriam—God delivered His people. When through unbelief these people refused to enter the Promised Land, they wandered for forty years in the Sinai Peninsula. During that time an entire generation died, and our scene opens with the twelve tribes now camped on the east side of the Jordan River, ready to begin the conquest of Canaan under the leadership of their new commander-in-chief, Joshua.

The first city the Israelites would have to take was Jericho, the City of Palms. It controlled a lush green valley. God had promised His people a land flowing with milk and honey, and the first city in their path was one that filled that description perfectly.

The valley was fertile and well-watered, overflowing with abundant crops and luscious fruits. The city itself was the strongest of the fortified cities in Canaan. The mud walls, about twenty feet high, seemed impregnable. Archaeologists tell us that there were actually two walls with a room-wide gap between them. If an enemy succeeded in scaling the first wall, he would be trapped in this no-man's-land, an easy target for the defenders. Jericho was well protected.

Over the gaps in these walls were houses at intervals around the city. Strong timbers supported these houses spanning the gulf between the two sets of walls. It was in one of these houses on the walls that Rahab lived.

Our story begins in Joshua 2:1:

> Joshua son of Nun secretly sent two spies from
> Shittim. "Go look over the land," he said, "especially
> Jericho." So they went and entered the house of a
> prostitute named Rahab and stayed there.

That's the setting: Israelite preparations for war,
spies, and questions of loyalty and patriotism. The spies
had come to Jericho. Where could they stay? How could
they learn what they needed to know? What better place
to go than to a house of prostitution? Visiting merchants
frequently asked directions to such places. We need not
be too surprised that the two spies from Israel ended up
at Rahab's house on the wall.

But had the spies succeeded in evading suspicion?
Read Joshua 2:2–7:

> The king of Jericho was told, "Look! Some of
> the Israelites have come here tonight to spy out
> the land." So the king of Jericho sent this message
> to Rahab: "Bring out the men who came to you
> and entered your house, because they have come
> to spy out the whole land."
>
> But the woman had taken the two men and
> hidden them. She said, "Yes, the men came to me,
> but I did not know where they had come from.
> At dusk, when it was time to close the city gate,
> the men left. I don't know which way they went.
> Go after them quickly. You may catch up with
> them."
>
> (But she had taken them up to the roof and
> hidden them under the stalks of flax she had laid

out on the roof.) So the men set out in pursuit of the spies on the road that leads to the fords of the Jordan, and as soon as the pursuers had gone out, the gate was shut.

Clearly, the spies had aroused suspicions among some of the people of Jericho and the king soon heard about them. He sent a delegation to Rahab's house to ask that the spies be turned over to the Jericho police force. Rahab was faced with having to make a split-second decision.

Would she do the patriotic thing and turn over the spies to the king? Or would she lie and become a traitor by sheltering the enemies of her people?

That is a big decision for anyone to make. And Rahab did not have several hours or several days to think it over or to consult with people she trusted. She had to make that decision quickly. You know from the text what decision she made. The spies, at least for the moment, were safe under the stalks of flax on her roof. The soldiers who had come to her door believed her story and went off to search for the spies on the road back to the fords of the Jordan River.

Think about Rahab's decision. What on earth convinced her that she would do better betraying her own people and risking her own life just to save the lives of two men whom she had never seen before and didn't know if she would ever see again?

Like many of the split-second decisions we make, Rahab's decision came out of who she was and what she believed about herself, about her world, and about God. What she believed gave her the courage to go against her people and her government when she was faced with a split-second decision.

Go with me in your imagination to that rooftop on the Jericho wall. Listen to what Rahab said to the spies after the soldiers left on their futile search. Sit with me under the stars as she chatted with the two men from Israel. Feel the warm spring breeze. Smell the rich scents of flowers on the night air. See the river sparkling in the moonlight to the east and the mountains looming strong to the west. Read what Rahab said to those two young men in Joshua 2:8–13:

> Before the spies lay down for the night, she went up on the roof and said to them, "I know that the LORD has given this land to you and that a great fear of you has fallen on us, so that all who live in this country are melting in fear because of you. We have heard how the LORD dried up the water of the Red Sea for you when you came out of Egypt, and what you did to Sihon and Og, the two kings of the Amorites east of the Jordan, whom you completely destroyed. When we heard of it, our hearts melted and everyone's courage failed because of you, for the LORD your God is God in heaven above and on the earth below. Now then, please swear to me by the LORD that you will show kindness to my family, because I have shown kindness to you. Give me a sure sign that you will spare the lives of my father and mother, my brothers and sisters, and all who belong to them, and that you will save us from death.

What fundamental belief caused Rahab to make that decision to hide the spies and betray her city? Rahab decided to bet her life and her future on Israel's God. She had become convinced, as she told the spies, that their God was "God in heaven above and on the earth below."

And that is the only way you and I can confront our culture or go against the tide of society around us. We find the courage to do that only when we are convinced that "the LORD [our] God is God in heaven above and on the earth below."

Do I really believe that God is sovereign not only in heaven above but also on the earth here below? Am I convinced that "my times are in God's hands," that God really does have "the whole world in His hands"? Can I be sure His hands are good hands and that He will cause justice to triumph and good to win out in the end?

The American poet James Russell Lowell wrote:

> Truth forever on the scaffold,
> Wrong forever on the throne.
> Yet that scaffold sways the future,
> And behind the dim unknown
> Standeth God within the shadow,
> Keeping watch above His own.

"Truth forever on the scaffold. Wrong forever on the throne." It seems like that sometimes, doesn't it? We look at our world around us and we see injustice triumph. We see the good guys lose and the bad guys win. We see a close friend having to cope with a broken marriage, not because she has been a poor wife, but because her husband has succumbed to the charms of another woman. We see an honest husband lose his job at the same time that a dishonest coworker is promoted. It doesn't look as if God is sovereign on the earth below. We don't have much to go on to believe that He is even sovereign in the heavens above. Is God really standing "within the shadow, keeping watch above His own"?

Whether you believe Lowell is right or wrong depends on what else you know about God.

Rahab knew enough about God to believe He would use His great power to benefit His own. She was willing to bet her life on it. She knew how thick the Jericho walls were. She lived on them. She knew how ferocious the Jericho soldiers were. As a prostitute she probably had listened to enough of them brag about their strength and prowess when they visited her. She could see how invulnerable Jericho was to any invader. But despite all of that, she had come to believe that the God of Israel would triumph, and that the Israelites were on God's side. She believed that so thoroughly that she was ready to bet her life on that reality. Rahab dared to stand alone against her culture because she had a strong faith in Israel's God.

We learn something important about Rahab's faith when we move over to the New Testament. To our surprise we find this prostitute held up as an example of outstanding faith. Look first at Hebrews 11:31: "By faith the prostitute Rahab, because she welcomed the spies, was not killed with those who were disobedient."

Here in this Hall of Fame for heroes of faith we find only two women—Sarah, the wife of Abraham, and the prostitute Rahab. Remarkable! But the writer of this letter to the Hebrews is not the only one who used Rahab's faith as an example. Look also at James 2:25: "In the same way, was not even Rahab the prostitute considered righteous for what she did when she gave lodging to the spies and sent them off in a different direction? As the body without the spirit is dead, so faith without deeds is dead."

Rahab's faith led not only to a strong statement about Israel's God: "Your God is God in heaven above and on the earth below." It also led to a strong action for the people of God. Someone has said that "faith is a *step*, not just a statement."

What demonstrated Rahab's faith? The writer to the Hebrews said that the fact that she welcomed the spies demonstrated her faith. James put his finger on the same thing: "she gave lodging to the spies and sent them off in a different direction"—away from the Jericho soldiers. Rahab's faith led her to action. Her decision to act grew out of her faith.

And what came of it? In betting her life on the reality and work of Israel's God, did Rahab choose well? If you grew up in Sunday school, you know the story better than I can tell it.

After having sent the Jericho soldiers off on a wild-goose chase, she had that wonderful conversation with the two spies on her rooftop under a star-studded evening sky. She confessed her faith in Israel's God. And she did one more thing. She asked that, in exchange for saving the spies' lives, the lives of her parents, brothers, and sisters be spared when God gave Jericho to the invaders.

"Our lives for your lives!" the spies assured her. On two conditions: she must not tell their mission to the authorities in Jericho, and she must bind a red cord in the window on the wall. Only those in that house at the time of the conquest would be saved. Everyone else would be destroyed.

They agreed all around on the conditions. She let them down over the wall by a heavy rope and told them to hide in the mountains until the search party had returned to Jericho empty-handed. She tied the red cord in the window. And she waited.

In Joshua chapters 3, 4, and 5 we read the story of a huge nation of people crossing a raging river and of the things that happened as they set up camp not far from Jericho. Meanwhile Rahab waited. Our story resumes in Joshua 6:1:

> Now Jericho was tightly shut up because of the Israelites. No one went out and no one came in.
>
> Then the LORD said to Joshua, "See, I have delivered Jericho into your hands, along with its king and its fighting men."

And with that God gave Joshua one of the strangest battle plans ever recorded. He was to organize a parade. At the head were some armed soldiers followed by seven priests carrying instruments made of rams' horns. Then came more priests carrying the Ark of the Covenant, followed by more armed soldiers. The seven priests were to blow the horns all the way around the city, but the Israelites lining the parade route were to be quiet. Once the parade was ended, everyone returned to the Israelite camp for the night. The people assembled and marched the first day. Again on the second day. The third day. The fourth day. The fifth day. Again on the sixth day.

What in the world would *you* have thought was going on, had you been a citizen of Jericho standing on the wall and watching them each day? Day after day after day? Would you have begun to wonder what kind of God would give such instructions to these people?

Or would it make you just a little bit nervous to watch the processional, all the while wondering what would happen next?

On the seventh day the parade formed as usual. The Israelites watched the armed soldiers, the priests with the horns, and the priests carrying the Ark line up in the customary formation. Everyone was quiet. They were supposed to be. But I suspect that even without such a command from Joshua, a lot of them would have been silent anyway. This was the big test. Would God come through for them, or would they end up looking as silly as they had looked all week?

One time around, twice around, three times around, four times, five times, six times, seven times. And suddenly Joshua gave the signal. The trumpets sounded. The people shouted. AND THE WALLS CAME A-TUMBLIN' DOWN. Those massive walls—twenty feet thick—collapsed in on the city. The armed Israelite soldiers were able to run up over the rubble and engage the Jericho militia in battle. The destruction of Jericho was total.

Or almost total. Left standing was a house on a section of the wall. From the window of that house dangled a red cord. People crowded around the window inside that house, watching in astonishment all that was happening.

Joshua called the two spies and gave them a good assignment: Go to Rahab's house and bring out everyone there and keep them safe. In Joshua 6:23 we read: "So the young men who had done the spying went in and brought out Rahab, her father and mother and brothers and all who belonged to her. They brought out her entire family and put them in a place outside the camp of Israel."

Safe! Rahab had bet her life on Israel's God. God had come through for her and for all who huddled with her inside that house on the wall of Jericho.

There is more to the story. In Joshua 6:25 the writer tells us that Rahab lived among the Israelites to the day the book of Joshua was written. She became one with the people of God. The fact that she had been a prostitute was no longer relevant. By faith she was joined to the community of God.

One of the remarkable things we see when we look at Jesus' contacts with women in the four gospels is that He often stooped down and lifted up "fallen women." Remember the woman with the alabaster jar of perfume in Luke 7 and the woman taken in adultery in John 8. Again and again, we see the compassion of Jesus reaching out to women who had broken the rules and had lived lives that "respectable" people looked down on.

Rahab reminds us that being joined to the family of God has nothing to do with our goodness. It has everything to do with God's grace. Through a prostitute God teaches us that we are saved by *grace*, not by being good.

But our story is still not over. Turn to Matthew 1— that dry, dull genealogy—and look at verse 5: "Salmon the father of Boaz, whose mother was Rahab."

Rahab the mother of Boaz? That means she was the great-great-grandmother of David, Israel's greatest king. Even more amazing, she was an ancestress in the genealogy of Jesus, the Lord of glory, the God-man, the Savior of the world.

Rahab, the prostitute. Wouldn't you think that God would be a bit more choosy about the lineage of His Son? For people for whom descent was everything, wouldn't

God take their scruples into consideration and choose a purer line for the Messiah? Apparently God wanted us to learn something else as we look at Rahab.

Rahab stands as a tribute to the possibilities within every one of us. God saw in her the possibility of an active and invigorating faith. Never mind what she was. He looked at what she could become.

It is the same for us. Our past is irrelevant. Our future alone matters to God. Faith can blossom in any environment. Roses can grow in manure piles. Whatever lies behind us is not nearly as important as what lies before us. The choices we have made in the past have brought us where we are today. The choices we make today, tomorrow, next week, or next year will determine our destiny.

Some of those choices will be split-second decisions. They will come out of who we are and what we believe about ourselves, our world, and God. Those decisions will determine the actions we take.

Rahab heard about Israel's God. She responded to what she heard by faith. She made a split-second decision to go with God by saving the two spies. Her faith gained her life in the midst of destruction. It gained her the salvation of her entire family. It gained her a place in Israel and marriage to Salmon, who, tradition tells us, was one of the two spies. It also gained her a place in the genealogy of Israel's greatest king and a place in the genealogy of our Savior, Jesus Christ.

What she had been was irrelevant. What she became through active faith was all that mattered.

What resources do you fall back on when you have to make split-second decisions in your life? Are your decisions grounded in your faith in a loving, compassionate God whose hand is on you for good? Do your actions show your faith as you go with God and with His people? Look up to Rahab. Look at this prostitute who modeled vibrant faith for Israel and for us today.

Questions for group discussion or personal reflection:

1. Describe some decision point you have faced.
2. What factors led you to make the decision you made?
3. As you look back at that decision, was it good or bad? Why?
4. How did your decision affect your life's direction?

Deborah: How to Lead
When Called by God to Do So

Few stories ignite my imagination and admiration as much as those from the lives of missionaries who are called to do extraordinary things for God. Among the exploits of great missionaries past and present, few are as astonishing as those of a small Scottish woman named Mary Slessor.

Mary had alone penetrated the jungles of Calabar, a region we now know as Nigeria in West Africa. God had called her to reach tribes no European or American missionaries had yet visited. Her life story is full of repeated acts of superhuman courage only because she was sure of her calling by an all-powerful God.

Leaving a fruitful ministry among the Efiks, she began contacts with the Okoyongs, deep in the rain forests of Calabar. Hearing drumming one evening, she went to the marketplace where everyone had gathered. Pushing her way through the crowd, she found masked Egbo men tightening the cords that tied a spread-eagled and terrified girl to stakes driven into the ground. For an assumed infraction of Okoyong law, the screaming girl had been sentenced to have boiling oil poured on her bare stomach. In *The Expendable Mary Slessor*, James Buchan describes the scene:

> The oil was boiling on a fire nearby and a masked man was ladling some of it into a pot. It

49

was a scene which would have daunted the bravest of people: the ring of seated chiefs, the masked men grotesque in the flicker of the fire and of the torches, the laughing, drunken warriors, the screaming, the drumming, and the sexual excitement and anticipation of the spectators. It is possible that if Mary had known what she was going to find, she would have thought it wiser to stay away . . . . But as she stood inside the circle and the chiefs saw her, it did not occur to Mary to turn back . . . . She walked out and got between the fire and the girl. What a film sequence it would have made. The hush as everyone stared at the small white woman. Then the explosion of chatter as the crowd babbled their amazement . . . . The masked man began to swing the ladle round his head and to caper towards Mary. She stood and stared at him. The ladle whistled nearer and nearer her head. The crowd looked on in silence. The Egbo man dodged from side to side, his eyes staring at her through the holes in the mask. He had the choice of striking her with the ladle or of retreating. Mary stared back at him. He retreated. Mary walked towards him on her way to where Edem [the chief] was sitting, and he almost fell over himself to get out of her way. Such a show of power from a mere woman astounded the crowd. They had never seen anything like it before . . . . The girl's punishment now became a trivial matter compared to this exhibition of the power of the white woman's God. The chiefs allowed Mary to take the girl into her own custody pending further consideration of her case. In a few days, in typical Okoyong fashion, the palaver was forgotten and the girl slipped quietly back to her husband.

How could anyone—woman or man—dare to stand up against an entire village? Buchan tells us that Mary "never doubted that she was living in the presence of God and that He was guiding her in the special work for which He had shaped her." Mary Slessor was able to lead tribe after tribe to Jesus Christ and to lead the way into the interior of Nigeria because she knew God had called her and had given her spiritual gifts and His presence to rely on as she carried out her mission.

For most of us life does not demand the fearless courage Mary Slessor showed again and again in a lifetime of work in Calabar. But wherever God has put us, we will handle the demands made on us better when we know we are called and equipped by God.

What is a woman to do if she finds herself called and equipped to serve God by leading others? A woman in the Old Testament found herself in that position. Her name was Deborah. We read about her in Judges 4:4–5:

Deborah, a prophetess, the wife of Lappidoth, was leading Israel at that time. She held court under the Palm of Deborah between Ramah and Bethel in the hill country of Ephraim, and the Israelites came to her to have their disputes decided.

Deborah, a prophetess. That's the first surprise. A prophet was a person who spoke the words of God.

Priests spoke to God for people. Prophets spoke to the people for God.

The words prophets spoke were of two major kinds. Some of the words were *foretelling*—predicting things to come in the future. Other words were *forthtelling*—preaching about sin, righteousness, and judgment to come so that people could choose to be on God's side. Prophets in both the Old and New Testaments resembled preachers.

The apostle Paul defined the task of the prophet in 1 Corinthians 14:3: "Everyone who prophesies speaks to men for their strengthening, encouragement and comfort."

That was the task God gave Deborah—to speak to men and women in Israel for their strengthening, encouragement, and comfort. He gave her knowledge of the future and insight into the ways she could bring that home to the Israelites. She was a prophetess.

The second thing we see in Judges 4:4–5 is that Deborah was the wife of Lappidoth. We know nothing about Lappidoth apart from the fact that he married Deborah. From that fact, however, we know that Deborah was not a single woman who could give her whole life to ministry for God. She was a wife. She had the responsibilities of a home. She had a husband to care for. She was not a free agent who could ignore the tasks that take up much of the time and energy of most women.

But note the order in the sacred text: she was first a prophetess, then a wife. She had a balancing act to practice day after day. She must have struggled with conflicts in her schedule. But she was God's spokesperson first. Hear me well: I am not suggesting that we all run out and put work for God ahead of our homes and our

Deborah

families. Most of us have not received the gift God had given Deborah. We don't have the same calling. But neither can we use our home and family as an excuse to avoid using God's gifts in the church.

The third thing we learn from the text about Deborah is that she was the leader of Israel. Other translations call her the *judge* of Israel.

What did that mean when Deborah lived? In early patriarchal times "capable men from all the people" were appointed to serve as judges (Exodus 18:25–26). As the tribes of Israel settled down in Canaan, most judges were primarily military leaders that came to power in times of national crisis. In one sense they were generals more than judges in the way we understand the word today.

But judges were also leaders who had risen to power because they had wisdom and were able to administer justice in the family, tribe, or nation. They ruled and protected with judicious military action.

When we look at the era in the Old Testament known as the period of the Judges, we see Israel operating as a loose confederacy of tribes whose common tie was their ancestor Jacob and who worshiped at the tabernacle in Shiloh. Israel was hardly a nation during this time, a period of about three hundred years stretching from the death of Joshua to the crowning of Saul as Israel's first king.

During those three centuries a pattern repeated itself many times. With no stable central government, the tribes each did their own thing. In fact, the last verse of the book of Judges tells us that "in those days Israel had no king; everyone did as he saw fit" (21:25).

It was a time of anarchy. It was also a time of apostasy. The Israelites absorbed many pagan worship practices from their neighbors. Human sacrifice, ritual prostitution, and many other pagan practices replaced the worship of Jehovah God. As a consequence, one tribe and then another was conquered by a foreign power and enslaved or forced to pay exorbitant tributes. After years of servitude, someone in the tribe would call out to God, institute reforms, and beg God for deliverance. A judge would rise up to organize a military campaign to throw off the oppressor. Then the tribe would live in peace until the people again wandered far from the law of God.

Some judges were better than others. If you want to spend a depressing afternoon, read through the book of Judges. You'll meet the characters you heard about in Sunday school—Gideon, Samson (and Delilah), and, of course, Deborah. You'll also meet some other, less savory characters. Some were better generals than leaders. But when we return to Judges 4, we find that Deborah combined the best qualities of the Old Testament judge. She was splendid in military strategy and she was superb as a judge adjudicating the problems people brought to her. We know she did well because Israelites came to her from all over the land to have her decide their disputes. Had they not had great confidence in her wisdom, they would have gone elsewhere for solutions to their problems.

Thus we meet good wife Deborah, prophesying to and judging for the people of God. What was the situation in which she found herself? We find that in Judges 4:1–3:

> After Ehud [the previous judge] died, the Israelites once again did evil in the eyes of the LORD. So the LORD sold them into the hands of Jabin, a king of Canaan, who reigned in Hazor.

Deborah

The commander of his army was Sisera, who lived in Harosheth Haggoyim. Because he had nine hundred iron chariots and had cruelly oppressed the Israelites for twenty years, they cried to the LORD for help.

We get a better idea how bad the situation in Israel was from chapter 5, verses 6–8:

> In the days of Shamgar son of Anath, in the days of Jael, the roads were abandoned; travelers took to winding paths. Village life in Israel ceased, ceased until I, Deborah, arose, arose a mother in Israel. When they chose new gods, war came to the city gates, and not a shield or spear was seen among forty thousand in Israel.

The situation was bad. It was so bad people couldn't even use the roads. They had to sneak around from village to village by hidden paths and clandestine trails. Village life ceased. Farmers had to thresh their grain in secret at night in caves. Life and property were worth nothing. People were hunted down like rabbits. Women were raped. It was a cruel and brutal oppression. And it went on for twenty years.

Note that not all of the land was under this oppression. When we look at the tribes who did not help in the war, we see that the oppression was localized in northern Israel.

Jabin's best weapon was his nine hundred iron chariots. They functioned best on level ground. Iron was heavy. Horses could pull the chariots with least difficulty on a flat plain, not in hill country. Deborah judged Israel at the beginning of the Iron Age, when the neighboring Canaanites had begun smelting iron before the Israelites learned that skill.

Meanwhile, back under her palm tree in the hill country of Mount Ephraim between Ramah and Bethel, Deborah dispensed justice and wisdom to all who came to her. At the same time she could not ignore the plight of her fellow citizens up north. She heard the stories of cruelty as she sat and listened day by day. One day she had heard enough and took action. Read what she did in Judges 4:6–7:

> She sent for Barak son of Abinoam from Kedesh in Naphtali and said to him, "The LORD, the God of Israel, commands you: 'Go, take with you ten thousand men of Naphtali and Zebulun and lead the way to Mount Tabor. I will lure Sisera, the commander of Jabin's army, with his chariots and his troops to the Kishon River and give him into your hands.' "

Deborah sent for Barak and gave him his marching orders. Note that Barak came when Deborah sent for him. This gives us some idea of the power and influence Deborah had in Israel. Note, too, that her instructions began with the words, "The LORD, the God of Israel, commands you." The prophetess at work. This was God's message for Barak, not Deborah's. That fact is important to understanding what followed. If the message had been just Deborah's idea of what might work, Barak would have had good reason to argue. But this was *God's* word to him. Barak responds in verse 8, saying, "If you go with me, I will go; but if you don't go with me, I won't go."

Preachers and commentators have described Barak as weak and cowardly. Not so. Barak was doing the normal thing, the natural thing, the expected thing. He didn't dispute God's instructions. He just wanted to be sure that he had the mouthpiece of God within earshot when the battle heated up and he needed instant instructions on the next tactic to follow.

But despite the fact that Barak was doing something prudent, Deborah the prophetess saw the fear and reticence he felt and added another prophesy in verse 9: " 'Very well,' Deborah said, 'I will go with you. But because of the way you are going about this, the honor will not be yours, for the LORD will hand Sisera over to a woman.' So Deborah went with Barak to Kedesh."

I like Barak. How many men do you know who would have listened to a woman like Deborah? His confidence in her tells us a lot about her. It also tells us about a man who was not ashamed to follow the leadership of a woman when he believed she spoke the very words of God.

What happened? In verse 10 we see that Barak pulled together an army of ten thousand men and, with Deborah, assembled on the sides of Mount Tabor. That in itself was tactically wise. The iron chariots had to stay on the plain. As long as Barak's army stayed on the slopes of the mountain, they were relatively safe.

Meanwhile, in verses 12 and 13, Sisera assembled his huge army on the plain between the Kishon River and his hometown of Harosheth Haggoyim. With the armies in place, it is clear that Barak and his rag-tag band of ill-equipped men were no match, humanly speaking, for Sisera's military machine down on the plain. Anyone looking at those two armies facing each other that day would have groaned for the Israelites and turned away to avoid watching the carnage. But that view of things discounts one crucial player in this drama: God. When Deborah spoke to Barak in verse 7, it was *God* she quoted with the promise that Sisera would be lured to the Kishon River and would lose the battle to Barak's band.

Things are seldom the way they look from our human perspective. For Barak on a slope of Mount Tabor, the contest must have looked dreadfully uneven. *Hopeless* might have seemed like a more accurate word. He may have had some qualms as he stood there. But the mouthpiece of God was beside him. Whatever else Barak experienced on that mountainside that day, he had faith. We know that from Hebrews 11:32, where we find Barak listed in the Hall of Fame of those with faith. His faith carried the day in the next moments. Read what happened in Judges 4:14–16:

> Then Deborah said to Barak, "Go! This is the day the LORD has given Sisera into your hands. Has not the LORD gone ahead of you？" So Barak went down Mount Tabor, followed by ten thousand men. At Barak's advance, the LORD routed Sisera and all his chariots and army by the sword, and Sisera abandoned his chariot and fled on foot. But Barak pursued the chariots and army as far as Harosheth Haggoyim. All the troops of Sisera fell by the sword; not a man was left.

What happened？ The timing was right. "Go!" yelled Deborah, and Barak by faith *went*. Trembling, perhaps. Weak in the knees, maybe. But he went. And God did the rest. Did you notice that as Barak advanced by faith, it was the *Lord* who routed Sisera and all his chariots and army? How did God do it?

We get some help understanding God's intervention in Deborah's song of victory in Judges 5:4: "O LORD, when you went out from Seir, when you marched from the land of Edom, the earth shook, the heavens poured, the clouds poured down water."

The historian Josephus tells us that as Sisera and his army marched east to encounter the Israelites streaming down Mount Tabor, a sleet storm hit the Canaanite army full in the face, blinding the archers and chariot drivers as well as the horses. Whether Sisera encountered sleet or rain, God unleashed the powers of the heavens.

Read on with me in Judges 5:19–21:

> Kings came, they fought; the kings of Canaan fought at Taanach by the waters of Megiddo, but they carried off no silver, no plunder. From the heavens the stars fought, from their courses they fought against Sisera. The river Kishon swept them away, the age-old river, the river Kishon. March on, my soul; be strong!

The rains descended and the floods came. As the plain turned into a muddy swamp, the iron chariot wheels sank into the muck and stuck fast. Sisera and his army had to abandon their mighty chariots of war and go on foot. At the same time the river Kishon, normally a trickling stream, swelled to a mighty torrent and swept many Canaanite soldiers along and out to sea. Hear the poetic rhythm of Deborah's song: "The river Kishon swept them away, the age-old river, the river Kishon. March on, my soul; be strong!"

I love that last line. When we see what God does with the insignificant, we take courage. We march on because we are strong in the strength of the Lord our God. The river Kishon—rarely a river, often just a dry creekbed—could fill and flood and sweep an army away to its doom.

When God is on the march, the stars fight on His side. The heavens do His bidding. All the forces of nature are under His control. No wonder we can march on and be strong!

Two more events that day joined human effort to divine work. Note, first, Judges 4:23–24: "On that day God subdued Jabin, the Canaanite king, before the Israelites. And the hand of the Israelites grew stronger and stronger against Jabin, the Canaanite king, until they destroyed him."

God gave the motivation through Deborah. God gave the supernatural help through nature. But Barak still had the task of carrying through, of finishing the job. He could have sat on a rock under a tree on Mount Tabor and said, "God, You're doing such a great job, please don't let me interrupt you." But he didn't. He did what he had to do. In the end, Jabin and his oppressive power were destroyed.

The second event of note that day is not one for the faint of heart. You may already know the story of Jael, the wife of Heber the Kenite. Recall that in Judges 4:9 Deborah had told Barak that he would not have the honor of killing the cruel Sisera. That honor would go to a woman.

How that happened is not a pretty story. Sisera, dog-tired from fleeing the battleground, came to the tent of the nomadic family of Heber the Kenite. Jael invited

Sisera inside to rest. He asked for water and she did even more by offering him yogurt. She covered him with a rug and promised to lie about his whereabouts if anyone came looking for him. But once he was asleep, she took a hammer and a tent peg and drilled him from temple to temple, fastening his head to the ground. The New English Bible is more graphic, with details of Sisera's brains oozing out on the ground and limbs twitching as he died.

At times I've recoiled from the story of Jael killing Sisera. First, she violated the Middle Eastern law of hospitality. Second, she did so in a cruel way. But as I have thought about Jael, I've realized that she did what had to be done with what were probably the only instruments she had at hand. A hammer and a tent peg were standard equipment in a nomadic family.

Did she have to kill Sisera? Someone had to do it! Sisera's cruelty was legendary. If he lived, he would find new ways to terrorize innocent people. Had Jael's husband, Heber, killed Sisera, we might not think too much of it. The Old Testament records countless stories of men turning with ease to violence. But a woman? With a tent peg and hammer?

Rabbinic tradition tells us that Jael's daughter had been cruelly gang-raped by Sisera and some of his cronies. We don't have biblical verification for that. But if the rabbis are on the right track, Jael had plenty of personal motivation to kill the man who had violated her daughter.

What we do know is that God's prophetic word through Deborah was fulfilled. Sisera met his end at the hand of a woman. In her song, Deborah sings, "Most blessed of women be Jael, the wife of Heber the Kenite, most blessed of tent-dwelling women" (5:24). Most blessed is Jael for doing God's work in destroying an evil man.

Our story of Deborah ends in Judges 5:31, where we learn that "the land had peace forty years." God's gift to Israel in an hour of terrible need was wrapped in the body and mind and heart of a woman. Deborah shatters some of our stereotypes about what leadership should be.

She had the spiritual gift of prophesy and used it to lead the people of God. She had the natural gift of wisdom, and perhaps the spiritual gift of wisdom as well, to judge wisely the people of God. She was God's spokesperson to whom generals and commoners alike listened. She was a strong leader whose word commanded the strongest in the land. Her power and influence were such that, had they not been tempered by her righteousness, she could have become a despot. She did not.

A wonderful humility enveloped Deborah's use of her gifts, her power, and her influence. Notice how often humility peers out around the corners of her life. She had the word from God on how the battle would end. She could have picked up a sword and marched in front of the Israeli army. But she stood aside and gave the task to Barak.

She made sure that Barak knew it was *God* who would give the victory in the battle. She took no credit for a brilliant military strategy.

In the opening lines of Deborah's song (Judges 5:2) she praised God for the people in Israel who were willing to take the lead and offer themselves for God's work. Clearly, Deborah didn't care who got the credit. She wasn't out to make herself look good.

Central to her use of her gifts, her power, and her influence was her unshakable faith in the Lord, the God of Israel. Her song in Judges 5 bubbles with her confidence in

God. She saw with clear eyes the shortcomings of her fellow citizens. She was not happy about the tribes that made no effort to help throw off the power of Jabin. But while she saw the foibles of the people she had to work with, beyond those foibles she saw the power and concern of God.

It was that unshakable confidence in God that enabled Deborah to use all that God had given her in public leadership. She knew that *God* had given her gifts and that *He* had called her to use them for the good of His people. She knew, from the history of Israel, that God delights in using the weak things of the world to shame the strong (1 Corinthians 1:27). She knew that if God is for us, none can stand against us (Romans 8:31). She *knew*. She had confidence. The same confidence that put steel in the spine of a small Scottish woman named Mary Slessor.

What is a woman to do today who has gifts from God that may put her up front? Do as Deborah did. Use those gifts. But hold them lightly on an open palm as God's gifts to you. This means not seeking the spotlight. It means not insisting on getting the credit for what you do. It means letting the One who is the giver of all good gifts give you a place to serve. It means letting God give you praise for your serving. It means letting Him shame the strong by using you in all your weakness. He is the One who raises up and puts down.

What is the woman to do today who does *not* have Deborah's up-front gifts? There isn't a woman in the church who does not have a sphere of influence. It may be a small circle of friends, a children's Sunday school class, or a place in a care group. Wherever God puts each of us, whatever He puts into our hands to do, the rules are the same: We must use His gifts to do our task. It is our choice whether or not to fulfill our calling by using all that God has given us for His glory. We do not seek the spotlight nor insist on getting the credit for what we do. We let the Giver of all good gifts give us a place to serve. Then we let Him give us praise for our serving. We let Him confound the mighty by using us in all our weakness. He is the One who raises up and puts down.

Questions for group discussion or personal reflection:

1. How do you feel about women in leadership positions in the church or in public life?
2. How should a woman who has leadership gifts use her abilities?
3. How does Jesus' parable of the talents in Matthew 25:14–30 apply to women with leadership gifts?
4. What attributes or spirit should characterize women using their spiritual gifts for Christ and His kingdom?

Ruth: How to See God in the Dailiness of Life

Do you enjoy reading? It is my greatest joy and sometimes my besetting sin. I can lose myself in a good book when I should be doing other things. Most of us who enjoy reading know that a good story can take us out of the humdrum sameness of our lives and transport us into the tension and drama of someone else's experience.

I have a second question: Do you ever sneak a peek at the ending before you get there? If you're into a detective story and it's time to cook dinner, you may think you can't wait to find out who dunnit. So you look. Or if it's a great romance and you can't stand the thought that the wrong girl gets the boy, you may glance at the last page to see who ends up in his arms.

If you have ever sat down to read the little book of Ruth in the Old Testament, were you tempted to sneak a peek to see how the story ends? If you did, you were probably disappointed. The final verses of Ruth chapter 4—the *climax* of the whole story—seem anything but climactic. What we find there is a genealogy: "Perez was the father of Hezron, Hezron the father of Ram, Ram the father of Amminadab, Amminadab the father of Nahshon, Nahshon the father of Salmon," and so on. Can you imagine a duller ending for a story? An author would have to work hard to come up with something more boring and anti-climactic than that.

Yet, when we look at this little book of Ruth, we see a very good storyteller at work. All the way through we watch the author dropping hints of things to come—clues that draw us in, that keep us aware that the plot is thickening. Things could turn out several different ways. Why would the writer want to blow a good story with a bad ending?

To understand that those dull verses at the end of the book really *are* the climax—and a stunning climax at that—we have to go back and look at the rest of the story. Then, suddenly, a boring genealogy comes alive and makes sense.

Our story is a play in four acts. The five principal actors on our stage are three women—Naomi, Ruth, and Orpah—and two men—Boaz and the nearer kinsman. The stage director is God.

When the curtain goes up on the first act, we find a bitter old woman on center stage. To listen to *her*, it is clear that the Stage Director does not know what He is doing. But that's getting ahead of the story. Begin with the description of the setting as we read it in the script in Ruth 1:1–5:

> In the days when the judges ruled, there was a famine in the land, and a man from Bethlehem in Judah, together with his wife and two sons, went to live for a while in the country of Moab. The man's name was Elimelech, his wife's name Naomi, and the names of his two sons were Mahlon and Kilion. They were Ephrathites from Bethlehem, Judah. And they went to Moab and lived there.
>
> Now Elimelech, Naomi's husband, died, and she was left with her two sons. They married

Moabite women, one named Orpah and the other Ruth. After they had lived there about ten years, both Mahlon and Kilion also died, and Naomi was left without her two sons and her husband.

The setting is in the time of the judges. This period of Israel's history was one of barbaric oppression and bloodshed. Between violent invasions, tribal civil wars, and unchecked lawlessness, the Jews had to contend with constant trouble. Now a famine added to their misery. In Bethlehem—the House of Bread—there was no bread. Elimelech chose to take his family to neighboring Moab.

While the trip to Moab was not a long one—not much more than thirty miles east of Bethlehem—distance in the Bible, as H. W. Morton observed, is often measured, not in miles, but in distance from God. Moabites worshiped the god Chemosh, not Jehovah. Elimelech and his family left the familiar for the unfamiliar, the known for the unknown.

While in Moab, the family faced first the loss of the father, Elimelech. Then the sons who had both married Moabite women also died. The play begins with three widows in a gloomy, hopeless setting. Naomi, on center stage, has heard that once again Bethlehem is really the House of Bread. The famine has passed. Food is plentiful in Judah. She and her two daughters-in-law prepare to move to Bethlehem. The dialogue in our play begins in verse 8:

> Then Naomi said to her two daughters-in-law, "Go back, each of you, to your mother's home. May the LORD show kindness to you, as you have shown to your dead and to me. May the LORD

grant that each of you will find rest in the home of another husband."

Naomi knew that Orpah and Ruth faced a bleak and uncertain future if they returned to Bethlehem with her. They must stay in Moab. She kissed them—a sign of release from any obligation to her. They had voluntarily stayed with Naomi after their husbands had died, but now they could not forfeit their own happiness just to care for her. Desperate, powerless to do anything for them, Naomi prayed that God would care for them and provide them with husbands who would care for them.

But note what Orpah and Ruth answered: "We will go back with you to your people." Whether out of loyalty to their dead husbands or out of love for their mother-in-law, Ruth and Orpah pushed on toward Bethlehem. But Naomi tried again:

> Return home, my daughters. Why would you come with me? Am I going to have any more sons, who could become your husbands? Return home, my daughters; I am too old to have another husband. Even if I thought there was still hope for me—even if I had a husband tonight and then gave birth to sons—would you wait until they grew up? Would you remain unmarried for them? No, my daughters. It is more bitter for me than for you, because the LORD's hand has gone out against me (1:11–13).

What is the tone of Naomi's argument to Orpah and Ruth? It isn't just another effort to persuade them not to stay with her. It is also a lament accusing God of botching up her life. It affirms God's direct involvement in her life and His accountability for her situation. Basically Naomi told Orpah and Ruth that if God was "after" her, to stay with her was to court disaster.

The second effort to persuade them had its effect on Orpah, who kissed her mother-in-law and started back to Moab. But Ruth still wasn't persuaded. In the next verses we hear her unshakable decision to stay with Naomi:

> Don't urge me to leave you or to turn back from you. Where you go, I will go, and where you stay I will stay. Your people will be my people and your God my God. Where you die I will die, and there I will be buried. May the LORD deal with me, be it ever so severely, if anything but death separates you and me (1:16–17).

With that Naomi gave up trying to talk Ruth into returning to Moab.

Can we fault Orpah for going back to Moab? Not at all. Orpah did the expected thing. It is Ruth who did the unexpected. We understand the reasonableness of Orpah's decision. We don't understand the incredible loyalty Ruth displayed. Ruth demonstrated what the Hebrews called *hesed*.

Hesed is a Hebrew word we can translate "loyal love." It is a love that goes well beyond the expected. David's mighty men showed *hesed* for their beloved leader a hundred years later when they left the wilderness and fought their way into and out of Bethlehem to bring David a drink of water from the town well. God shows us *hesed* in sacrificing even His own Son to redeem us, to buy us back from sin. Ruth was a shining example of *hesed* as she stood at a crossroad between familiar Moab and unfamiliar Judah.

Her loyal love made the choice—for Naomi's people and for Naomi's God. We see her making that choice with no husband and no prospect of marriage, devoting herself to an old woman. She might have wished for a crystal ball as she stood on that dusty road so many years ago. It would have been nice to see how her choice would work out. But she had none. She had to choose for God and Naomi with no guarantees.

The scene continues. In verse 19 we see the two women arriving in Bethlehem where everyone came out to greet them. "Can this be Naomi?" It had been more than ten years since she had left. Suddenly hearing her name, *Naomi*, reminded the old woman of the irony of that name. *Naomi* means "pleasant" or "lovely." "Lovely?" she exclaimed. "Don't call me *Lovely*! Call me *Mara* [bitter]!"

As Naomi continued speaking, her anger at God spilled over once again. "The Almighty has made my life very bitter. I went away full, but the LORD has brought me back empty."

Throughout this first act we hear Naomi talking about God. She was conscious of His work in the universe and in her life. But as she talked about God, we see that she misjudged Him and she misjudged life. She stated that she went out of Judah *full*. But did she? The very thing that caused her family's migration to Moab was a famine. They went out empty. Life was tough or they would not have left Bethlehem in the first place.

Naomi also stated that God had brought her back *empty*. But had He? It was true that she had lost her husband and both sons. But in their place God had given her the incredible devotion of Ruth, who pledged to stay with her to death's door and beyond.

Naomi misjudged her situation when she misjudged God. She focused on the negative and became bitter. Calling herself *Mara* (bitter), she looked at God and looked at life through dirty windows.

Like Naomi, we can be religious. We can talk about God. We can offer prayers to God. But if we misjudge Him and His work in our lives, we easily misjudge all that touches us.

As act one and chapter one end, the curtain slowly descends on two women: loyal Ruth and bitter Naomi. The last words of the last verse of this chapter give us a clue to what is to follow in the next act. Ruth and Naomi had arrived in Bethlehem as the barley harvest began. What did this presage for two poor widows newly arrived in town?

As the curtain rises on act two, we discover that Naomi had a relative in town who was wealthy and influential. Was he destined for some crucial role in our play?

Meanwhile Naomi and Ruth had nothing to eat. Ruth decided to glean, that is to follow the reapers during the harvest and to pick up from the ground any grains left behind. In this act Naomi moves to the stage wing and Ruth moves to center stage.

In Ruth 2:3 we read that "as it turned out, she found herself working in a field belonging to Boaz." That statement makes it sound as if all that followed was purely accidental. But the author is actually hinting at a cause for this "chance" happening. Behind what appears to be human luck lies divine purpose. Even in the "accidents" in life, the hand of God is at work on our behalf.

Now look at verse 4: "Just then Boaz arrived from Bethlehem."

Surprise! One more coincidence! The wealthy, influential relative of Naomi owned the field and happened on the scene while Ruth was there!

Noticing Ruth, he asked about her and learned that she was from Moab and had come back with Naomi. Now comes the moment of truth. "Chance" had thrown Ruth and Boaz together in the same field. What would Boaz do?

Obviously, things are turning out well. Boaz, in short, gives Ruth "most favored gleaner" status in his fields. By following his instructions carefully, Ruth would be protected from young men who might try to bother her. She would also glean much more grain than would normally be the case.

Not only did Boaz make Ruth's gleaning easier, but he also invited her to eat with his harvesters and saw to it that she had an adequate meal. At the end of her first day of gleaning, she returned to Naomi with a shawl full of winnowed grain. The Bible tells us that she took home an ephah of barley—about twenty-nine pounds of grain. Ruth's success on her first day of gleaning far exceeded her expectations when she set out that morning.

What happened when she returned to Naomi that evening? Of course, the older woman wanted a full recounting of all that had happened that day. Such a huge shawl full of grain meant that she had gleaned in a good place. Where had she gone? In whose field had she gleaned?

Notice Naomi's reaction when Ruth answered her questions. Hearing about Boaz, she exclaimed, "The LORD bless him! . . . That man is our close relative; he is one of our kinsman-redeemers."

Ruth

What does that mean? Why is that important? The
curtain descends slowly on our second act. But Naomi's
statement about a kinsman-redeemer lets us know that
the play is not over.

Act three is about to begin. It turns out to be the
turning point in the play. God has provided food for the
two widows. But that is only a short-term solution to
their needs. Ruth needs a husband. Naomi needs a son to
preserve her inheritance and to carry on the family name.
As the barley and wheat harvests end, Naomi cooks up a
scheme that is bold, brash, and a little bit dangerous for
Ruth. Read her plan in Ruth 3:1–4:

> One day Naomi her mother-in-law said to her,
> "My daughter, should I not try to find a home for
> you, where you will be well provided for? Is not
> Boaz, with whose servant girls you have been, a
> kinsman of ours? Tonight he will be winnowing
> barley on the threshing floor. Wash and perfume
> yourself, and put on your best clothes. Then go
> down to the threshing floor, but don't let him
> know you are there until he has finished eating
> and drinking. When he lies down, note the place
> where he is lying. Then go and uncover his feet
> and lie down. He will tell you what to do."

Thus Naomi began to answer her own prayer for
Ruth back in Ruth 1:9—"May the LORD grant that each
of you will find rest in the home of another husband." In
one way Naomi models for us the way God works
through human actions. We are not to wait passively for
events to happen. When an opportunity presents itself,
we may need to seize the initiative. Naomi did just that.

But we also recognize that in Naomi's plan lay real risk for Ruth.

Boaz and Ruth would be in a secluded spot where they could talk privately. In Old Testament times, however, threshing floors were associated with licentiousness. Naomi was gambling on the character of Boaz, that he would not take unfair advantage of Ruth. Naomi was asking Ruth to enter an uncertain, compromising situation with a great deal hanging in the balance.

What *was* hanging in the balance? Was Ruth being asked to seduce Boaz there on the threshing floor?

The Levirate Law required that if a man died without an heir, his brother was to marry the widow. The first son born to them then became the legal heir of the deceased husband and continued his name, inheriting his property. If no brother were available to marry the widow, she could ask a more distant relative to do so. Here we see Ruth using a strange old custom to propose marriage to Boaz. The meaning of what she did was to ask for Boaz's total protection.

I've always been glad for many reasons that I was born a woman. One reason is that as a woman in our culture, I never had to risk rejection by having to propose marriage to a man! But Ruth lived in a different time and place. She had to take that risk.

She didn't propose as someone might today. Rather, she asked Boaz to spread his garment over her as a kinsman-redeemer. That act symbolized his intention to protect her. It was like giving and receiving an engagement ring today.

Did he do it? Yes and no. He replied, "Mmmm, yes. I'd like to do that. But I'm not your nearest kinsman-redeemer. There is another man who is closer to Naomi by family ties. He has first choice. It's up to him."

So, no. They were not engaged that night. But Ruth knew that Boaz would marry her if the nearer kinsman reneged. Boaz would settle things properly and leave the outcome to God.

Ruth remained quietly at Boaz's feet throughout the night, then just as quietly went back to Bethlehem before dawn. The curtain descends on our third act as Ruth tells Naomi everything that happened.

Even the schemes of men and women can be used by God to accomplish His purposes. This scheme did not turn sour, not because the circumstances were not right for hanky-panky, but because of the character of Ruth and Boaz. Boaz was concerned for Ruth's reputation. She was safe. Naomi staked the scheme on Boaz's integrity. He proved to be a man of honor. But the question now in the air is, Which guy will get the girl?

The curtain rises on act four. We see Boaz at the city gate, where he knew he would find the nearer kinsman. It was certain that Ruth would soon have a husband. What was *not* certain was who it would be. What up to this point had been a private matter between Naomi, Ruth, and Boaz now had to become public. This was a family matter to be worked out between the kinsmen in a public meeting.

Assembling ten witnesses, Boaz addressed the nearer kinsman about redeeming the property of Elimelech. Easy enough! "Sure," replied the kinsman, "I'll redeem that." It looked easy enough. He knew he would have to marry the widow to do that, but he assumed that Naomi was too old to have children and he would end up with the property with no heir to claim it. Financially the investment was a bargain without risk. How could he lose?

Boaz sprang the clincher: Ruth comes with the property. If the nearer kinsman bought it, he bought her as well. The kinsman would be obliged to father a son by Ruth to perpetuate Elimelech's name over his inheritance. In other words, the kinsman would not be allowed to keep the property when the son was old enough to claim his inheritance.

Suddenly the picture changed for the nearer kinsman. He quickly waived his prior rights of redemption. Boaz would get Ruth! The crowd cheered and Boaz took his bride home.

What follows in this act ties up all the loose ends in our story. It isn't enough that the guy gets the girl or the girl gets the guy. All of that is for a larger purpose.

One purpose lies in perpetuating Elimelech's name over his inheritance. For that Naomi must have a son. But she's too old for that! Not by Jewish law. When her kinsman Boaz and Ruth, her daughter-in-law, produce a son, we see an interesting procession winding through the streets of Bethlehem. The women of the town are carrying this tiny baby and placing him in the arms of Naomi. Naomi now has a son. The bitter woman who complained in the first act about being empty is now *full*. Not only is she well fed. She has a son to carry on her husband's name. This son is Elimelech's legal heir.

Does our story end here? No. We still have that strange genealogy as the climax of our story. What do we learn from it? Pick up reading where I left off earlier: "Salmon the father of Boaz, Boaz the father of Obed, Obed the father of Jesse, and Jesse the father of David" (4:21–22).

David! Suddenly the simple, clever human story of two struggling widows takes on a new dimension. This bitter old woman and this foreign Moabitess become bright threads woven into the fabric of Israel's national history.

God provided bread through Ruth's gleaning. God provided security through Ruth's marriage to Boaz. God provided posterity for Elimelech and Naomi. Even more, God provided a great king for the nation Israel through a foreign woman. God used the faithfulness of ordinary people to accomplish great things.

We find the same genealogy in Matthew 1:3–6:

> Perez the father of Hezron, Hezron the father of Ram, Ram the father of Amminadab, Amminadab the father of Nahshon, Nahshon the father of Salmon, Salmon the father of Boaz, whose mother was Rahab, Boaz the father of Obed, whose mother was Ruth, Obed the father of Jesse, and Jesse the father of King David.

This genealogy does not stop with David. After many more unpronounceable names, we read in verse 16: "and Jacob the father of Joseph, the husband of Mary, of whom was born Jesus, who is called Christ."

Not only did the faithful Ruth and the upright Boaz serve as great-grandparents of Israel's greatest king. They also stand in the line of those through whom God chose to send His Son into the world to bring us salvation.

Many times on a dreary Tuesday afternoon we may find it hard to believe that God is really at work in our lives. God seems hidden from us. Like Naomi in the first act, we can misjudge life because we are not sure God is actively involved in our lives.

Things happen that look like accidents—like Ruth gleaning in the fields of Boaz. Life can seem haphazard and accidental. But over all the seeming accidents in our lives God is at work, making divine appointments with us through the things that happen to us. God is the stage manager in control of all the players on the stage. In the midst of what seems terribly ordinary, He is doing something extraordinary.

It has been said that what we are determines what we see. We may look for God and miss Him because we confuse Him with shining angels. God is found not just in the miraculous and the extraordinary. He is at work in us and through us in the dailiness of life. On a dreary Tuesday afternoon we can get the idea that life is all up to us. But if we belong to God, even when we don't see Him at work, we can be sure that God is moving events on our behalf.

Ruth made a choice on a dusty road between Moab and Bethlehem. She chose to give her loyalty to God and His people. That choice may have seemed insignificant, but it changed Naomi and it changed history.

When you and I choose God and His people, we may hear no bells ringing. But the silence does not mean the choice is not life-changing. As Christian women we are involved in an incredible drama. There are no ordinary days. There are no insignificant choices. If we saw our life as God sees it, we'd be overwhelmed. On a dreary Tuesday afternoon we can remind ourselves that as we choose for God and His people, God will use that choice in ways that exceed our imagination.

Ruth

Questions for group discussion or personal reflection:

1. Describe some event in your life that looked coincidental.
2. What happened that made you look back and conclude that the coincidence was really God at work?
3. How has this affected the way you now look at other "coincidences"?
4. What do you believe about God's concern for your life?

Hannah: How to Deal With Depression

Depression. It happens to the best of people.

In her book *Some Run With Feet Of Clay*, actress Jeannette Clift tells of a conversation she had with a good friend:

> The other day I called one of the most productive Christians I know. "How are you," I asked, thinking it was a somewhat needless question. She was always fine, and had nineteen Scripture verses to prove it! I didn't get her usual answer, though. Instead I got a long pause, and then words all capsulated in one breath.
>
> "Oh, Jeannette, I'm awful! I've been so depressed I don't know what to do. I've had to quit teaching my Bible classes. I'm not doing anything. I don't go out, I don't see anybody. It's all I can do just to get up in the morning, and some days I can't even do that. I'm so ashamed of myself I don't think I can stand it!"

Jeannette explains,

> This was no erratic spiritual novice; this was a mighty Christian soldier! I had seen her in action and praised God for her accuracy as she taught or

counseled. My heart hurt for her. This dear friend was not only down in the depths, but ashamed of herself for being there . . . . Any Christian who is truly shocked by another Christian's depression has not dealt honestly with the possibility of her own.

In the past year I have spent many hours with each of two close friends trapped in the web of paralyzing depression. One woman is the college friend whose faith and commitment to Christ brought me into a personal relationship with God. She and her husband have ministered effectively in Christ's name in East Africa for more than thirty years. During this furlough, however, she has been plunged into severe depression.

My second friend was our colleague in ministry in France. Gifted with a splendid mind, she has not always found doors open to the use of her gifts. Focusing her energies on her family, she and her husband have successfully parented two model sons. Now that the boys are grown, she has not been able to find outlets for all that she has to give. She has lived for several years now in a miasma of depression.

Cynthia Swindoll, executive director of Insight for Living, looked back over the fifteen years in which her life was darkened by depression. In the preface to Don Baker's book, *Depression*, she described her experience:

[It was] black as a thousand midnights in a cypress swamp.

[It was] loneliness that is indescribable.

[It brought] confusion regarding God.

[I experienced] frustration with life and circumstances.

Hannah

[It was] the feeling that you have been abandoned, that you are worthless.
[I felt] unlovable.
The pain was excruciating.

Depression. Did you notice the feelings Cynthia Swindoll had? She felt lonely, confused, frustrated, worthless, unlovable. The pain, she said, was excruciating.

Depression comes in many forms with many symptoms. Perhaps you experience some of them right now. Dr. Timothy Foster lists seven main symptoms of depression in his helpful book, *How To Deal With Depression*.

1. We lose emotional feeling and call it "the blahs." This is that drop in mood in which we say, "I don't feel particularly bad; I don't feel particularly good. I just don't feel much of anything." (Foster reminds us that every emotionally-caused depression starts with a case of the blahs that hangs on and gradually deteriorates.)
2. We become overly self-conscious. Most of the time we do scores of things "on automatic pilot" —we drive the car, cross our legs, scratch our noses or eat dinner with no conscious thought about our actions. But suddenly we have to think about what are usually unconscious decisions. We become self-conscious.
3. Our sleep patterns change. If we normally sleep through the night, we may experience sleeplessness. If we usually function well on seven or eight hours of sleep at night, we may find that we want to sleep all the time.

4. Our eating patterns change. If we have always kept our weight under control with disciplined eating, we may find ourselves reaching for food constantly. Or we may lose our normal appetite and cannot force ourselves to eat.

5. Our crying patterns change. This, too, can take two forms. If we cry regularly, we may find something holding back normal tears. We can't cry. Something blocks the flow of our emotions. Or we may constantly feel that we need to cry. The tears are always only an inch below the surface.

6. We lose confidence in our ability to function. With this we may experience a loss of energy or a lack of initiative.

7. Our mood drops. We feel sad. Depression often starts with feeling "nothing" or the blahs, but eventually the mood drops and a combination of sadness and not caring sets in. Foster states that the presence of only one or two of these symptoms should not alarm us. But if we experience three or more of these symptoms, we may be in depression.

Where does depression come from? In most cases it can be traced to the way we think about ourselves.

Some depressions—about 5 percent of them—are due to a biochemical imbalance and must be treated with medications for life. It is estimated that the other 95 percent of depressions are rooted in emotional factors.

Depression is one way of handling stress. Some people handle stress by becoming physically ill. Others handle stress by over-achieving. Still others handle stress with a drop in mood, by checking out from full participation in life.

Many depressions are caused by some traumatic event in our lives. We can point to those events and explain why we are depressed. Perhaps we feel rejected by someone we value. Or we've just come through a devastating divorce. Or perhaps someone close to us has recently died. Maybe it's a job loss with the threat of losing our house. Depression from loss is the easiest kind to understand.

Other depressions can't be tied to anything specific that has happened to us. We feel down "for no reason at all."

Stress often moves in with us when we focus on ourselves negatively. It comes when we feel powerless to change our situation. We see no alternatives from which to choose. Wherever we turn, we see closed doors or roadblocks shutting us off from happiness. What is merely a minor barrier for one woman becomes an insurmountable obstacle for another.

For many women in their middle years, depression comes when they realize that they will never become what once they dreamed of being. Psychologists call this *involutional melancholia*. Helplessness gradually becomes both a cause and an effect of depression.

All depressed people experience a decrease in self-confidence. If I have low self-esteem, I am much more vulnerable to depression. Something happens to me that confirms my idea that I'm no good. The scenario might look like this:

I work at Denver Seminary where I edit the seminary magazine *Focal Point*. Suppose my boss stops by my office and asks me if I have finished writing a certain article for the next issue. I haven't. So I feel his disappointment in me. I begin to translate that into all kinds of feelings he, in reality, isn't having. If my self-esteem is low, I may conclude that he is disgusted with me for not getting my work done. In fact, I assume, he is getting so disgusted that he will probably fire me. I believe that I deserve whatever he throws at me because I am not a capable person. I am really a failure. Because I am so worthless and really am a handicap at the office, the best thing I can do for Denver Seminary is to quit my job so my boss can hire someone else who will do the job correctly.

Have you ever played that kind of scenario in your head? I have. What happens is that I file this incident away in my memory where I have already filed many other incidents of "rejection." My level of self-confidence sinks a bit lower each time under the weight of this heavy file-drawer full of my failures.

As my self-confidence drains away, I withdraw from people around me, from life in general, and often from God. I'm probably not conscious of my reasons for withdrawing. But the more I withdraw, the more I blame myself. This merely increases the problem. Each time I do this, my self-confidence hits a new low. A vicious cycle begins to spin, leading me into more withdrawal and more feelings of guilt and worthlessness.

Caught in the cycle, I feel totally helpless. Nothing that I do is worth anything. I'm at the mercy of forces that overwhelm me in my inadequacy. I feel myself being sucked down, down in a spiraling whirlpool of depression.

Negative thoughts about ourselves quickly become automatic. We don't have to work at thinking negative thoughts. They become well-ingrained habits strengthened by years of practice. We do not arrive at negative thoughts through logic. We reach most of them with no objective evidence at all. But that doesn't stop us.

Depression creates a frame of mind in which almost everything we experience reminds us of our miserable, helpless condition. This is one reason depression is so painful. We really believe we are to blame for whatever we think is wrong. We hold ourselves responsible for everything bad that happens around us. We emphasize failures and we ignore successes or brush them aside as accidental.

Most of the time, depressed people anchor their sense of self-worth to a very narrow idea of what success is. Unrealistic expectations and impossibly high goals lead us to an overwhelming sense of failure and worthlessness. We set ourselves up to fail. The mental habit of inflating others and deflating ourselves is typical of depression. We end up with distorted perceptions of other people that leave us feeling hopelessly inferior. We see ourselves as stupid, unattractive, untalented, or unspiritual.

So much for a clinical description of depression. It can be helpful to review symptoms and the syndrome. But this isn't a medical journal and depression is not a virus. It is always personal. It happens to real people. We may understand it better if we look at a case study in depression.

Our case study is a woman named Hannah. Her story can help us as we walk with her through and out of her depression. We meet her in 1 Samuel 1. As we get acquainted with her, we discover that she had several sources of stress.

First, she lived at a stressful time in Israel's history. The nation was merely a loose confederacy of tribes united around the worship of Jehovah at the shrine at Shiloh.

Invaders harassed one tribe, then another. Over a period of several hundred years one or another strong leader called a judge would deliver God's people from foreign rule, only to find another Israeli tribe oppressed by a different group of outsiders. As we flip on the news or pick up *Time* or *Newsweek*, we can understand how the tensions in the world and in our town can affect the way we feel.

Not only was Hannah's nation oppressed by neighbor nations, but the religious life of the people was being corrupted by bad priests. The two sons of the high priest made a mockery of the sacrifices, and to make bad matters worse, they were sleeping with the women who served at the entrance to the tabernacle. It was not a time to inspire faith and devotion to God.

Yet, in the midst of religious hypocrisy we find a pious family living in Ramah in the hill country allotted to the tribe of Ephraim. Elkanah, the husband in our story, was a Levite, or a priest. Every year he and his family made the ten-mile journey on foot to the tabernacle or shrine at Shiloh to worship.

Hannah lived at a stressful time both politically and religiously. But she also had to live with stress in her family. In 1 Samuel 1:2 we learn that Elkanah had two wives—Hannah who was beloved but barren, and Peninnah who was less loved but who was very fertile. Some of Hannah's stress came from living in a polygamous marriage.

Polygamy was a fact of life in ancient Israel. Wives were a means of securing children. In Hannah's case it is likely that she was Elkanah's first wife. But because she was infertile, he took a second wife to insure that the family name would not be lost because he had no children.

Hannah

In Hannah's day a woman who failed to produce children was considered to be a useless link in the chain leading to the promised Messiah. Hannah's situation was depressing. Year after year Peninnah produced children. Year after year Hannah suffered emotionally from her infertility, her hopes for a pregnancy receding with every menstrual period. Hannah's stress in the family came not only from being in a polygamous marriage. It also came from her infertility as she lived next to a co-wife who had no trouble conceiving and bearing children.

Hannah's stress, however, was compounded by the fact that Peninnah never stopped needling her about her childlessness. In verse 6 we read that her rival, Peninnah, "kept provoking her in order to irritate her." We know from verse 7 that this had been going on for a long time—"year after year."

One of the most trying times for Hannah appears to have been that annual pilgrimage to Shiloh. Imagine having to walk for ten miles with someone who never stops picking at your inadequacy all the while her children keep bumping into you, wiping their noses on your skirt or asking you to carry them. No wonder Hannah arrived at Shiloh under a black cloud of depression.

How do we know she was depressed? What were some of her symptoms? Elkanah's questions to his wife in verse 8 give us some clues:

Why are you weeping?

Why don't you eat?

Why are you downhearted?

Think back to Foster's seven major symptoms of depression. He said that any three indicated depression. Hannah was depressed. Elkanah's well-intentioned effort to console her did not succeed. Nothing seemed to make any difference. Her despair was overpowering. She withdrew from the comfort of her husband. She withdrew from the family circle.

If you have ever been in the black hole of depression, you can sympathize with Hannah. She was depressed, and she had much in her life to cause her depression. In the midst of it all, however, Hannah had not lost her grip on God. Watch what happens next. In verses 9 and 10 we read:

> Once when they had finished eating and drinking in Shiloh, Hannah stood up. Now Eli the priest was sitting on a chair by the doorpost of the LORD's temple [tabernacle]. In bitterness of soul Hannah wept much and prayed to the LORD.

Note that while we have learned a lot about Hannah in the Bible story up to this point, we only now hear Hannah herself speak. We have had no indication whether she answered Peninnah's jeers or whether she tried to help Elkanah understand her misery when he attempted to console her. Until she speaks in verse 11, she has been a silent suffering figure, very much like many women suffering from depression today. Depression has a way of robbing us of the ability to communicate with the important people around us. We may feel that no one will understand.

In bitterness of soul she wept. But she did something else. She prayed to the Lord. The first time we hear her speak, we hear her addressing God:

> She made a vow, saying, "O LORD Almighty, if you will only look upon your servant's misery and

remember me, and not forget your servant but give her a son, then I will give him to the LORD for all the days of his life, and no razor will ever be used on his head."

Hannah's vow was called a Nazirite vow. Samson, an earlier judge of Israel, was also a Nazirite, "set apart to God from birth," one who would "begin the deliverance of Israel from the hands of the Philistines" (Judges 13:5). Jews believed that anything that had not been touched, plowed, or cut belonged to the Lord. A field was the Lord's until it was plowed. Once a farmer dug it up, it was his and not the Lord's. A person dedicated to the Lord from his birth could not have his hair cut. Once it was cut, he no longer had the same relationship to the Lord. This explains what happened to Samson when Delilah wheedled the secret of his strength from him and a razor was used on his head.

Listen to Hannah as she bargained for a son. Feel her desperation and the urgency of her petition. "Look at my misery! Remember me! Don't forget me! Give me a son!" We hear the heaviness in the words she prays. We see it in the way she prays. Read verses 12 through 16:

As she kept on praying to the LORD, Eli observed her mouth. Hannah was praying in her heart, and her lips were moving but her voice was not heard. Eli thought she was drunk and said to her, "How long will you keep on getting drunk? Get rid of your wine."

"Not so, my lord," Hannah replied, "I am a woman who is deeply troubled. I have not been drinking wine or beer; I was pouring out my soul to the LORD. Do not take your servant for a wicked woman; I have been praying here out of my great anguish and grief."

Added to Peninnah's jibes and Elkanah's ineffective effort at consolation came a sharp rebuke from the high priest. In the midst of her misery, Hannah also had to deal with unjustified criticism from one who misunderstood her.

In the prayer in verse 11 she made a vow that if the Lord gave her the desire of her heart, she would give that son back to Him to serve Him all the days of his life. But that vow and her pleas do not account for all the time Hannah stood praying. In verse 10 we read that "in bitterness of soul Hannah wept much and prayed," and in verse 12, "she kept on praying."

Sympathetic to Hannah's words, Eli told her in verse 17 to "go in peace, and may the God of Israel grant you what you have asked of him." Note that Eli did not know what Hannah had asked God to do. He merely added his prayer to hers to the God of Israel. Yet something happened to Hannah as she stood there praying. Whatever it was, it produced the result we see in verse 18: "Then she went her way and ate something, and her face was no longer downcast."

Hannah joined in the worship of the Lord the next morning, went back to Ramah with Elkanah, and *voila!* before long she was pregnant and gave birth to Samuel whose name means "heard of God." She asked. God heard her and answered her prayer. No wonder her depression lifted! She had the baby she asked for.

Is that really what happened? If our story ended with 1 Samuel chapter 1, we might think that the only way out of depression is to have God intervene in some miraculous way to fill up the empty places in our lives. But the story doesn't end with chapter 1. The key to understanding Hannah's dramatic turn-around in verse 18 lies in her song, or psalm, that we find in 1 Samuel 2:1–10.

Hannah's depression lifted when she took her focus from herself and her situation and put her focus on God. In the midst of her misery she was able to focus on three important facts about God. She underlined these three facts in her song.

The first thing she knew about God is found in 1 Samuel 2:2: "There is no one holy like the LORD; there is no one besides you; there is no Rock like our God." She recognized God's holiness.

What could the fact of God's holiness mean to a woman in depression? Far from being consoling, that could only intensify the feelings of worthlessness and guilt that are often part of depression.

If we define holiness negatively—as a separation from all that is unclean—that may make us feel worse about ourselves. But God's holiness is much more. Charles Ryrie suggests an analogy that may help us understand this word *holy*. Ryrie asks, "What does it mean to be healthy?" It means the absence of illness. But we all know that being healthy is a lot more than simply not being sick. It also means having energy, being physically able to meet the demands of our daily lives.

Holiness is not merely the absence of evil. It is also the presence of positive right. It is God at work doing what is positively right for us. It is the part of God's nature that keeps Him from doing anything in our lives that is not in our best interest. His love is a holy love, a pure love, committed to our best good.

The second thing Hannah knew about God is found in 1 Samuel 2:3b: "For the LORD is a God who knows, and by him deeds are weighed." The New American Standard Bible translates this verse, "For the LORD is a God of knowledge."

Not only does God's holiness keep Him committed to our best good; His perfect knowledge keeps Him from doing anything in our lives that is not perfectly right for us.

Someone has said that "God does not waste His strokes in our lives." That is true. It is true because God *knows* what is best for us. No trial and error. No foul balls or strikeouts. The Lord is a God of knowledge. That gives us confidence in His actions in our lives.

The third thing Hannah knew occupies much of her song. God has power. We see this in 1 Samuel 2:6–7 and in verse 8b:

> The LORD brings death and makes alive;
> he brings down to the grave and raises up.
> The LORD sends poverty and wealth;
> he humbles and he exalts . . . .
> For the foundations of the earth are the LORD's;
> upon them he has set the world.

The Lord of Creation has all power. He can do whatever He wants to do.

That fact without the first two facts might terrify us. If God had all power and we did not know anything else about Him, we'd have reason for a massive depression. We'd all cower in dark corners to escape His wrath or His caprice. But God tempers His power with His commitment to our welfare. He controls His power with His knowledge of what is best for us.

Hannah

My husband, Randy, and I have four adult children. We have always wanted the best for our children. But often we didn't know what was best for them. Which schools would be best? Which activities would be most wholesome? Which church would nurture them? As our children grew up, we made thousands of decisions with their interests at heart. But we were not always sure that our choices were wise.

Not only have Randy and I often lacked knowledge of what was best for our children; there were times when we knew what was best but didn't have the power to make that decision stick. We're finite, fallible parents who have made lots of mistakes along the way. We wanted what was best for our children, but we lacked the knowledge and the power we needed.

God is not finite. God is not fallible. He not only *wants* what is best for us and *knows* with perfect knowledge what is best, He also has the power to make the best happen in our lives. God's holy commitment to us, God's knowledge of what is best for us, and God's power to make the right things happen in our lives are all linked together for our good.

What snapped Hannah out of her depression? She saw God as He really is. God backed His commitment to her welfare with His knowledge and His power to do what needed to be done in her life.

Hannah's story had a happy ending. Samuel was born. She gave him to the Lord, and God gave her three more sons and two daughters. Yet in 1 Samuel 1:18, when she stopped praying, ate some food, and stopped looking sad, she didn't know at that moment how the story would end. She was able to do that because she had met with God and understood who He was and what He could do.

At the beginning of this chapter, I mentioned that psychologists believe depression is related to the way we think about ourselves. It is also true that depression is related to the way we think—or fail to think—about God. Once we bind ourselves to a God-sized God, we have a resource for dealing with depression. We can focus on God—His holiness, His knowledge, His power. We can face our fears and anxieties in the light of His character and His commitment to us.

If depression results from the way we think about ourselves, then it can be lifted by the way we think about ourselves in relation to a holy, knowledgeable, and powerful God who is committed to us.

Robert Browning reminds us that " 'tis looking downward that makes one dizzy." I'm an acrophobe. I don't like being up high on the top of things like fire towers or monuments or skyscrapers. Looking down terrifies me. Browning is right: " 'tis looking down that makes one dizzy." The downward look is the one that leads to depression. The upward look takes away our fear. Look to the God of Hannah, the one who dispelled her depression with a new understanding of His love, His knowledge, and His power.

Questions for group discussion or personal reflection:

1. What does the loving holiness of God mean to you as you face tough places in your life?
2. What does God's complete knowledge of everything mean to you as you live out each day?
3. What does it mean to you that God has complete power to do whatever He wants to do?
4. How do these three facts about God help or hinder you when you are in depressing circumstances?

Abigail: How to Live With a Difficult Husband

Have you ever walked down your street and looked at each house and wondered about the way the people living in that house get along with each other?

Or have you looked at a woman sitting ahead of you in church and thought, "Wow! No question about it, she's got it all! Her handsome Christian husband is a leader in the church. And he treats her like a queen. Their obedient kids never seem to give them any trouble. They have enough money to do whatever they want to do and go where they want to go. I wonder what it would be like to be in such a perfect Christian family."

Sometimes we look at others around us and allow ourselves to slip into a little pity party, thinking how much better other people's lives are than our own.

That's the problem of judging from the outside. What goes on behind the closed doors of a Christian home may be quite different from what *should* go on in a family. The "too perfect" family in the next pew may turn out to be anything but perfect.

A few years ago I spoke at a women's retreat in a south-central state. The women were from a strict church where everyone knew exactly how to cross each "t" and dot each "i." They filled their notebooks, appearing to write down virtually everything I said. But I wondered as I spoke if any of them were *real*. If they were cut, would they bleed?

On Saturday evening, after my third talk, the answer came. Three women approached me after that service. Each one had essentially the same story to tell. Here is one woman's account.

As she walked toward me, it was clear that she was terribly frightened. I could see the fear in her eyes and the nervousness in her twisting fingers. She appeared to be held together with little more than rubber bands. As I tried to put her at ease and probe for the cause of her distress, little by little she told me her story.

She had been married for thirteen years to a man who was a seminary graduate and who had pastored three churches during their marriage. He had recently left the ministry and was trying his hand at selling real estate. The couple had three school-age children. She worked full time as a psychiatric nurse and was bringing in the only regular paycheck at that time. I'll call this couple Jack and Jane.

Jack is an abuser. Yes, he has been a pastor. He is a Christian. He is a seminary graduate. But he is also an abuser. He beats his wife.

Jane is a battered woman. She is intelligent and works in psychiatric nursing. But she is still a battered wife.

Jack has been beating Jane since the first year of their marriage. The beatings take many forms. They start when his rages burst out and he throws everything he can lay hands on at her. Then he pounces on her, pummeling her, pulling her hair out by handfuls.

After this kind of beating, she knows he will return in the night and start in again. So she lies awake all night, "feeling the lion prowling around the house," not knowing how or when he will attack her again. The second attack may be another beating, or it may be a bucket of cold water dumped on her in the dark.

If Jack goes into a rage while they are driving in the car, she fears for the lives of the entire family. Once when she was pregnant, he reached across her, opened her car door and pushed her out into the street from the moving vehicle.

After these attacks Jack becomes very contrite. In public, especially in the church where he is looked up to as a strong leader, he hugs Jane and tells people to look at his beautiful wife. Outside the home he carefully cultivates the impression of being a loving, doting husband.

Jack's rages seem to be precipitated by a number of things. If he catches Jane reading a book, he snatches it away, telling her that if she wants to learn anything, she must ask him and he will teach her.

He has regimented the family into a rigid daily schedule of memorizing verses of Scripture. He has, in fact, devised a system that many families in their church use regularly. In it he chose a key verse for every chapter in the Bible and created a complex memory system for learning these verses. Members of his family also must spend a certain amount of time each day listening to Christian tapes. Anytime a member of the family has not learned the verse perfectly or cannot answer all his questions about the tape, Jack gets very upset.

Several years ago Jane persuaded Jack to see a counselor with her. But the Christian counselor merely lectured her on her duty to be submissive.

As Jane talked to me, it was clear that she had been the brunt of Jack's rages for years. But she found the courage to speak to me only because she now feared for the safety of their three children. She had been taught so well by the church to be submissive that she thought she had no alternative but to stay in the home, take the abuse, and risk being killed as Jack's rages escalated. In fact, as is often true of battered women, Jane actually took the blame for Jack's abuse. He insisted that if she were different, he would not beat her. He did not see himself as an abuser.

That is Jane's story. Two other Janes talked to me that same evening in that south-central state.

Battered women are a fact of life in American society today—and a fact of life within our evangelical churches. One out of every eight women in our country is physically abused. One out of every four is sexually abused. In the United States a woman is beaten every eighteen seconds. One-fourth of these are pregnant. In fact, the battering pattern often begins with a woman's first pregnancy.

Furthermore, nine out of every ten battering incidents are not reported to the police. Legal experts call wife-abuse the "silent crime," one of the most unreported or under-reported crimes in our country.

Many women are not physically battered but are still abused. A major source of depression, for instance, is low self-esteem that comes from being constantly put down by the people closest to us—those who should build us up.

I have a close friend whose husband hardly ever sits down at the dinner table without telling her what food she *should* have cooked and how the food she did cook *should* have been cooked. For more than twenty-five years my friend has endured this torrent of criticism at virtually every meal. No wonder her self-confidence is zero. There are few things, from combing her hair to cleaning the house, that she can do to please him. He picks away at her day and night. He, too, is an abuser. She, too, is an abused woman.

Abuse can be physical. It can be verbal. It can be non-verbal. In whatever form it comes, many Christian women accept this abuse in the name of submission. They are convinced that as Christian women they have no alternative but to take the abuse as God's will for their lives.

A case study in handling an abusive man comes to us in 1 Samuel 25. There we meet a man named Nabal married to a woman named Abigail. As the chapter opens we read in verses 2 and 3:

> A certain man in Maon, who had property there at Carmel, was very wealthy. He had a thousand goats and three thousand sheep, which he was shearing in Carmel. His name was Nabal and his wife's name was Abigail. She was an intelligent and beautiful woman, but her husband, a Calebite, was surly and mean in his dealings.

Nabal was a hard man to live with. God described him as surly and mean. The force of the Hebrew words is that he was harsh and overbearing, a heavy-handed evil-doer.

The servants in Nabal's household would certainly agree with God's description of this man. In verse 17 we overhear a servant talking to Abigail about his master and her husband: "He is such a wicked man that no one can talk to him."

Again, the Hebrew text is very strong. Nabal is "an evil man, a son of Belial," the worst possible statement of contempt that the servant could use. Nabal was a hard man, a difficult man, a severe man. He was impossible to reason with.

The servant was not alone in that opinion. Abigail describes her husband to David in verse 25: "May my lord pay no attention to that wicked man Nabal. He is just like his name—his name is Fool, and folly goes with him."

Nabal was a wicked, difficult man. God said so. The servant said so. Abigail agreed.

Abigail probably got into that unpleasant marriage through no choice of her own. In Abigail's day marriages were arranged by the parents. Nabal was one of the wealthiest men in the region. In verse 2 we learned that he had a thousand goats and three thousand sheep. He was a man of importance and influence. To arrange a marriage with such a man was probably considered a good catch. The fact that Abigail might not be happy in such a marriage was irrelevant.

Unfortunately, today many women by their own choice get into marriages every bit as miserable as Abigail's. The handsome prince turns out to be a toad. The fine Christian leader turns out to be an abuser.

How did Abigail handle her situation, locked in a marriage to a wicked man, blatant in his evil, one whom no one could talk to or reason with? Can we learn anything from her that can help us or help women we know who are trapped in such a situation?

At the very least we need to make the best of a bad situation. Better, we need to find a way to turn a bad situation into something good. When we first meet

Abigail, we see a woman doing everything possible to limit the damage her husband has done. And Nabal had done real damage, so much so that the entire household was in danger of extermination. Let's review the story.

It opens during the time of year when Nabal's three thousand sheep were being shorn. That is a lot of sheep, a lot of shearers, and a lot of work for everyone concerned.

Sheepshearing season in Nabal's day was also a festive time. It was customary for the sheep owner to provide a feast when the job was done. At that feast he would give gifts to everyone who had helped in any way during the year. This was a token of thanks to God and a gesture of goodwill to his neighbors. When David sent his young men to collect what was due to them for the protection they had provided Nabal's shepherds during the year, they had every reason to expect Nabal to be generous.

But instead, in verses 10 and 11, we see Nabal insulting David's men in two ways. First, he should have responded generously to them for the help they had given his shepherds. Second, oriental custom required him to be polite to them even if David had been a deadly enemy. Not only did wicked, surly, mean Nabal refuse to give anything when he should have given freely, but he also scorned David's character in front of his men.

David understood the insult well. His answer, found in verses 12 and 13, was essentially, "Okay, men, put on your swords. We're going to clean up on this guy and on every man and boy in his household." With four hundred armed men David set out to destroy Nabal's household.

At the same time a wise servant ran to Abigail to report what had happened. Read his summary of events in verses 14 through 17:

David sent messengers from the desert to give our master greetings, but he hurled insults at them. Yet these men were very good to us. They did not mistreat us, and the whole time we were out in the fields near them nothing was missing. Night and day they were a wall around us all the time we were herding our sheep near them. Now think it over and see what you can do, because disaster is hanging over our master and his whole household. He is such a wicked man that no one can talk to him.

Abigail had a bad situation on her hands. Four hundred men were on their way to kill not only Nabal but most of the household. She had to act quickly to limit the damage her husband had done.

Knowing yourself, what would you have done in Abigail's place? Would you have run off to save yourself? Would you have organized the servants to fight David's men? Would you have tried to reason with Nabal? Would you have resigned yourself to being killed? Would you have panicked?

In verses 18 through 23 we watch Abigail take decisive independent action:

Abigail lost no time. She took two hundred loaves of bread, two skins of wine, five dressed sheep, five seahs of roasted grain, a hundred cakes of raisins and two hundred cakes of pressed figs, and loaded them on donkeys. Then she told her servants, "Go on ahead; I'll follow you." But she did not tell her husband Nabal.

As she came riding her donkey into a mountain ravine, there were David and his men descending toward her, and she met them. David had just said, "It's been useless—all my watching over this fellow's property in the desert so that nothing of his was missing. He has paid me back evil for good. May God deal with David, be it ever so severely, if by morning I leave alive one male of all who belong to him!" When Abigail saw David, she quickly got off her donkey and bowed down before David with her face to the ground. She fell at his feet and said . . . .

Quick-thinking Abigail hurried to head off trouble at the pass. But what do you think of what Abigail did? As a Christian woman, do you think she acted correctly?

What was really happening as she scurried around to get all the bread baked, the raisins and figs packed, and the wineskins loaded on the donkeys?

First, she did exactly the opposite of what Nabal wanted done. He had turned David's men away, but she prepared large quantities of food for them.

Second, she did this behind his back. The text points out that she did not tell her husband what she was doing.

Do her actions seem right to you?

Look at David's evaluation of what Abigail did in verses 32 and 33:

> David said to Abigail, "Praise be to the LORD, the God of Israel, who has sent you today to meet me. May you be blessed for your good judgment and for keeping me from bloodshed this day and from avenging myself with my own hands."

David saw Abigail's independent action, contrary to Nabal's wishes, as being from God. Abigail stands before us as a model of a wise woman in a difficult situation. She acted in the best interests of her household, and of her husband. The first person to feel the sharp edge of David's sword would have been Nabal. In going against Nabal's wishes, Abigail was saving his life. She had his best interests in mind.

Not every situation women face in bad marriages is a matter of life and death. In Abigail's case it was. In Jane's case it was getting there. A Christian woman's obligation to be a submissive wife ends where people's lives are at risk, either physically or spiritually. A woman is wise who does what she can to limit the damage caused by a difficult man in the home.

Such a woman may have to take immediate steps to ensure safety for herself and her children. If the situation is physically dangerous, she must first get herself and her children out while she can. She must act in the best interests of everyone concerned. This includes her husband's best interest, but it also includes her own and that of any children involved.

It is important to know that a woman is not a failure as a wife and she is not disobedient to God if she takes active steps to preserve life in an abusive situation.

The second step that women must take is to work to turn bad situations into good ones. A person with a cancer may undergo radiation treatment or chemotherapy to keep the cancer from spreading. That is a way of limiting the damage. But if the cancer is operable, the surgeon will also elect to remove it so that the patient can return to full health.

A woman who is twenty-five pounds overweight may work hard to keep from gaining more weight. But she is still carrying around twenty-five pounds too many for her heart. She has to turn a bad situation into a good one by losing those extra pounds. We want to do more than limit the damage. We want to turn a bad situation into a good one.

Abigail successfully headed off David's army from slaughtering Nabal's household. But to keep from having to repeat the rescue operation in another situation, she had to do more than that. Read what Abigail did next in verses 36 and 37:

> When Abigail went to Nabal, he was in the house holding a banquet like that of a king. He was in high spirits and very drunk. So she told him nothing until daybreak. Then in the morning, when Nabal was sober, his wife told him all these things, and his heart failed him and he became like a stone.

It wasn't enough to avert one danger. Nabal had to be confronted with his way of handling life. He had to understand the consequences of his churlish behavior.

One of the things we see in verse 36 is that Abigail chose the right time to talk to Nabal. Often when we confront a difficult person, we choose the wrong time and the wrong place. Abigail wisely waited until the banquet was over, the drunken stupor was passed, and Nabal was sober.

Even though Abigail chose her moment wisely, she took great risks in confronting Nabal. Recall that God had described him as harsh and overbearing, a wicked evil-doer. The servant had called him a hard, severe man that no one could reason with. Abigail had no assurances that Nabal would listen to her. She had no way of knowing whether he would become furious and harm her. But she knew that she had to confront Nabal even though it might not turn out well.

For Nabal, at least, it did *not* turn out well. The shock of his close brush with David's wrath put him into cardiac arrest. We don't know from the passage whether Nabal's attack was brought on by anger over Abigail's meddling in his affairs or if he was enraged that David had gotten the better of him. Perhaps it was sheer terror that struck him when he realized how close he had come to death. Whatever caused the stroke or heart attack, in ten days' time it proved to be fatal. Nabal died.

We also do not know from the biblical text *how* Abigail talked to Nabal on that fateful morning. We know only that she "told him all" that had happened. She took the next necessary step to turn a bad situation into a better one. She confronted him with the consequences of his actions.

In a difficult relationship, don't simply try to limit the damage. Work to make a bad situation good by helping the difficult person see what he is doing to himself and to the important people in his life. Love sometimes has to be tough, because it seeks what is best for everyone involved. A man who abuses his wife or is difficult to live with has his own set of problems. They keep him from being the joyful, fully-functioning person God designed him to be. In the words of David Augsburger's book title, "Care enough to confront." Confront to redeem, not to destroy.

Many women locked in abusive marriages find confronting almost impossible to do. The reasons are many. Often such women have come to believe the husband's reiterated statement that if they were different women, they would be treated differently. Or they have an unbiblical understanding of submission. Or their self-esteem has been destroyed and they have no inner strength to resist the abuse. To take that next necessary step of confronting for change, an abused woman must be sure of her own value before God so that the difficult person does not beat her self-esteem down to nothing. Life with Nabal could not have been happy. Yet Abigail did not allow Nabal's nastiness to make her bitter. This beautiful, intelligent woman was strong enough inside to withstand Nabal's unreasonableness.

How does our story of Abigail end? In verse 38 we learn that ten days after Abigail's talk with Nabal, he died. In verse 39 we discover that David wasted no time once he heard the news of Nabal's death. He proposed marriage to Abigail, and by verse 42 she had already climbed back on her donkey, accompanied by her five maids, to go to David and become his wife. She was a fitting companion for Israel's great and future king.

Abigail's story ended "happily ever after." But that is not the way Jane's story has ended. Nor is it the way the story ends for many other Christian women locked in a difficult marriage. Often we are not released from misery but must learn new ways to cope with misery and turn it into something good.

Not long ago I received another letter from Jane. Up to that time we had exchanged letters through her work address at the hospital. This was the first letter giving me her home address.

I had sent Jane some materials about abusers and battering. Let me share with you her letter starting with her reaction to a "violence index" I had included:

In reviewing all the materials, I believe the most frightening part was taking the violence test and realizing our violence index was into the dangerous level. I had never seen it in black and white before, or had thought about the specific questions that were asked. It sobered me further . . .

In June and July, Jack's behavior or attitude became more hateful and oppressive. More frequently he involved the children, sometimes blaming them for his outburst. He threw a glass at the kitchen sink with such force that the glass shattered all over the kitchen, the counters, floor, etc. Then Jack wanted Mickey, our twelve-year-old, to pick it up. I refused to let Mickey clean up Jack's mess, so it stayed that way for two days. Sherry (age 11) had been away. She walked in and asked, "Was this an accident, or did Dad get mad?" She was told the truth. Stanley (age 9) began getting hysterical every time Jack raised his voice, and that would make Jack more mad.

Let me interrupt Jane's letter for a moment. A year earlier Jane would not have thought to oppose Jack's command to Mickey to clean up the glass. She would not have told Sherry the truth about the shattered glass. Jane had gradually gained inner strength to face Jack with what he was doing. The letter continues,

In the middle of July, I involved another party, Chuck and Margaret . . . . Without Jack knowing about it I took an afternoon off and talked with them. Margaret and I had already been talking some. Chuck is an attorney in town and he is well respected by Jack in every way. They have been friends in our church for years. As you would expect, Jack hit the roof when I told him, the same day, that I had gone. He started with the same accusations of betrayal all over again. I thank God for the courage to have spoken again.

Chuck, Margaret, Jack, and I meet about once a week for 2–3 hours. The first session was the worst, but Alice, the last six weeks have been wonderful. Chuck confronts issues and Jack has not resisted the accountability. Through tears and pain and sorrow he has committed himself to me different from ever before. He has faced the issue as sin and as totally unacceptable. He is genuinely striving for a holy walk. The sessions are difficult because of the painful things we go over, but *so* productive. Once more I have hope.

The children know we are going and are glad, too. Even Sherry's defensive spirit has improved in the last month. There is *so* much work to be done. Daily I still see reflections of the "down with women" attitude, but I have a freedom to discuss it with him later or save it for our time with Chuck and Margaret. Jack has admitted to not giving me any freedom, being jealous of even phone conversations with other women. He doesn't understand why, but he now sees it as abnormal.

Alice, I think there is hope. Please continue to pray with me. I know the road ahead will not be without bumps, perhaps major ones. But my support has widened. Therefore, my base is stronger and so is Jack's.

Please continue to share with other women the need for openness and for friends, that life does not have to be endured but can be lived and even enjoyed. I look forward to see what God has tomorrow for me. Please feel free to share my life with others if it would help. And keep in touch.

Love, Jane

Each time I reread Jane's letter, I remember the terrified woman who for thirteen years had not said one word to one person about all she endured with a difficult man. I thank God that she found the courage to talk to me. I am glad that she found even greater courage to seek out a support system in her hometown. She now has hope. She had none a year ago. I thank God that Jane did what Abigail did. She first took steps to lessen the damage to herself and to her children. She opened up to a trusted friend, who became the beginning of a local support group for her. She gained the courage to refute Jack's unreasonable accusations and to counter his selfish demands.

Little by little, she has forced him to take responsibility for his actions. Now in these weekly sessions with Jack, Chuck, and Margaret, she continues the confrontation that is healing her marriage.

Do you live with a difficult man? Do you have a friend caught in a punishing marriage? Take Abigail as a good role model. Work to make the best of a bad situation. Better, work to turn the bad into good. Let God work in you and through you by His power to redeem a bad relationship.

Questions for group discussion or personal reflection:

1. What do you think the Bible teaches about submission?
2. How does submission apply when a husband is difficult or abusive?

3. Can a woman have a submissive spirit and still take independent action?

4. What biblical principles do you think should guide her?

The Widow of Zarephath:
How to Cope
When Times Are Tough

When I was a little girl, my favorite part of every fairy tale was the last line after the handsome prince had rescued the beautiful damsel and had whisked her off into the sunset. The stories always ended the same way: "And they lived happily ever after."

Most of us, if we are honest with one another, hope for a storybook romance that will have exactly the same ending. And perhaps it *will* be true for you. But if statistics can be believed, for many of us "happily ever after" will be merely a fairy tale.

One reason is that women live longer than men. According to actuarial tables, the average life span for American males is 71.1 years, whereas the average life span for females is 78.3. From childhood up to young adulthood, boys outnumber girls, but around age 24 this starts to balance out and move the other way. From the 1984 population figures for the United States we learn that while currently there are 1.5 million widowed elderly men in the USA, there are 7.8 million widowed women over age 65. Among senior citizens over 65 there are only 67 men for every 100 women.

I have to face the fact that the chances are statistically high that I will outlive my husband. I may have to finish my days alone as a widow.

Another reason "happily ever after" may not happen to some of us is that of all the women who marry during this year, 50 percent of them will end up in a divorce court. We all have friends who have to juggle a necessary job, children, taxes, house repairs, and both mothering and fathering because their marriages dissolved in divorce.

In some cases our friend received the abrupt shock that there was another woman for whom her husband was leaving his family. In other cases our friend finally found the courage to walk out on a man who was physically or emotionally abusive. For the sake of her physical safety and her sanity, she had to get out.

What are the chances that a woman, widowed or divorced, may remarry and live "happily ever after"? Figures from two recent studies differ. The most depressing of the studies reported that a woman of thirty today stands only a 20 percent chance of marrying or remarrying. The more optimistic study reports that a thirty-year-old woman has a 66 percent chance of marrying or remarrying. But that number drops to 41 percent when she reaches thirty-five, to only 23 percent when she reaches forty, and to 11 percent at forty-five. For a superannuated grandmother like me, the percentages would be almost zero.

The reason the figures drop so quickly is clear. There are simply more women in the world than men. We women comprise 51.6 percent of the world's population. Men make up only 48.4 percent. Women outnumber men in the United States by more than five million.

All of this is to warn us that the likelihood of "happily ever after" may be slimmer than we'd like to think. You who live alone may have some excellent advice for those of us who still enjoy a good marriage.

The Widow of Zarephath

Several years ago I taught a weekly Sunday class for women that was made up almost entirely of women going through the shocks and aftershocks of divorce. Deep bonds were forged between us as we cried together and prayed together about the trauma most of them were passing through. I still get together regularly with women from that group. Joann, a divorcee with two teenage sons, struggles to feed, clothe, and shelter her boys on a limited income. As I think about her, I remember another woman alone who also struggled to care for her son. Her story is recorded in 1 Kings 17.

Let me sketch in the background so that you will understand how tough the times were in which this woman lived and nearly died. If you are familiar with the history of Israel, you know that after Moses died, Joshua led the people of God in the conquest of Canaan. Although the Israelites saw the hand of God at work for them, giving them the land through a host of miracles, they quickly turned from God to the pagan practices of neighboring tribes. From time to time godly leaders like Deborah and Samuel came on the scene and brought the conscience of the people back to their God. But most of the time the people were far from Jehovah, the Lord God of Israel.

Then came Israel's greatest kings—David and Solomon. Under their leadership the nation expanded and grew rich and strong. After Solomon's death, however, the tribes split apart into two separate nations, Israel in the north and Judah in the south. Particularly in the north the people were quick to leave their worship of Jehovah, the Lord God of Israel, and to turn to the worship of pagan idols.

Our story opens in the reign of a king in the north named Ahab. The Bible tells us that "Ahab son of Omri did more evil in the sight of the LORD than any of those before him" (1 Kings 16:30). We learn that Ahab married a foreign princess named Jezebel, who introduced the worship of Baal into Israel. Ahab also erected the Asherah, leading the biblical writer to conclude that "Ahab . . . did more to provoke the LORD, the God of Israel, to anger than did all the kings of Israel before him" (v. 33).

As we move into 1 Kings 17, we meet one of the most extraordinary characters in the Bible, Elijah the Tishbite from east of the Jordan River in Gilead. Elijah was a prophet. We first hear him as he delivers a prophetic word to the evil king Ahab:

> As the LORD, the God of Israel, lives, whom I serve, there will be neither dew nor rain in the next few years except at my word (1 Kings 17:1).

The Bible does not tell us how Elijah got into the palace in Samaria in the first place, or what the king said when he heard Elijah's words, or if Jezebel was present. We hear Elijah's prophecy. Then we watch the prophet following God's directions by leaving from the first exit and heading for a hiding spot east of the Jordan by the brook Kerith. There he stayed in a brushy ravine as the drought began. The Bible tells us that God took care of the prophet by sending him ravens to serve him with bread and meat every morning and evening. With water from the brook he survived until "the brook dried up because there had been no rain in the land" (verse 7).

Now what? Would the ravens start bringing Elijah water as well? No. God had another plan. In verse 9 we read His command to the prophet:

The Widow of Zarephath

> Go at once to Zarephath of Sidon and stay there. I have commanded a widow in that place to supply you with food.

What a *strange* command from God! Go to Zarephath which belongs to Sidon? Zarephath was a village attached to the major city of Sidon. It was a kind of suburb of Sidon, Jezebel's hometown. Elijah was hiding out east of the Jordan River in an impenetrable ravine to avoid the wrath of Ahab and Jezebel. Crossing Ahab's territory and taking up residence near Jezebel's home city seemed very risky. But that was God's game plan for Elijah.

It is also strange that God promised Elijah that a *widow* would take care of him. A widow? How could a widow help the prophet?

God seldom does only one thing at a time. He wasn't merely taking care of Elijah. The next step for Elijah also involved the way God would take care of a destitute widow in a foreign land. When things happen in our lives that in some way "don't make sense," it is likely that we merely do not understand how many complex designs God is weaving, working not only in our lives but in the lives of others as well.

One of the impressive things about Elijah is that he did whatever God told him to do. Period. We have no record that he argued with God or dilly-dallied around, killing time in the hope that God would change His mind and issue a more reasonable command. Elijah acted on the word of God as soon as it came to him. Off he headed for Zarephath, about a hundred-mile journey on foot. If Ahab and Jezebel had a price on the prophet's head, he probably made the journey by back roads and rarely-used mountain paths.

We finally meet the poor widow, responsible for a young son and herself, as Elijah nears the village of Zarephath:

> When he came to the town gate, a widow was there gathering sticks. He called to her and asked, "Would you bring me a little water in a jar so I may have a drink?" (1 Kings 17:10).

A widow was there gathering sticks. No name. No details about her age or her appearance or her station in life. A widow gathering sticks.

As she worked, she was undoubtedly startled when a strange man called out to her and asked her to get him a drink of water.

Without question Elijah must have been both thirsty and hungry after his long trek from east of the Jordan River. If Kerith had dried up, then it was likely that other brooks along the way to Sidon were also dry.

Note in passing that Elijah suffered from the drought as much or more than the evil king Ahab suffered. Innocent people all over Canaan suffered. We'd like to think that hurt comes only to evil people and that good people are spared from suffering. This is not so. We live in a fallen world, a world shot through with sin. We *all* have to live with the consequences of a fallen world. We *all* experience the evil things that come because evil people make evil decisions. Elijah suffered. The widow suffered. Hundreds of other people suffered because Ahab had forsaken the Lord his God and had introduced Baal worship to Israel.

Thus we see a weary, hungry, thirsty prophet asking help from a widow bent over picking up a few sticks.

The Widow of Zarephath

"Please? Would you get me a drink?"

As she turned to go after some water for him, he called after her, "And bring me, please, a piece of bread."

Watch the drama unfold now as our nameless widow speaks for the first time in verse 12:

> "As surely as the LORD your God lives," she replied, "I don't have any bread—only a handful of flour in a jar and a little oil in a jug. I am gathering a few sticks to take home and make a meal for myself and my son that we may eat it—and die."

Elijah! Did you hear what she said? Don't ask this poor woman for her last bit of food!

Elijah, perhaps you asked the wrong widow. Maybe this isn't the one God has commanded to provide for you. How could she? She has nothing! She and her son will die of starvation after they eat this last morsel of bread she is preparing to bake.

Read Elijah's reply in verses 13 and 14:

> Elijah said to her, "Don't be afraid. Go home and do as you have said. But first make a small cake of bread for me from what you have and bring it to me, and then make something for yourself and your son. For this is what the LORD, the God of Israel, says, 'The jar of flour will not be used up and the jug of oil will not run dry until the day the LORD gives rain on the land.' "

What a test of faith this widow faced! She had to make a quick decision. On what basis would she decide?

She was a foreigner. She probably had not grown up hearing about Israel's God. What would she think of Elijah's word that the Lord, the God of Israel, would see to it that the jar of flour would not be used up and the jug of oil would not run dry? In that moment she had to decide either to trust God's word through this stranger and do as he asked, or decide that he was a fool and ignore his request. We see her decision in verse 15:

> She went away and did as Elijah had told her. So there was food every day for Elijah and for the woman and her family. For the jar of flour was not used up and the jug of oil did not run dry, in keeping with the word of the LORD spoken by Elijah.

As you think about the widow's decision to share her last bit of food with Elijah that day, what do you think prompted her action?

She might have concluded that she and her son would die anyhow and might as well share what little they had with a stranger in need. After all, she lived under the Middle Eastern obligation of hospitality to strangers.

Or she may already have had a strong prompting in her soul that God, the God of Israel, had sent this prophet to her. In her day to house a prophet under one's roof was a great honor. Perhaps something good *would* come of it if she gave the little she had to this man of God.

Or she may have latched onto Elijah's promise that if she gave what she had, Israel's God would see to it that her needs and the needs of her son would be met as long as the drought lasted. Was it with faith that she reached out to the promise?

The Widow of Zarephath

Sometimes when we have no faith of our own, someone else's faith can become contagious enough to infect us as well. Elijah's certitude about God's promise and His ability to deliver on that promise were strong. Perhaps his faith infected her. Whatever happened, she was willing to stake her life and her son's life on that word.

We don't know what went on in that widow's mind that day in Zarephath nearly three thousand years ago. We do know that she *acted* on the word of God. She heard God's word and she obeyed it. She did what Elijah asked her to do.

Sometimes when our backs are against the wall, we have to decide whether to obey the Word of God or choose to do what appears to be in our best interest. Particularly is this true for a woman alone. Often resources are short and needs are great. We may have to live through thirty-one-day months with twenty-one-day paychecks. When God asks us to go the extra mile and share the little we have with someone even needier, it may be hard to decide what to do. Should we do what God asks of us, or should we guard the little we have for ourselves?

The next time you are tempted to ignore God's word to you and do the self-protective thing, remember the widow of Zarephath. What would have happened to her and to her son that day had she refused to obey the word of the Lord?

If our story ended here, we might conclude that things work out for us when we choose to believe God's word and God sends a prophet our way and works a miracle. After all, because the widow chose to share what little she had with God's messenger, every day as long as the drought lasted there was flour in the jar and oil in the jug. Every day she, her son, and the prophet had bread to eat. God provided for their physical needs.

But that's not the end of the story. Look at the rest of it in 1 Kings 17:17–24:

> Some time later the son of the woman who owned the house became ill. He grew worse and worse, and finally stopped breathing. She said to Elijah, "What do you have against me, man of God? Did you come to remind me of my sin and kill my son?"
>
> "Give me your son," Elijah replied. He took him from her arms, carried him to the upper room where he was staying, and laid him on his bed. Then he cried out to the LORD, "O LORD my God, have you brought tragedy also upon this widow I am staying with, by causing her son to die?" Then he stretched himself out on the boy three times and cried to the LORD, "O LORD my God, let this boy's life return to him!"
>
> The LORD heard Elijah's cry, and the boy's life returned to him, and he lived. Elijah picked up the child and carried him down from the room into the house. He gave him to his mother and said, "Look, your son is alive!"
>
> Then the woman said to Elijah, "Now I know that you are a man of God and that the word of the LORD from your mouth is the truth."

That's the end of the story. We hear no more about this nameless widow. But before we leave her, we can profit from examining this second major test of faith in her life.

The Widow of Zarephath

In the first episode with Elijah, she was tested in the area of her present needs—food for the next meal. Now in this second incident she was tested in the area of her future. Her son was taken from her. This was the boy who would care for her in her old age, who would provide for her when she could no longer do so. Her future was wrapped up in him. Now he was gone.

In the first test she had to make a choice and *act*. In the second test she had no choices to make. There was nothing she could do. She was absolutely helpless in the face of this disaster.

Life comes at us both ways, doesn't it? Sometimes we can make decisions and act and make provision for the next day, the next month, or the next year. Other times we are confronted with tragedies that leave us helpless and unable to act. There is absolutely nothing that we can do. This was the case for the widow in Zarephath.

But God had not left her without resources. She had God's presence in the person of His prophet, Elijah. Elijah, a man in touch with God and a man of faith, interceded for the widow when she had no place to turn. God heard the prophet's prayer and He restored life to the widow's son.

It was another miracle. Their daily needs were met with one miracle—the jar of flour and the jug of oil that did not fail. Now her future needs were met with another miracle—the resurrection of her son to life.

God seldom comes to us through a great prophet like Elijah. Nor does He usually supply our needs with obvious miracles. But the fact that we do not see Elijah and experience dramatic supernatural interventions does not mean that God isn't just as concerned about our lives and our needs.

One early evening while we were still living in Vienna, Austria, my husband, Randy, phoned home while he was out on pastoral visitation. A family in our church had just moved that day and could not get their stove hooked up to cook some dinner. Could we feed them that evening?

"Of course," I answered. Then I went to the kitchen to see what was there that could feed four adults and two teenage boys with massive appetites. I found enough meat for the entree and enough fresh vegetables for a salad. But no potatoes. No pasta. Only one cup of rice. The food stores were already closed for the night. We'd have to make do with what was there.

I filled the largest cooking pot I owned with water and put it on to boil. Then I held the cup of rice above the boiling water and prayed, "Lord, this one cup of rice has to feed Reid and Bette and Brad and Reidy—and Randy and me." With a little bit of faith, a lot of doubt, and some resignation because I had nothing else in the house to cook, I poured the rice into the water, put the cover on the pot, and went about preparing the rest of the meal.

That evening we had a great time with our guests. The rice filled my largest serving bowl. Everyone had plenty. There was rice left over.

I don't know what happened inside that cooking pot that night. I do know that God used our resources to do His work and some small miracle took place.

Now hear me well. I am not advocating that we set aside our brains and neglect our plain duty to work so that our daily needs will be met. But I do know that at times when we have done everything possible and God asks one more thing of us, He will be there to provide.

I cook rice often. I get precisely the amount of cooked rice that the package tells me I'll get from the amount of raw rice I pour into the cooking pot. That's because God has already provided me with the means to buy groceries. We do not lack. God usually works through the jobs He has provided and through the intelligent use of our resources. But when our backs are against the wall, when it looks as if we have no way out of our dilemma, God is there in the dilemma and will see us through it.

Did you notice in 1 Kings 17 what has happened to the widow's faith? In verse 12 she spoke of "the LORD your God." He was not her God. But somehow there was enough faith to act on Elijah's statement that the Lord, the God of Israel, would provide for them every day throughout the long drought.

When her son died, however, the widow accused Elijah (verse 18) of coming to remind her of some past sin and to punish her by taking her son away. She called him a messenger of God's vengeance. She really did not understand that he was also a messenger of God's love.

Her present needs were cared for and her future was assured as her son was returned to life. Then the widow made the declaration of faith with which the chapter ends: "Now I know that you are a man of God and that the word of the LORD from your mouth is the truth."

If the widow had never been tested, her faith would not have grown. Her understanding of who God was would not have progressed. She would have remained ignorant and untrusting.

It is through the horrible tests in life—tests in which we have to make hard decisions and times in which we have no decisions we can make—it is in these difficult moments that faith grows.

Most of the time we don't *see* God at work. We rarely experience His dramatic obvious miracles. The jar of flour *does* get used up. The jug of oil *is* empty. Our future is ripped away from us in one way or another. We may stand shorn of everything we count important. We may sit bereft of all that gives meaning to our lives.

But like the widow of Zarephath, when our backs are against the wall, we are not alone. We may *feel* alone. But with faith—sometimes faith borrowed from someone else—we begin to realize that God *is* there. In the shadows, perhaps. But He does keep watch over His own.

Ponder the words of our Lord Jesus Christ in Matthew 6:25–31:

> I tell you, do not worry about your life, what you will eat or drink; or about your body, what you will wear. Is not life more important than food, and the body more important than clothes? Look at the birds of the air; they do not sow or reap or store away in barns, and yet your heavenly Father feeds them. Are you not much more valuable than they? Who of you by worrying can add a single hour to [her] life?
>
> And why do you worry about clothes? See how the lilies of the field grow. They do not labor or spin. Yet I tell you that not even Solomon in all his splendor was dressed like one of these. If that is how God clothes the grass of the field, which is here today and tomorrow is thrown into the fire, will he not much more clothe you, O you of little faith? So do not worry, saying, "What shall we eat?" or "What shall we drink?" or "What shall we wear?" For the pagans run after all these things, and your

heavenly Father knows that you need them. But seek first his kingdom and his righteousness, and all these things will be given to you as well.

Life boils down to our perspective, doesn't it? God, who saw a pitiful pagan widow in a dusty coastal village called Zarephath, also sees you and sees me. God taught her about Himself by bringing her to the end of herself and the end of her resources. He often teaches us to trust Him best when we have come to the end of ourselves and our self-sufficiency.

When the chips are down and our backs are against the wall, the God of Elijah and the God of the widow of Zarephath is still our God. He is there. We can trust and not be afraid.

Questions for group discussion or personal reflection:

1. How do you handle life when you have a twenty-one-day paycheck that has to stretch over a thirty-one-day month?
2. How does God enter into the picture when things are not going well?
3. What spiritual resources do you think exist but you find hard to tap into?
4. What do you think would make a difference to help you trust God more when things are tough?

Huldah and Miriam: How to Use Your Spiritual Gifts Wisely

Do you have a close friend or relative in a distant city to whom you send a gift on her birthday or at Christmas? If you care about that person, you probably put a lot of time into choosing the gifts you send. You may also read at least two hundred cards at the card shop as you look for exactly the right one to send.

Let's assume you've been sending cards and gifts to this special friend for the past ten years. Now the opportunity has come up to visit that friend after all these years. While your head is full of all the things you want to do when you get there, you also look forward to seeing your gifts in her home.

After excited greetings at the airport, you find you can hardly wait to arrive at her home. As you enter, you glance surreptitiously around the living room, the dining room, the kitchen, the bathroom. You don't see any of the things you've purchased and wrapped so carefully over the years. No sign of the needlepoint pillow you spent months making. Nor of the bone china cup and saucer you knew she would love.

When you open the guest room closet, however, you spot them. All of your packages are still wrapped in brown paper, sitting in a row on the closet shelf.

How does that make you feel? What do you think of this friend on whom you have lavished so much time and thought and money?

We all know that such a scenario is not likely to happen. When gifts arrive, most of us tear off the paper to see what a thoughtful friend has given to us. Do you think it is even possible that someone could have given us wonderful gifts that we've left unopened?

Is it possible that God has given us gifts that we have stacked carelessly on the shelf of our lives—unopened, unused? Have we received spiritual gifts we've never bothered to unwrap? Or perhaps we've unwrapped them, but, because we didn't know what to do with them, we've tossed them on a guest room closet shelf.

A number of women in the Old Testament received spiritual gifts. We will look at two who used them. One of them was nearly destroyed by her spiritual gift. As we look at these two women, we may learn how to unwrap and use our gifts wisely.

HULDAH

In 2 Kings 22 we meet a remarkable woman named Huldah. She lived in Jerusalem at a solemn time in Israel's history. The great kings of Israel, David and Solomon, had passed from the scene. The nation split into two rival groups. Ten tribes in the north called themselves "Israel," and the two remaining tribes in the south were known as "Judah." Idolatry, Baal worship, ritual prostitution, and human sacrifice had crept into the religious worship of the people. The Lord God of Israel was sometimes seen as only one god among many. Sometimes He was not worshiped at all. The leaders of Israel were so evil that in 722 B.C. the northern ten tribes were taken captive by the Assyrians and were carted off east of the Euphrates in exile.

In the south the little nation of Judah fended off invaders. But it was only a matter of time before it, too, would be taken captive. Judah's kings were evil men. The nation was corrupt.

In the midst of this a prince named Josiah was born. His grandfather Manasseh had been one of the most evil kings in Judah. His father Amon wasn't much better and was murdered by his officials when Josiah was eight years old.

This young boy suddenly found himself on the throne of Judah at the ripe age of eight. One good thing happened. Somewhere, perhaps from his mother Jedidah or from his tutors, Josiah learned to walk in the law of the Lord God and to follow the example of his ancestor, King David. In the midst of generations of totally corrupt rulers came a young boy whose heart was turned toward God.

When Josiah was twenty-six years old and had been reigning for eighteen years, he ordered some renovations on the great temple Solomon had built. Money had been collected and it was time to get on with the repairs.

God's house had been desecrated with pagan worship and was in shambles. The amount of work that needed to be done was staggering. The work started. Carpenters, masons, and builders swarmed over the temple. Timbers and dressed stonework were hauled in for the job.

In the midst of all this activity a workman stumbled across an ancient scroll. What was it? What did it say? What did it mean? No one knew. Does it strike you as strange that even Hilkiah the high priest did not know the meaning of this sacred writing? He reported the find to Shaphan the secretary. Shaphan the secretary passed the word to Josiah the king.

When Josiah listened to the words Shaphan read him from the scroll, his reaction was immediate. He tore his robes and ordered everyone within shouting distance to find out about this book. Whatever Shaphan read to Josiah, it clearly spoke of the destruction God would bring on His people if they departed from His ways. There was no doubt in Josiah's mind that, if these things were true, his kingdom was in great danger. Read Josiah's reaction in 2 Kings 22:13:

> Go and inquire of the LORD for me and for the people and for all Judah about what is written in this book that has been found. Great is the LORD's anger that burns against us because our fathers have not obeyed the words of this book; they have not acted in accordance with all that is written there concerning us.

Josiah was frightened. But he was also a man of action. He ordered all the leaders in the kingdom to find out what this book meant. To do this they would have to find a prophet, someone who could discern the meaning behind the written words.

A number of prophets lived in Jerusalem at that time. From Jeremiah 1:2 we know that Jeremiah had been receiving prophetic messages from God for Judah for at least five years at the time the scroll was found. In Zephaniah 1:1 we discover that Zephaniah was also prophesying in Judah during the reign of Josiah. Does it seem strange, then, that in 2 Kings 22:14 we read that Hilkiah the priest and the rest of the king's counselors turned to a *woman* for an explanation of the word of the Lord? They sought out Huldah, a prophetess who

134

was the wife of Shallum, the keeper of the royal wardrobe.

Sometimes we hear the statement that God is forced to use women to do men's work when no men are available. People use that reasoning to excuse work that women have done on the mission field. It is hard to support that idea from our text. God had given a special spiritual gift to the woman Huldah, and then God used her to speak His message both to the high priest and to the king.

We know very little about Huldah. Verse 14 tells us that she lived in the Second District. The King James Version of the Bible interprets this to mean that she lived "in the college." On some old maps of Jerusalem, the Second District is called the university district. Jewish tradition tells us that Huldah was probably a teacher.

What we do know about her is that she was a prophetess. She received God's word and delivered it to men and women. The fact that Hilkiah the high priest and the other officers from the palace sought her out without hesitation tells us that she was well known for her discernment and her piety. She could be trusted to tell them the true words of God sharply, clearly, accurately.

What were those words God gave her for a high priest and a king? Look at what Huldah told that impressive group of men from the palace in verses 15 through 20:

> This is what the LORD, the God of Israel, says: Tell the man who sent you to me, "This is what the LORD says: I am going to bring disaster on this place and its people, according to everything written in the book the king of Judah has read. Because they have forsaken me and burned incense to other gods and provoked me to anger by all the idols their hands have made, my anger will burn

against this place and will not be quenched." Tell the king of Judah, who sent you to inquire of the LORD, "This is what the LORD, the God of Israel, says concerning the words you heard: Because your heart was responsive and you humbled yourself before the LORD when you heard what I have spoken against this place and its people, that they would become accursed and laid waste, and because you tore your robes and wept in my presence, I have heard you, declares the LORD. Therefore I will gather you to your fathers, and you will be buried in peace. Your eyes will not see all the disaster I am going to bring on this place."

So they took her answer back to the king.

Strong words. What did you notice in Huldah's prophetic announcement? One thing is clear: she did not mince words. She spoke decisively and to the point. She did not beat around the bush. She didn't couch her word from the Lord in apologies. She didn't refuse to answer because she was a woman and didn't want to offend the men. Huldah simply used her gift. Period. We don't hear of her again. She was on stage and off stage in one quick, dramatic scene.

Another thing is clear from Huldah's words: Her message was from the Lord, the God of Israel. Four times she underscored that. "This is the word of the LORD, the God of Israel." She knew that God was speaking through her. She didn't hem and haw, saying, "Well, if you want my opinion about this scroll," or "My idea about this book is . . ." She knew she was God's spokesperson.

The high priest, Hilkiah, and the rest of the crowd from the palace also knew that. They didn't stand around discussing whether they should get a second opinion. They took her message back to the king. Because they and he believed Huldah's message to be from God, the king instituted a religious reform in Judah that was the most sweeping ever during the time of the divided kingdoms.

There stands Huldah, the prophetess, a woman of distinction who used her God-given spiritual gift for the benefit of a nation.

MIRIAM

A second prophetess in the Old Testament is one you probably know better than you know Huldah. Her name is Miriam and her career was very different from Huldah's. Huldah was a married woman, probably a teacher, who lived quietly in Jerusalem. Miriam, on the other hand, is the first unmarried mature woman we meet in the Bible. Possibly the slaughter of Hebrew boy babies by the Egyptians while she was growing up meant that there weren't enough men to go around when she reached adulthood. Or it may be that her prophetic vocation was a full-time calling that caused her to forego marriage. As we meet Miriam at three key points in her life, we see her as a vigorous leader with a quick and creative mind.

We begin with Exodus 2:1–10, where we meet her in a setting most familiar to all of us:

> Now a man of the house of Levi married a Levite woman, and she became pregnant and gave birth to a son. When she saw that he was a fine child, she hid him for three months.
>
> But when she could hide him no longer, she got a papyrus basket for him and coated it with tar and pitch. Then she placed the child in it and

put it among the reeds along the bank of the Nile. His sister stood at a distance to see what would happen to him.

Then Pharoah's daughter went down to the Nile to bathe, and her attendants were walking along the river bank. She saw the basket among the reeds and sent her slave girl to get it. She opened it and saw the baby. He was crying, and she felt sorry for him. "This is one of the Hebrew babies," she said.

Then his sister asked Pharaoh's daughter, "Shall I go and get one of the Hebrew women to nurse the baby for you?"

"Yes, go," she answered. And the girl went and got the baby's mother. Pharoah's daughter said to her, "Take this baby and nurse him for me, and I will pay you." So the woman took the baby and nursed him. When the child grew older, she took him to Pharoah's daughter and he became her son.

This familiar story about Moses hidden in the bulrushes is one most of us learned when we were very young. We know how the courageous and resourceful older sister, Miriam, saved the life of Israel's greatest leader and law-giver.

Think about the courage it took for a Hebrew slave girl to walk up to the princess, the daughter of a hostile ruler, and suggest that she be allowed to run and find a nurse for this tiny Hebrew baby. Imagine the alert mind that enabled Miriam to come up with a scheme that would not only save her little brother from death but would also allow his own mother to have him back to care for openly.

Miriam had strong natural gifts. But she had something more. Look at her eighty years later in Exodus 15:20:

> Then Miriam the prophetess, Aaron's sister, took a tambourine in her hand, and all the women followed her, with tambourines and dancing. Miriam sang to them: "Sing to the LORD, for he is highly exalted. The horse and its rider he has hurled into the sea."

Miriam the prophetess. Moses, after forty years in the Egyptian palace and then forty years in the desert of Midian, had become the reluctant mouthpiece of the Lord, the God of Israel. He had confronted Egypt's ruler not once but ten times, demanding the release of the Hebrew people. God overruled Pharaoh in a series of miracles, and now the Israelites stood on the east side of the Red Sea. They were free after centuries of slavery. They were safe.

As Moses and all the people sang a song of praise to God for delivering them dramatically from the power of the Egyptians, Miriam led the women in singing and dancing. It was a great scene! It may have been a high point in Miriam's life.

We don't know much about how Miriam used her spiritual gift as a prophetess. We do know that God gave her a leadership role in the nation Israel. The prophet Micah tells us that in Micah 6:4: "I brought you up out of Egypt and redeemed you from the land of slavery. I sent Moses to lead you, also Aaron and Miriam."

Miriam worked with her two brothers to lead the people of God. We don't know the specifics of her leadership role. We know only that she was more than just a sister of two famous brothers. She was part of the team.

It would be nice to close the book on Miriam while she was successful. But we can't do that. We have to move on to scene three. We find this in Numbers 12:1–2:

> Miriam and Aaron began to talk against Moses because of his Cushite wife, for he had married a Cushite. "Has the LORD spoken only through Moses?" they asked. "Hasn't he also spoken through us?" And the LORD heard this.

Oh-oh. Instead of staying on Moses' team, Miriam and Aaron got on Moses' back. Look carefully at what was happening.

The subject of their complaint was that Moses had married a Cushite woman. It may have been that Zipporah, his first wife, daughter of Jethro, had died and he had remarried. That is not clear in the text. What is clear is that a Cushite is not a Hebrew. Cush was the land south of Egypt. This woman was not "one of them." She was a foreigner.

Note that while the subject of their complaint was Moses' marriage to this woman from Cush, the questions they were asking gave away their real complaint: "Has the LORD spoken only through Moses? Hasn't he also spoken through us?"

What does that sound like? Could it be that such spiritually-attuned people like a high priest and a prophetess were envious? Were they jealous? God apparently thought so. Note His response to them in Numbers 12:6–8:

> When a prophet of the LORD is among you, I reveal myself to him in visions, I speak to him in

dreams. But this is not true of my servant Moses; he is faithful in all my house. With him I speak face to face, clearly and not in riddles; he sees the form of the LORD. Why then were you not afraid to speak against my servant Moses?

God decided it was time to make clear to both Miriam and Aaron that while they had spiritual gifts, power and prestige, they were *not* in the same category as Moses. Miriam may have had visions and dreams as a prophetess. But God dealt with Moses even more directly than that.

This brilliant woman Miriam blew it. She let her selfish ambition get the best of her. She thought Moses had no monopoly on divine communication. God set her straight because He does not look at arrogance and presumption as small sins.

The moment I begin looking at someone else in leadership and start comparing myself and my gifts to what God has given her, I open myself to envy and selfish ambition. The New Testament writer James talks about not only the danger in this kind of thinking, but the source behind it. We find his counsel in James 3:13–17:

Who is wise and understanding among you? Let [her] show it by [her] good life, by deeds done in the humility that comes from wisdom. But if you harbor bitter envy and selfish ambition in your hearts, do not boast about it or deny the truth. Such "wisdom" does not come down from heaven but is earthly, unspiritual, of the devil. For where you have envy and selfish ambition, there you find disorder and every evil practice.

Miriam succumbed. She had trouble accepting the position God marked out for *her*. She had a lofty place in Israel. She was one of the nation's three leaders. She had a dramatic spiritual gift. But she lost her perspective, insulted her brother Moses, and in the process, she insulted God.

Milton, the English poet, commented that hell is a democracy while heaven is a theocracy. No one gets to vote on God. Angels don't decide what roles they want to play, whether they are seraphs or cherubs. God makes those decisions.

It is the same for us. He is the same God who gives us our gifts and marks out the place where we use them. He knows what gifts we need and how we can best fit His kingdom plans. We move into a dangerous mindset when we decide that we are better judges of our gifts, place, and service than God is. Miriam overlooked that.

God dealt with her swiftly and surely. She became leprous—covered with leprosy, the most loathsome disease known in the ancient world. Contagious and now quarantined from the Israelites, she was shunned by the very people she had impressed with her importance.

As you read the account in Numbers 12, does it strike you that both Aaron and Miriam had complained against Moses, but only Miriam was stricken with leprosy? Does that seem fair?

Notice in verse 1 whose name comes first: Miriam's. The Hebrew text actually reads, "Miriam and Aaron, *she* began talking against Moses." Miriam was the ringleader. Perhaps Aaron was once again the pliable man who at Mount Sinai had let the people talk him into making the golden calf.

In Miriam's punishment we see her stature. To those to whom much has been given, Jesus reminds us, much will be required. Miriam was the strong person. She deserved a strong punishment.

From Numbers 12 we learn how the story ended. For seven days Miriam was banished outside the Israelite camp. For seven days all progress toward the Promised Land halted. For seven days the people of God waited. Miriam had misinterpreted her gifts and her calling, and in the process had harmed the progress of the people of God. Only after she had seven days to think things over and straighten out her attitude did God hear Moses' prayer and heal her.

When we receive spiritual gifts from God, we cannot misuse them without bringing harm to the people of God. Whatever gifts we have, we must use them with the right spirit. Or we may do more damage than good.

Spiritual gifts come from God. He means for us to use them. From Huldah we learn that when we have spiritual gifts from God, we are to use them without excessive modesty, without apologies, without hemming and hawing around. *God* has given us these gifts. Heaven isn't a democracy where we are asked to vote on our gifts. We take what a sovereign and good God gives us.

How do you feel about the spiritual gifts God has given *you*? Are you comfortable with them? Perhaps you have gifts that puzzle you. Is your gift teaching? Where can you use that? Begin by using your gift in the opportunities God gives you. Learn from Miriam's mistake not to overestimate your gift. Don't insist on using your gift only in places of obvious leadership. Perhaps God wants you to use that gift with three-year-olds for a while. Prove your gift where God opens the door for you. Start where you are allowed to start. When you have proved your gift in one place, another door will open.

The first step all of us must take is to accept our gifts as from God to benefit His people. We must take them off the shelf of our lives, unwrap them, and put them to use. We are to use them, not with selfish ambition, but humbly for God's glory. With a godly attitude and a willingness to use our gifts freely and fully, we will be amazed by all that God can do through us.

You may think that God has made a mistake and has given you a gift you know you cannot use. If you believe that God is both sovereign and good, then you must believe that He purposes to use a gift for which you think you have no aptitude or interest. The problem may be simply a question of practice to develop skill in the use of that gift.

For many years I taught little fingers to play the piano. I know that practice makes perfect. The converse is true as well: No practice makes very imperfect music. Many spiritual gifts must be honed by constant practice before we feel comfortable using them. We practice to become skillful in using our gifts.

I have two friends who are now concert pianists. Both began piano studies with the same simple two-finger songs and endless scales. They arrived where they are today because they cared enough about music to put in the endless hours of practice. Can we expect to find shortcuts to skilled service for God? No. Practice makes perfect.

At the same time, as we use our gifts for God's people, God's power will work through our gifts. These gifts are, after all, the expression of God's power and presence in our lives. They are the evidence of God's work within us. They can transform us as we put them to work. That is reason enough to unwrap them and put them to use.

Choose to use your gifts. Use them as Huldah did—unself-consciously, without apologies, without excuses. Use them where and how God calls you to use them. Use them for God's glory alone.

Questions for group discussion or personal reflection:

1. What spiritual gifts have you received from God?
2. How do you know you have them?
3. Describe how you have honed your gifts for more effective service.
4. Describe ways you have found to use your gifts.

Esther: How to Use Power to Benefit Others

Are you ready for a quick trip on a magic carpet to the ancient land of the Arabian Nights? We're off to Persia when it was the greatest empire on earth, greater than any empire that had ever existed before. So hang on tight as we fly through the air with the greatest of ease to the lavish, luxurious capital of Persia called Susa (or Shushan in some Bible translations).

As we make the descent to Susa, known as "the City of Lilies," we can see the magnificent summer palace gleaming in the Mesopotamian sunshine. Gliding to a soft landing in the outer court of the palace, we are first struck by the great marble pillars surrounding us. Cords of fine white linen and purple material in great silver rings are attached to the pillars. They hold back sumptuous blue and white linen curtains so that we get the long view of this summer playpen for the mightiest ruler on earth. His name in the King James Version is Ahasuerus. The New International Version gives us his historic identification as Xerxes.

From our history books, inscriptions, and Persian writings, we know quite a bit about Xerxes. He was not a particularly nice person to be around. As a matter of fact, you could not be certain of your own future if you got close to Xerxes and then made one wrong step. He was a capricious tyrant. His will was absolute. He held the power of life and death with a nod of his head.

For example, when Pythius, one of his leading officials, offered him four million dollars to pay for one of the Persian military campaigns, Xerxes was so pleased that he refused the money and gave Pythius a gift instead. However, when Pythius later suggested that perhaps his oldest son might be excused from fighting in that campaign, Xerxes was so angry that he hacked the boy in half and marched his army between the pieces. To say the least, Xerxes was temperamental.

Another time a storm at sea destroyed three hundred of his ships. Xerxes grabbed a strap, went down to the seashore and beat the sea three hundred times—once for each ship —to punish it.

Xerxes was a despot, an absolute ruler who could be generous one minute and vindictive the next. His temper was frequently out of control. He was the greatest autocrat of his time, a man whose most foolish afterthought was a command, and into whose presence it was a crime to come unbidden.

As our story unfolds in the book of Esther, a huge banquet is in progress in the Susa palace. Satraps or princes, nobles, and officials from the 127 provinces of Persia, stretching from India to Ethiopia, gathered at the tables. For half a year Xerxes had displayed all the wealth of his kingdom and the splendor and glory of his majesty (1:4). Now a seven-day banquet was in progress.

The guests reclined on silver and gold couches. They drank from golden goblets, each with a different design and filled with whatever the guest requested. Can you imagine their condition after a seven-day open bar?

On the seventh day, drunk Xerxes had an idea. Why not show off his gorgeous queen, Vashti? She was, in the words of Esther 1:11, "lovely to look at." So the seven eunuchs who watched over Xerxes' harem ran to get her. We now meet the second character in our story, Xerxes' magnificent queen, Vashti.

You and I meet her, but Xerxes' guests did not. Vashti did the unthinkable. She refused the king's summons. Xerxes saw this as a rebellion that had to be nipped in the bud. Otherwise a woman's insurrection might spread throughout the kingdom. Vashti was immediately uncrowned and banished from her position as queen. Read the conclusion of the proceedings in Esther 1:16–22:

> Then Memucan replied in the presence of the king and the nobles, "Queen Vashti has done wrong, not only against the king but also against all the nobles and the peoples of all the provinces of King Xerxes. For the queen's conduct will become known to all the women, and so they will despise their husbands . . . . This very day the Persian and Median women of the nobility who have heard about the queen's conduct will respond to all the king's nobles in the same way. There will be no end of disrespect and discord.
>
> "Therefore, if it pleases the king, let him issue a royal decree and let it be written in the laws of Persia and Media, which cannot be repealed, that Vashti is never again to enter the presence of King Xerxes. Also let the king give her royal position to someone else who is better than she. Then when the king's edict is proclaimed throughout all his vast realm, all the women will respect their husbands, from the least to the greatest."
>
> The king and his nobles were pleased with this advice, so the king did as Memucan proposed

. . . proclaiming in each people's tongue that every man should be ruler over his own household.

Exit Vashti. Vashti, a woman who had the courage to refuse an indecent command from her husband. The national custom was that a woman did not appear unveiled in the presence of men, especially drunken, reveling men. Vashti lives in history today, not because she was beautiful, but because she had character. She had respect for herself. She knew the cost. She realized she would face dismissal from the court, possibly even death. But she loved honor more than life itself. Exit Vashti. We honor her memory as a woman of courage.

Now what? Xerxes already had a fabled harem or seraglio filled with beautiful women. He could have a different one as his bed partner night after night. But he tired of that and agreed that it was time to replace Vashti.

How was that to be done? Why not a beauty contest? He ordered his officials to go throughout all 127 provinces in Persia and find the most beautiful virgins. They were to be brought to the palace at Susa to undergo the beauty treatment required before presentation to the king. And what a beauty treatment it was: a full year of care beginning with six months' anointing with oil of myrrh followed by six months' treatment with perfumes and cosmetics.

The contest was underway. The most beautiful women in the empire were brought to Susa. It is now that we meet a Jew named Mordecai who had a beautiful foster daughter called Hadasseh in Hebrew or Esther in Persian.

This orphaned Jewish girl, adopted and reared by her cousin Mordecai, was "lovely in form and features." She was chosen for presentation to the king. During her year of preparation in the harem, she made a splendid impression on Hegai, the eunuch in charge of the harem. When her turn came to spend a night with King Xerxes, he, too, fell in love with this lovely Jewish girl.

What would you feel if you were in Esther's position? If you knew about Xerxes and his evil temper and capricious ways? If you knew what had happened to Vashti? If you weren't particularly happy about being part of a harem?

When Esther found herself in the king's palace, she accepted it with grace. She made the best of a situation she might have preferred to avoid.

Xerxes placed the crown of the realm on Esther's head, gave a great banquet in her honor and proclaimed a holiday throughout the empire to recognize her accession to the throne. But don't get the idea that Esther was a real sovereign in her own right. Remember what happened to Vashti. Esther understood that she had little power.

Before we can get on with our story, we have to meet one more character, an Agagite named Haman. An Agagite was an Amalekite, and Haman was a man with a long history of hatred for the Jews. He was also a man who didn't know when to stop. Furthermore, he was the second-from-the-top man in the Persian court.

As Haman came and went each day between his house and the palace, he passed the Jew Mordecai, Queen Esther's cousin, sitting at the palace gate. Xerxes had commanded that everyone bow down and pay homage to Haman, but Mordecai had a different idea. In Esther 3:5–6, we read:

> When Haman saw that Mordecai would not kneel down or pay him honor, he was enraged.

Yet, having learned who Mordecai's people were, he scorned the idea of killing only Mordecai. Instead Haman looked for a way to destroy all Mordecai's people, the Jews, throughout the whole kingdom of Xerxes.

Haman's evil mind began to concoct a plan. Arranging to have a lot cast each day to indicate the most propitious moment, Haman finally spoke to Xerxes:

> There is a certain people dispersed and scattered among the peoples in all the provinces of your kingdom whose customs are different from those of all other people and who do not obey the king's laws; it is not in the king's best interest to tolerate them. If it pleases the king, let a decree be issued to destroy them, and I will put ten thousand talents of silver into the royal treasury for the men who carry out this business (3:8–9).

The king agreed almost casually that on December 13 of that year all Jews in the Persian empire would be killed. With the press of Xerxes' signet ring sealing the documents, Haman's plan became fixed as law. And the law of the Medes and Persians could not be rescinded. The decree to "destroy, kill and annihilate all the Jews—young and old, women and little children" was carried by couriers to the farthest corners of the empire. Esther chapter 3 closes with the statement that "the king and Haman sat down to drink, but the city of Susa was bewildered."

In the midst of all this, Esther, the beautiful queen, sat secluded in the palace, seeing no suffering, no disruption, unaware of the fate hanging over her people—and perhaps herself. Then one day she heard that Mordecai was seated at the palace gate in sackcloth and ashes. Hurrying a servant bearing decent clothing out to him, she learned in return of Haman's scheme and the king's edict sealing the fate of all Jews in the kingdom. Mordecai sent to her a copy of the king's edict and urged her to go to Xerxes on behalf of her people. What follows is the core of our story. It is recorded in Esther 4:9–17:

> Hathach went back and reported to Esther what Mordecai had said. Then she instructed him to say to Mordecai, "All the king's officials and the people of the royal provinces know that for any man or woman who approaches the king in the inner court without being summoned the king has but one law: that he be put to death. The only exception to this is for the king to extend the gold scepter to him and spare his life. But thirty days have passed since I was called to go to the king."
>
> When Esther's words were reported to Mordecai, he sent back this answer: "Do not think that because you are in the king's house, you alone of all the Jews will escape. For if you remain silent at this time, relief and deliverance for the Jews will arise from another place, but you and your father's family will perish. And who knows but that you have come to royal position for such a time as this?"
>
> Then Esther sent this reply to Mordecai: "Go, gather together all the Jews who are in Susa, and fast for me. Do not eat or drink for three days,

night or day. I and my maids will fast as you do. When this is done, I will go to the king, even though it is against the law. And if I perish, I perish."

So Mordecai went away and carried out all of Esther's instructions.

Esther had to make a choice. She could continue to conceal her Jewishness. She could probably spend the rest of her days as the first lady of Xerxes' harem. She could live in splendor and luxury.

Or she could take her life in her hands and do what she could to find a way around the king's law to save her people. Esther came to understand that her position was not a privilege to be enjoyed but a high responsibility to be used to save others. Her people were in peril. Their problem became her problem. It was her duty to save them because she was in the best position to do so.

Where has God brought you in your life today? Certainly not to the harem of a Persian court. It is also unlikely that you have the destruction of an entire race of people hanging on the decisions you make today or next week. Wherever you are, whatever you are facing, hear Mordecai's words because they have relevance for us today as well: "Who knows but that you have come to [your] position for such a time as this?"

Sometimes as women we deplore the smallness of our challenges and the limits of our influence for good. We may feel we have limited usefulness to God. We must remind ourselves that the sovereign God has His hand on our lives and knows what we are able to do. Whatever God is putting into your hands to do today, tomorrow, or next week is never without meaning, never without significance. God has brought you to your present position and place in life for His own purposes.

When Esther understood Mordecai's words, she rose to the challenge: "I *will* do what I need to do, and if I perish, I perish." We can almost see her spine stiffening as she stands taller and straighter. Her firmness is surprising in light of her training to be a submissive and sensual harem girl. But like other Hebrew women whose stories we know, Esther found inner strength to do the right thing at the right time.

All of us know people who seem to have no fear. They do whatever they need to do without flinching, without a backward look. We admire them, but we know we cannot emulate them because we have so many fears of our own. We could never be like them.

We *do* identify with someone who has fear. Esther feared. We can hear it in her responses to Mordecai. We see it in her insistence that the Jews in Susa spend three days fasting before the Lord on her behalf. We understand it in her realistic appraisal of the situation: "If I perish, I perish."

When we see someone *with* fear able to rise above that fear and make the great life-risking decision, we go beyond admiration for such a person. We think, "Yes, maybe, just maybe even I could get beyond my fears and do what I know God is putting in my hands to do." Courage does not mean we will not have fear. It means that we refuse to take counsel from our fears.

How would *you* have acted if you had been in Esther's place? If you knew that to go to the king without being invited would almost certainly mean your death? Suppose you already suspected you had lost favor with him because he had not invited you for thirty days now?

You would probably think through your strategy very carefully. At least you should! Esther did. She prepared herself carefully and also prepared a sumptuous dinner for three.

Then, in her royal robes, she walked slowly from the women's quarters, through the great colonnades, under the great blue and white linen curtains, until she came to the inner courtyard. She stopped outside the doorway to the throne room, standing where Xerxes could see her.

Can you feel what she must have felt in that moment? Heart pounding? Cold chills chasing up and down her spine? Hands perspiring? If you can feel what she felt, then you can feel her great relief when Xerxes raised his golden scepter and extended it to her. For the moment, at least, she was safe.

When Xerxes asked what she wanted, instead of blurting out the bad news about his edict and her people, she merely invited him and Haman to a banquet. Xerxes quickly summoned Haman and the three went off to the feast Esther had prepared.

Again Xerxes asked Esther what she wanted. Again she invited him and Haman to a second dinner the next day. Was she procrastinating? Or was she preparing the scene with great care? She and God's people had fasted and prayed for her encounter with the king. In some way God led her to know the right moment. That first banquet was not it.

You've had those experiences, haven't you, when you somehow knew deep inside that the timing wasn't right for something that needed to be done. So you waited. Later you understood why you had waited. Something happened as you waited that turned the situation around. That happened to Esther.

Remember Haman? He left the banquet that day in high spirits. But as he passed through the palace gates, he came down to earth with a thud. In Esther 5:9 we read that "when he saw Mordecai at the king's gate and observed that he neither rose nor showed fear in his presence, he was filled with rage against Mordecai." In the next two chapters of Esther we see what can happen when we focus on an irritant rather than on the good things we have.

From the Mediterranean Sea to the Persian Gulf there was nothing that Haman could not have had for the asking. Women? Precious stones? Exotic foods? Haman could have it all. Somehow none of that mattered when he thought about Mordecai's insult. He forgot everything he had and focused his mind on the one thing he could not have. He allowed that one thing to destroy his happiness. It later ruined his family and cost him his life.

On the advice of his wife and friends, he had a gallows seventy-five feet high built on which to have Mordecai hanged.

In his anger, he decided that on the next day he would ask Xerxes for permission to have Mordecai executed. He could not wait until December 13 to see Mordecai put to death with all the other Jews.

Meanwhile, back at the palace, Xerxes was having a sleepless night. What better way to be put to sleep than to have the chronicles of the king's realm read out loud to him? As the attendant read the chronicles, he came to the notation that the Jew Mordecai had discovered a plot against Xerxes and had reported it to the king through Esther.

"What has been done for this man to honor him?" the king demanded. "Nothing," came the reply. Just then

Haman entered the outer court to speak to the king about hanging Mordecai. "Bring in Haman," the king commanded, "and let him tell me what should be done for a man the king delights to honor."

Haman thought the king was talking about him, so he suggested a showy procession to honor such a man. Can you imagine how he felt when he learned that he was to carry out such a procession for Mordecai, of all people? What a wretched twist of fate!

Now the time was right. *Now* the stage was set. Xerxes needed to be reminded of Mordecai's loyalty and willingness to save the king's life *before* Esther talked about the edict against the Jews. At that second banquet, when Xerxes asked Esther what she would like, she pled for two things: her life and the lives of her people who "have been sold for destruction and slaughter and annihilation."

Xerxes exploded. Who would dare do such a thing? Esther's answer came quickly: "The adversary and enemy is this vile Haman." Infuriated, Xerxes got up and went out into the palace garden to think over his next step. At that Haman blundered one last time. He threw himself at Esther's feet, "falling on the couch where Esther was reclining." Returning, Xerxes misread the scene. "Will he even molest the queen while she is with me in the house?" With that Haman was led off, hooded, for immediate execution on the very gallows he had prepared for Mordecai.

Haman was finally off the scene, gone forever. But the edict still stood. The law of the Medes and Persians could not be rescinded. The Jews were still bound for slaughter unless . . .

Unless Xerxes came up with another edict permitting the Jews to defend themselves, and even more, to destroy, kill, and annihilate any army that might attack them. The second edict was quickly drawn up and sent to the governors of all the provinces in the empire: The Jews could not only defend themselves but could attack their enemies and destroy them.

December 13 dawned, and in Esther 9:1 we read, "On this day the enemies of the Jews had hoped to overpower them, but now the tables were turned and the Jews got the upper hand over those who hated them."

Read chapter 9 for the grisly details if you wish. Esther's victory was far from gentle that day. More than seventy-five thousand enemies of the Jews died. December 13 became a national Jewish holiday, Purim, a day to celebrate God's deliverance from Persian enemies.

Where do you find yourself today? To what small kingdom has God brought you for such a time as this? You may be in a tough spot on a path bristling with problems. The load seems too heavy to continue carrying. These factors may be the very reasons God put *you* where you are and not someone else with less strength or less understanding. Perhaps He has put you where you are because He knows you can be trusted to see your task through with honor.

Esther is the one book of the Bible in which the name of God does not appear in any form. But that does not mean that God was not there. His purpose was still carried out—through a king's insomnia, an attendant's reading of a certain chronicle of the kingdom, a young Jewish orphan being chosen as queen. No book of the Bible teaches God's sovereignty and providence more clearly than Esther.

James Russell Lowell captured this truth when he wrote,

> Behind the dim unknown
> Standeth God within the shadow
> Keeping watch above His own.

Do you know that? Can you face each day secure in the reality that the difficult places in your life are in God's hands? He may seem invisible, but He never lets go of the helm of the universe. God's cause is always safe. The drama of our lives is God's drama.

Haman was *big*. He was powerful. He almost won. But he didn't. Xerxes was *big*. He was more powerful than Haman. But even in his capriciousness, he could not destroy the people of God. Esther needed a God-sized God to take her into the king's presence. She needed to rely on a God-sized God if she was to request the deliverance of her people. She succeeded because she *did* have a God-sized God.

Like Esther, we need a God-sized God as we face the difficulties of life. The good news is that we *have* a God-sized God. He is there. He cares. He will work on our behalf. As we move through each day, we can do so purposefully because we know, with the poet, that

> Behind the dim unknown
> Standeth God within the shadow
> Keeping watch above His own.

Esther

Questions for group discussion or personal reflection:

Sometimes as Christian women we find ourselves in situations where we have to make difficult decisions.

1. Is it better to try to change difficult situations or just grit our teeth and bear them? Explain your answer.
2. If we decide to try to change difficult situations, what factors should we keep in mind?
3. How should we view God's will when we are in tough places?
4. What does it mean to put our trust in God when we are in tight places?

The Proverbs 31 Woman: How to Keep Your Priorities Straight

What do you feel when someone mentions the Proverbs 31 woman? I've seen women's eyes glaze over. Others have muttered, "Don't throw the Proverbs 31 woman at me! I don't need that!"

There is something about this paragon of feminine virtue that makes most of us uncomfortable. When preachers use her—especially on Mother's Day—as a template laid over our lives, few of us measure up. That's the problem most of us face when we read about the Proverbs 31 woman.

Turn to Proverbs 31 and see what you're up against! You find this woman described in verses 10–31:

> A wife of noble character who can find?
> She is worth far more than rubies.
> Her husband has full confidence in her
> and lacks nothing of value.
> She brings him good, not harm,
> all the days of her life.
> She selects wool and flax
> and works with eager hands.
> She is like the merchant ships,
> bringing her food from afar.
> She gets up while it is still dark;
> She provides food for her family
> and portions for her servant girls.
> She considers a field and buys it;

out of her earnings she plants a vineyard.
She sets about her work vigorously;
her arms are strong for her tasks.
She sees that her trading is profitable,
and her lamp does not go out at night.
In her hand she holds the distaff
and grasps the spindle with her fingers.
She opens her arms to the poor
and extends her hands to the needy.
When it snows, she has no fear for her household;
for all of them are clothed in scarlet
[or in lined or doubled clothing].
She makes coverings for her bed;
she is clothed in fine linen and purple.
Her husband is respected at the city gate,
where he takes his seat among the elders of the land.
She makes linen garments and sells them,
and supplies the merchants with sashes.
She is clothed with strength and dignity;
she can laugh at the days to come.
She speaks with wisdom,
and faithful instruction [or the teaching of kindness]
is on her tongue.
She watches over the affairs of her household
and does not eat the bread of idleness.
Her children arise and call her blessed;
her husband also, and he praises her:
"Many women do noble things,
but you surpass them all."
Charm is deceptive, and beauty is fleeting;
but a woman who fears the LORD is to be praised.
Give her the reward she has earned,
and let her works bring her praise at the city gate.

The Proverbs 31 Woman

Well! How does *that* make you feel? Superwoman herself. When we read about the Proverbs 31 woman, we often turn away from her, sure that she couldn't be for real.

She can do *everything*. She supervises all household work. She cares for her children. She keeps her husband happy. She helps him get ahead in the world. In addition, she deals successfully in real estate and runs her own manufacturing business. As if that weren't enough, she sews her own clothes, always speaks wisely and kindly, and never fails to trust the Lord. How's that for a tall order!

Down deep inside, most of us would *like* to be able to do all that. We'd like the strong self-esteem and confidence we'd feel if we were like that. But what happens to many of us is that we get so tied up trying to be everything to everyone, juggling family life, social life, and commitments outside our homes, we end up in a heap, feeling like total failures. We're sure that people around us neither understand nor appreciate all we have tried to do for them.

Natasha Josefowitz described a modern American Superwoman like this:

> She is a perfect mother
> the model wife
> the best housekeeper
> the greatest cook
> the most available daughter
> the most effective worker
> the most helpful friend.
> She is wonderful at
> juggling home and career
> with a constant smile

and an even disposition.
She is everything
to everyone.
But who is *she*?

Those of us who may have lost sight of our *selves* in our mad rush through the Superwoman Syndrome may be able to learn something valuable from the Proverbs 31 woman. Far from being an impossible model, she may turn out to be a liberating guide to those of us who need her help.

We can take a *small* bit of comfort from the fact that the writer introduces her by asking the question, "Who can find an excellent wife, a wife of noble character, a woman of worth?" At least it is encouraging to know that she is rare. If every other woman in my neighborhood were a full-fledged Proverbs 31 woman and I were the only one who didn't measure up, that would be even more depressing.

But the fact that she may be rare should not keep us from learning from her. After all, she is in the Bible. We could pretend she's not there and ignore her. But as Christian women who want to take our Christian vocation seriously, we cannot sidestep this passage. Instead, we need to take a closer look at a model woman who may help us keep *our* priorities straight in life.

What we see as we step closer for a second look is a woman who is characterized by what the Hebrews called *hachmah*—wisdom. It is not that she had a high IQ. She may have had that. But she possessed something more. She had *hachmah*—a skill for living. She knew how to order her priorities to concentrate on what was important.

Hachmah. As we look at this interesting word in Exodus 31, we see that it means a skill that comes from God. Bezalel had *hachmah* in all kinds of crafts. The Spirit of God had filled him with skill "to make artistic designs in gold, silver and bronze, to cut and set stones, to work in wood, and to engage in all kinds of craftsmanship" (4–5). Another Israeli, Oholiab, also had *hachmah*, a God-inspired skill to weave the intricately designed cloth for the priestly garments and the tabernacle.

Hachmah is the key to our Proverbs 31 woman as well. She had a skill for living. She had lived long enough and well enough to have gained insight into how to live wisely.

This isn't something that comes automatically with age. Some people never develop it. It is a skill that we develop as we practice it. We have to want it and we have to be willing to practice to perfect it. It is *hachmah*, a skill for living.

What does this skill for living look like in action in our Proverbs 31 woman? In the first place, a woman of worth is a wise *manager*. Her skill for living enables her to manage her time well, manage her resources well, and manage her own gifts and abilities well. Let's look at each of these briefly.

First, she manages her time well. Some of what we read about her may put us off a bit. For example, in verse 15 we read that she gets up while it is still dark and provides food for her family.

Not being a morning person, I do not rise joyfully. I have to be at my desk at Denver Seminary by 8:00 a.m. each day. In all the years I have worked there, that is probably the greatest challenge I face each morning— getting to work on time! I'm simply not into early rising.

But I *do* know that managing my time well means getting started in the morning.

It's easy to read Proverbs 31 and conclude that our woman of worth never stopped working. But that isn't the case. Clearly she had a splendid relationship with her husband. We read in verse 11 that he had full confidence in her because, in verse 12, she brought him good, not harm, all the days of her life.

She also had a good relationship with her children. In verse 28 we learn that they rise up and call her blessed. She wasn't just a well-dressed dynamo in perpetual motion. She took time to build relationships, and kindness was on her tongue.

At the same time she used her free time wisely. She *invested* time. She did not simply waste it. If you find time slipping through your fingers so that you come to the end of each day wondering what you accomplished, you may want to monitor the way you use time. You may conclude that you can use your time more wisely simply by cutting out some television viewing or cutting down the time you spend on the phone. A wise woman manages her time well. She knows the value of her time.

Second, she manages her resources well. She knows that what really matters is not how much we have but how well we manage what we have. Her husband could trust her not to blow them away financially by charging too much on the credit cards. She was not afraid of hard work to make ends meet with a little left over for some shrewd investment. She learned skills that made wise management easier.

Perhaps you need to manage your resources better. If money is tight, the first step, of course, is to stop spending. That is, declare a moratorium on *all* spending.

Challenge yourself to see how long you can go without spending *any* money at all. You might surprise yourself.

A second step is to examine what you can do to economize. You may need to buy generic foods and drugs, cook from scratch instead of from prepared packaged foods, learn to sew, take up walking instead of golf. When you must do it, there is *always* a way to cut back. The Proverbs 31 woman of worth manages her resources wisely.

Third, our woman of worth manages her own gifts and abilities wisely. Sometimes as we read through Proverbs 31, we are so overwhelmed by all our woman of worth does that we ignore what she does *not* do. It sounds as if she does it all. But she doesn't. She has servant girls, according to verse 15. This enables her to concentrate her efforts in the areas of her skills. We see her entrepreneurial side as she moves out of the house and gets into real estate and manufacturing. This Proverbs 31 woman has gifts that she uses outside her home. She left much of the housework to the servant girls and used her skills where they most benefited her family.

This woman of worth knows what she is about:

She sets about her work vigorously;
her arms are strong for her tasks (verse 17).
She sees that her trading is profitable (verse 18).
When it snows, she has no fear for her household
(verse 21).
She is clothed with strength and dignity;
she can laugh at the days to come (verse 25).

We cannot set our priorities and live by them if we don't know who we are and what our abilities and gifts are. We all have to take some time to ask what is really important to us. We can't do it all. We have to pick and choose where to put our strokes. What we choose should be in line with what defines *us*, not what defines our neighbor or our best friend.

We can gird ourselves with strength and dignity only when we have a good handle on who we are and what we are about. We must concentrate our strength where it can make a difference for the important people in our lives. Clearly our Proverbs 31 woman of worth could best help her husband and provide for her family by buying fields, planting grapes, and making and selling sashes.

What are your natural gifts? Where are you most comfortable? In what spheres are you most successful and fulfilled? What flips your switch? What turns you on? Where do you feel God most often uses you? What skills do you have that you would like to develop?

Part of being a Proverbs 31 woman is to know yourself. Several years ago at a Columbia University seminar, I heard for the first time about the "Rule of Good Enough." I wish I had known about it when I was young. I've spent most of my life trying to do everything *perfectly*. Of course, I didn't succeed. No one does. It is important to learn that there are a great many things in life that are not central to who I am. I don't have to do those things perfectly. Perhaps I don't need to do them at all.

When you know who you are and what is really important for you to do, you can apply the Rule of Good Enough to everything else. That is a good management principle. It is one that our Proverbs 31 woman of worth used. She left tasks to the servants they could do better than she. She spent her time doing what was most in line with her abilities and most likely to enhance her family.

Our woman of worth is a wise *manager*. But she is more. She is also a wise *counselor*. In verse 26 we learn that "she speaks with wisdom, and faithful instruction [or the teaching of kindness] is on her tongue." No wonder her husband had full confidence in her.

Many women give counsel. Some of that counsel is wise. Abigail gave wise counsel to David and to Nabal. Deborah gave good advice to Barak. Huldah was God's mouthpiece of wisdom to King Josiah through the high priest and the king's counselors.

Other women give poor counsel. In the Old Testament we also meet women like Jezebel, who gave Ahab evil advice. Rebekah persuaded her son Jacob to deceive his father, Isaac. Earlier in the book of Proverbs we see warnings about the bad advice a young man could receive from a nagging contentious wife or from a seductive strange woman. In contrast, the Proverbs 31 woman speaks with wisdom as a wise counselor.

It is one thing to learn principles of wise management of time, resources, and gifts. It is another thing to learn to be a wise counselor. Where can we go to learn that? The key lies in the last part of verse 30: "a woman who fears the LORD is to be praised."

How does that fit? Turn back to Proverbs 9:10—"The fear of the LORD is the beginning of wisdom, and knowledge of the Holy One is understanding."

Our woman of worth "feared the LORD." That was the source of her *hachmah*, her wisdom, her skill for living, which she could pass on in wise counsel.

What does it mean to "fear the LORD"? The *fear* of the Lord is a reverent understanding of who He is and where we stand in relation to Him. The single most important thing you and I can know is who God is. There is nothing that matters more than that. We must know that God exists and that He is our creator and the creator of the world we inhabit.

We must see ourselves in relation to His greatness, His majesty, His power. We must see ourselves as creatures dependent every day of our lives on our Creator. That is why the woman of worth could laugh at the days ahead. She knew what we must know, that our times are in God's hands. She knew that God's hands are good hands and that He does only what is best for us. She knew what Jesus knew, that our heavenly Father knows what we have need of and has committed Himself to meeting our needs.

This kind of fear or reverence or awe of God's mighty power on our behalf gives us a different way of looking at ourselves and at our problems. We work hard. We use all our gifts, abilities, and skills to meet needs—our own, our family's, and the needs of others outside our family circle. But while we work as skillfully as we can, we also work knowing that God is working in us and through us.

God is our source of *hachmah*, wisdom. He works with us as we seek to manage our time well, to manage our resources well, and to manage the use of our gifts and abilities well. God is with us. That gives us a perspective and the strength to keep on.

What does it mean to be a Proverbs 31 woman of worth? It does *not* mean being Superwoman. It does not mean being Mrs. America. It does not mean doing it all and doing it perfectly.

It does mean bringing God's perspective to the choices we make every day of our lives.

It means choosing to manage our time in light of eternal values. What will *really* matter when this life is done?

It means choosing to manage our resources wisely for the benefit of people around us—for our families and for those whose needs we can help meet.

It means choosing to leave undone or applying the Rule of Good Enough to the things that are less important. It's knowing what doesn't have to be done at all.

It means being a wise counselor as we live life with the skill that comes from bringing a godly perspective to all that we do.

In short, it means "practicing the presence of the living God," as Brother Lawrence put it. It means seeing the hundreds of choices we all make every day from God's vantage point. It means making those choices with the long view. It means living before the eternal God.

"Charm is deceptive, and beauty is fleeting; but a woman who fears the LORD is to be praised." *That* is what it means to be a Proverbs 31 woman of worth. To be a woman who fears the Lord is a noble goal. It is a choice we make. The good news is that with God's help we can become women who live life with godly skill.

Questions for group discussion or personal reflection:

1. How do you feel about the Superwoman Syndrome? How would you describe it?
2. Do you feel that people expect you to be a superwoman? If so, how do you react to that kind of pressure?
3. What kind of problems do you have getting and keeping your priorities straight?
4. What do you think the Bible teaches about the way you use your time?

Mary: How to Bring Christ to Your World

Women and their choices. It all started with Eve, a flawless woman in a flawless world with a flawless relationship to her Creator God and to her husband, Adam. Eve—the complete woman, the one who had it all. She was free to be all that any woman could ever wish. When we look at Eve, we see what we were created to be, what God had in mind for each of us.

But in Eve we also see what humanity chose to become. Eve's choice didn't seem like much at the moment—just a decision about a piece of fruit. But her choice demonstrates for us part of what it means to be created in the image of God. We are free to put *our* will above God's will for us. We are free to thumb our nose at our Creator. We are free to live without God and to dispense with His Word and His will.

The consequence of that choice for Eve was alienation. She and Adam were separated from God. All of us since then have been distanced from God. The most important of all relationships, the vertical one with our Creator, was broken.

The second alienation came between Eve and Adam. The struggles we have today trying to relate perfectly to the important people in our lives show us how devastating that second alienation is. Statistics on divorce, physical and sexual abuse, and the need many of us have to consult a counselor demonstrate that

175

horizontal relationships are seldom all we want them to be.

The third alienation is one we simply live with: the rupture between us and nature. We battle weeds in our gardens and pain in our bodies. We create dams and reservoirs to overcome the shortage of necessary water. We shovel mountains of snow in the winter and we try to keep cool in the summer. In short, we accommodate ourselves to a world that is not always kind to us. We live with a basic alienation from nature.

All of this has come because one beautiful morning Adam and Eve chose to put their wills above God's will. In the process they gained what they were promised: an experiential knowledge of good and evil. They had known the good in Eden. They learned about toil and pain and loss and death. Eve's anguish must have been greater than anything we can imagine. She knew the good as no one since has known it. That must have made the evil that much more stark in its awfulness.

God gave Eve one tiny ray of hope on that dreadful day on which they were driven out of Eden. God buried a promise in the curse He placed on the serpent. He said He would put enmity between Satan and the woman, between his offspring and hers. At some future time, however, her offspring would crush Satan's head even though Satan would first strike the offspring's heel. This promise, called the *protoevangelium* or the first announcement of the gospel, is one that no Old Testament women saw fulfilled. Rachel and Leah didn't see it. Miriam didn't see it. Ruth didn't see it. Esther didn't see it. Thousands and thousands of years passed. Women and men struggled with alienation from God, from each other, and from the physical world around them. It must have seemed to many that God would never fulfill His promise. Had He forgotten? Had He changed His mind? Would nothing ever change?

Then in a tiny fifth-rate hill village called Nazareth, in a third-rate country called Israel, the curtain went up on a scene that has changed the course of history and has changed the lives of millions of men and women. It is the familiar story that we find in Luke 1:26–38:

> In the sixth month, God sent the angel Gabriel to Nazareth, a town in Galilee, to a virgin pledged to be married to a man named Joseph, a descendent of David. The virgin's name was Mary. The angel went to her and said, "Greetings, you who are highly favored! The Lord is with you."
>
> Mary was greatly troubled at his words and wondered what kind of greeting this might be. But the angel said to her, "Do not be afraid, Mary, you have found favor with God. You will be with child and give birth to a son, and you are to give him the name Jesus. He will be great and will be called the Son of the Most High. The Lord God will give him the throne of his father David, and he will reign over the house of Jacob forever; his kingdom will never end."
>
> "How will this be," Mary asked the angel, "since I am a virgin?"
>
> The angel answered, "The Holy Spirit will come upon you, and the power of the Most High will overshadow you. So the holy one to be born will be called the Son of God. Even Elizabeth your relative is going to have a child in her old age, and

she who was said to be barren is in her sixth month. For nothing is impossible with God."

"I am the Lord's servant," Mary answered. "May it be to me as you have said." Then the angel left her.

Put yourself in Mary's place. For thousands of years the Jews had talked about God's promised Redeemer. They had the words of the prophets and knew that the Messiah would be born in Bethlehem south of Jerusalem. They knew He would be born to a woman who was a virgin. They knew He would be born to a descendant of the great king, David. *Someday* He would come. But now? Through a simple peasant girl who lived several days' journey north of Bethlehem in a Galilean town called Nazareth?

Mary knew the promises as all Jews knew them. She might even have nurtured the secret hope, as many women must have nurtured it, that God would choose *her* to bear the Messiah. But when the angel appeared to her that day, her shock must have been enormous. Can you imagine what she felt?

I have no idea in what form Gabriel came to Mary that day. When the same angel came to Daniel nearly five hundred years earlier, Daniel described his reaction in these words: "As [Gabriel] came near the place where I was standing, I was terrified and fell prostrate" (Daniel 8:17). The second time Gabriel appeared to Daniel, the prophet described the scene in Daniel 10:5–17:

> [He was in the form of] a man dressed in linen, with a belt of the finest gold around his waist. His body was like chrysolite, his face like lightning, his eyes like flaming torches, his arms

and legs like the gleam of burnished bronze, and his voice like the sound of a multitude.

I, Daniel, was the only one who saw the vision; the men with me did not see it, but such terror overwhelmed them that they fled and hid themselves. So I was left alone, gazing at this great vision; I had no strength left, my face turned deathly pale and I was helpless. Then I heard him speaking, and as I listened to him, I fell into a deep sleep, my face to the ground.

A hand touched me and set me trembling on my hands and knees.

Daniel then recounted some of Gabriel's message to him, in the midst of which,

While he was saying this to me, I bowed with my face to the ground and was speechless. Then one who looked like a man touched my lips, and I opened my mouth and began to speak. I said to the one standing before me, "I am overcome with anguish because of the vision, my lord, and I am helpless. How can I, your servant, talk with you, my lord? My strength is gone and I can hardly breathe."

I'm with you, Daniel. If an angel of God appeared to me looking like Gabriel that day, I, too, would be speechless, breathless, and scared to death. Whatever form God's angel took in appearing to Mary that day, she was clearly troubled. She needed the word of comfort that followed: "Do not be afraid, Mary, you have found favor with God." Thereupon followed the announcement that she would become the mother of God's promised Redeemer, who was to be called Jesus.

Note Mary's first reaction in verse 34: "How will this be since I am a virgin?" She did not contradict Gabriel's message by saying, "Impossible!" She merely wondered "how."

The answer came: God Himself would father the child. Proof that God could do the impossible lay in the fact that Mary's cousin Elizabeth had become pregnant in her old age.

Before Mary lay a choice. She could say, "No, sorry, Gabriel. Joseph would never understand such an arrangement. The people in this small town would gossip. That would create too many problems for the child as well as for us. I don't think I really want the troubles this would create for all of us."

Mary could have said all that. But she didn't. We hear her submission to God's will in verse 38: "I am the Lord's servant. May it be to me as you have said." End of conversation. Gabriel left.

If you had been Mary that day, what would you have thought after Gabriel left you alone? Possibly you would have sat still for a while, stunned at the awesome experience of an angelic visitation and even more stunned at the message that *you* had been chosen by God to bring the Messiah into the world.

Mary, when she had digested the experience and the reality of this extraordinary pregnancy, immediately got ready and hurried to visit her cousin Elizabeth, who lived in the hill country of Judea. It was a couple days' journey south by foot or about eighty miles from Nazareth.

Whether Mary thought of visiting Elizabeth only because the angel had mentioned the older woman's

pregnancy or because the two women were already good
friends is not clear. Obviously it was important to Mary
to spend some time with Elizabeth. We know nothing
from Scripture about Mary's family. She may have been
an orphan staying with relatives in Nazareth. Her sudden
departure to the hill country of Judea for a three-month
visit with Elizabeth does not appear to have caused
family problems in Nazareth.

In any event, Mary arrived at Elizabeth's house, and
even as she passed through the door, Elizabeth was filled
with the Holy Spirit and exclaimed in Luke 1:42–45:

> Blessed are you among women, and blessed is
> the child you will bear! But why am I so favored,
> that the mother of my Lord should come to me?
> As soon as the sound of your greeting reached my
> ears, the baby in my womb leaped for joy. Blessed
> is she who has believed that what the Lord has
> said to her will be accomplished!

"Blessed is she who has believed that what the Lord
has said to her will be accomplished!" Eve had heard the
word of the Lord about the tree but had *not* believed. Mary
heard the word of the Lord from His messenger Gabriel
and she *had* believed. She believed against everything that
seemed rational, natural, or humanly possible. She could
submit to God's will because she had believed.

Mary responded to Elizabeth's inspired greeting with
what is known as the Magnificat. It is recorded in Luke
1:46–55:

> My soul glorifies the Lord, and my spirit
> rejoices in God my Savior, for he has been mindful

of the humble state of his servant. From now on all generations will call me blessed, for the Mighty One has done great things for me—holy is his name.

His mercy extends to those who fear him, from generation to generation. He has performed mighty deeds with his arm; he has scattered those who are proud in their inmost thoughts.

He has brought down rulers from their thrones but has lifted up the humble. He has filled the hungry with good things but has sent the rich away empty. He has helped his servant Israel, remembering to be merciful to Abraham and his descendants forever, even as he said to our fathers.

Much in the Magnificat takes us back to Hannah's song in 1 Samuel 2. Mary must have known not only the stories but the songs of her Jewish history. Hannah's words came easily to her lips as she praised God.

Mingled in Mary's praise is a clear understanding that the world in which she lived—and the world in which we live today—is not the world God designed for us to occupy. It is a world shot through with sin and death, a world in which all of the alienations stemming from Eve's and Adam's choice had been at work for thousands and thousands of years. Mary's world was one of Roman domination. It was a world in which a cruel and capricious king, Herod, ruled Palestine. It was a world in which even the religious leaders in Israel "devour widows' houses and for a show make lengthy prayers" (Matthew 23:14).

Mary's praise to God includes her awareness of the poor, the hungry, and the afflicted. Mary saw the miracle of her conception as *God on the move*. *God* was about to begin the long-overdue tasks of scattering the proud, of bringing down rulers, of lifting up the humble, of filling the hungry with good things and sending the rich away empty. In short, Mary saw that God was moving to fulfill His promise to His people. A promise first made in a garden thousands of years before. A promise made to the two whose choice had begun the alienations that twisted people's minds and put callouses on their hearts and made the world an ugly, despotic, and painful place in which to live.

It is probable that Mary stayed with Elizabeth for three months until the birth of John the Baptist. Then three months pregnant, Mary returned to Nazareth. She had lived for three months with the wonder, excitement, and thrill of being the God-bearer. Now she had to face the scorn and rejection of Joseph and the hometown people.

Again, put yourself in Mary's place. She was clearly in an embarrassing situation. Joseph, too, was in a tough spot. A Jewish engagement often lasted a year and was a kind of marriage without sex. If Mary got pregnant during this period, tongues would wag. If Joseph, knowing that he was not the father, decided to break the engagement to Mary, she could be stoned to death. If, on the other hand, Joseph went ahead with the wedding to Mary, people would think that he had violated the strict customs of chastity during the engagement period.

Follow the struggle Joseph had within himself as soon as he learned that Mary was pregnant. The story is recorded in Matthew 1:18–25:

> This is how the birth of Jesus Christ came about: His mother Mary was pledged to be

married to Joseph, but before they came together, she was found to be with child through the Holy Spirit. Because Joseph her husband was a righteous man and did not want to expose her to public disgrace, he had in mind to divorce her quietly.

But after he had considered this, an angel of the Lord appeared to him in a dream and said, "Joseph son of David, do not be afraid to take Mary home as your wife, because what is conceived in her is from the Holy Spirit. She will give birth to a son, and you are to give him the name Jesus, because he will save his people from their sins."

All this took place to fulfill what the Lord had said through the prophet: "The virgin will be with child and will give birth to a son, and they will call him Immanuel"—which means, "God with us."

When Joseph woke up, he did what the angel of the Lord had commanded him and took Mary home as his wife. But he had no union with her until she gave birth to a son. And he gave him the name Jesus.

Put yourself in Joseph's place. We don't know from the Bible whether Mary tried to explain her pregnancy to Joseph. Even if she had, had you been Joseph, would *you* have believed that story about an angel and a divine conception? Or would you more likely have thought that Mary had been untrue to her vows? Joseph, too, needed an angelic visitor to convince him of the truth concerning his present circumstances.

Joseph was in a wretched situation. He needed supernatural proof to believe in the supernatural birth of

Jesus. He, too, needed to believe the word of God through an angel and then act in obedient faith on that word. Joseph by faith became willing to pass himself off as the father of Mary's baby even though the townspeople would believe he had taken advantage of her during their engagement. It was the only way to protect her.

During Jesus' later ministry we hear the Pharisees asking with a sneer, "Where is your father?" (John 8:19). Did they question whether Joseph was really Jesus' father? Further in the same chapter (John 8:41), they tell Jesus, "*We* are not illegitimate children," implying that Jesus was. Clearly both Mary and Joseph were compromised. They could not explain what was happening and clear their names and reputations. Both Mary and Joseph had to live with reproach in a society with the highest standards of sexual purity in the world at that time. They both knew what they would have to live with. There was no other way. Mary and Joseph had to have complete faith in God and in each other to make that marriage work.

Another trial still lay ahead of this obedient pair. For that we go to Luke 2:1–3:

> In those days Caesar Augustus issued a decree that a census should be taken of the entire Roman world. (This was the first census that took place while Quirinius was governor of Syria.) And everyone went to his own town to register.

Anyone familiar with Christmas knows the story. Mary, now nearly ready to deliver, had to go with Joseph to Bethlehem, the city of David, their ancestor, to register for the census. The trip was nearly ninety miles. It had to be made either on a donkey or on foot. Either way it was a long and arduous journey. We can easily imagine how tired Mary must have been, possibly already in early labor, when they arrived at Bethlehem's inn. Turned away because the inn was packed with others who had also come to register for the census, they climbed down the steep hillside on which the inn had been built and found shelter in the cave under the inn, where animals were stabled. There, Mary gave birth to Jesus, the Holy One of God, and wrapped Him in swaddling clothes, and laid Him in a cattle food trough.

An insignificant couple arrived as strangers at the end of a long and tiring journey. A simple peasant girl faced the delivery of her first child virtually unattended, with no material comfort, no conveniences. It could have passed completely unnoticed. But it didn't. God had other plans.

Once again an angel of the Lord brought terror when he came calling. A band of shepherds in a nearby field learned of the birth of this insignificant baby to insignificant parents in an insignificant stable in an insignificant town on the eastern rim of the Mediterranean Sea. Suddenly all that seemed insignificant was transformed as God stamped that event with life-changing, world-changing significance.

"Today," the shepherds were told, "in the town of David a Savior has been born to you; he is Christ the Lord!" (Luke 2:11). A Savior. The Christ. The Lord. Immanuel, God with us. Jesus, the One who would save His people from their sins. The One promised to Eve and Adam in Genesis 3:15. The One whose coming would restore for each of us the possibility of a personal relationship with God our Creator. The One who would heal our alienation, not only from God but from one another.

Mary made a choice. Like Eve, she had the freedom to choose. Eve had chosen for herself against God. In that choice she found bitterness and sorrow. She brought sin and alienation into the world.

But when Mary made a choice, she chose to bow to the will of God, despite the problems it could cause. In making that choice, she became the God-bearer, the one through whom the Savior came into the world. When faced with the choice of how she would use her life, she chose for God. She chose well. She found blessedness in bringing the Savior into the world. She found joy in accepting God's will for her life.

Upon each of us rests the awesome responsibility of choice. It is part of what it means to be created in the image of God. We can choose for our Creator or against our Creator. We can choose to let Him work through us wherever He has placed us. Or we can choose our own will, our own comfort, and our own convenience. The choice is ours. God does not force any of us against our will. The power of choice may be God's most awesome gift to each of us.

Where has God put you?

What is He asking you to do?

You can hear His voice in the Scriptures. You can hear His voice through the teachings of His ministers. You can hear His voice in prayer and meditation. As you listen to His voice, what do you hear Him asking you to do?

Before you stands a choice. You can choose, as Eve did, to ignore God's will for you. Or you can choose, as Mary did, to embrace the will of God regardless of public opinion. If you choose as Mary did, you, too, will be blessed. You will know the presence of God with you. You will know the blessing of God on your work. You will know the favor of God when you one day stand before Him. You will hear those thrilling words, "Well done, good and faithful servant!"

Questions for group discussion or personal reflection:

1. The freedom to choose is perhaps God's most awesome gift to each of us as human beings. How do you feel about that gift?
2. What are the things you find most difficult about being a woman who must make many choices?
3. What are the things you like most about being a woman who must make many choices?
4. In what practical ways do you find that God enters into the choices you make?

Jesus: How to Be a Disciple of the Master Teacher

In 1980 my husband and I moved back to the United States after nearly two decades of overseas missionary service. One of the first things that struck me as we settled into the American version of the Christian community was the strong emphasis on discipling. It seemed that every Christian we met was either discipling a newer Christian or was being discipled by an older Christian.

Younger women approached me and asked me to disciple them. Their requests had the feel of something programmed, cut-and-dried. I hated to admit it, but I didn't have a clue what I was supposed to do. So I listened, asked questions, and read books. I discovered an exploding literature on how to disciple or be discipled.

Much that I found, however, was formula-driven: do these five things in this order and you'll automatically be the growing Christian God wants you to be. These looked neat and efficient, and we Americans like things that way. If we can reduce a process to a formula (preferably one that either alliterates or forms an acronym!), we can convince ourselves that we have the process under control.

In many areas of life that works. Formulas do get some processes under control. Every recipe is a formula: take these ingredients in these proportions and combine them in this way and voilà!—cornbread or pot roast or chocolate mousse. Any woman who walks into her kitchen to prepare a meal works with formulas. She either already knows them in her head or knows where to find the ones she will use. If we've been at the business of cooking very long, we don't need to reach for a recipe book every time we make a cream sauce or pie crust.

To learn to cook well, we start out following the formulas (recipes) carefully. As we become more skilled, we may alter the formulas to our own taste. But whether we have five well-used recipe books open on the counter every time we prepare a meal or we work out of cooking experiences accumulated over the years, we are combining certain ingredients in certain proportions in a certain way. We're using formulas. Good cooks and bad cooks alike use formulas. They merely differ either in the formulas they use or in the ways they use them.

Is discipleship the same as cooking? Can I be guaranteed that if I combine certain ingredients (joining a Bible study group, spending a specified amount of time each day in prayer, attending three church services a week, witnessing to non-Christians on schedule) in certain proportions and in a certain way, I will become a mature Christian?

To find that answer I decided to follow Jesus Christ through the four gospels and look at what the master disciple-maker said to those who followed Him as disciples. What I found was that His contacts with men and women didn't seem to fit any particular formula. He is, in C. S. Lewis's words, "not a tame lion." He never seemed to approach people in the same way twice. He suited His method to each person's unique need.

Jesus went out of His way to encounter a preoccupied Samaritan woman and engage her in a conversation that brought her and many in her village to faith. Yet He distanced Himself from His own mother to move her to a different relationship to Himself. He tested a Syrophoenician woman by refusing her request as a way of leading her on to great faith, but He lavished unsolicited grace on a widow whose son had died. Sometimes He talked in riddles to those who wanted answers; other times He gave answers to questions people had not asked. He refused to endorse Martha's notion of what Mary should be doing, just as He refused to answer Peter's question about the task He would give John.

I thought of the scores of women I had worked with in Europe. Whether singly or in small and large groups, these women were individuals. Each one brought her own unique life experience, her own fears and dreams, her own baggage to the Christian life. I can buy a dozen eggs and assume that all twelve eggs are pretty much alike and will act the same way in an angelfood cake. I cannot assume that a dozen women stirred together in a Bible study group will act the same way.

Cookie-cutter discipleship programs reminded me of the near-impossibility of two women—one a size 8 and the other a size 18—sharing the same size 13 dress pattern. Without a great many major adjustments to the pattern, neither woman will end up with a wearable dress.

No two of us are the same. Not only do we vary in height, weight, and hair color, we vary in interests, gifts, and skills. Just as Jesus molded His response to individuals around their specific needs, so we learn to follow Jesus as His disciples out of our own individuality.

When I was growing up, people had to know their sock size. Today we can buy one size that fits all. We don't have to remember sock sizes any more. But following Jesus isn't like buying a pair of socks. One size doesn't fit all.

Instead, it is more like a rug I hooked many years ago. I had seen the picture of that rug in a magazine and could imagine it under our coffee table in the living room. Six feet in diameter, it was a single round flower with scores of oval petals in every shade of blue and green. What struck me was that, while the general contours of the petals were similar, no two petals were alike. If they were close in size, they were completely different in color or shade. It was that variety that gave the rug its vibrancy.

As I watched Jesus reach out and touch individual women and men in the Gospels, I discovered that God always works with originals, not with copies. Who could doubt the originality of Mary of Magdala or of Martha and her sister Mary? Like the petals of my hooked rug, there are no two alike.

This is not to say that Jesus did not have specific goals for those who follow Him. He made six statements that help us recognize His disciples when we see them. Luke records three conditions Jesus laid down for His followers: "If anyone comes to me and does not hate his father and mother, his wife and children, his brothers and sisters—yes, even his own life—he cannot be my disciple" (14:26); "Anyone who does not carry his cross and follow me cannot be my disciple" (14:27); "Any of you who does not give up everything he has cannot be my disciple" (14:33). John then gives us three proofs of a disciple: "If you hold to my teaching, you are really my disciples" (8:31); everyone "will know that you are my disciples if you love one another" (13:35); "bear much fruit, showing yourselves to be my disciples" (15:8).

That's a daunting list of requirements for disciples. It appears that Jesus set the bar higher than any of us can jump on our own. We not only must hold to His teachings, love one another, and bear much fruit; we must give up everything, carry our cross, and make all human relationships secondary to following Jesus. No wonder "many of his disciples turned back and no longer followed him" (John 6:66).

Meeting the requirements of such a list would be nearly impossible if being a disciple were nothing more than a formula, an abstract concept. It's tough to give up everything for an abstraction. But Jesus doesn't ask us to give up anything for an abstraction. He invites us into a relationship that so changes our priorities that what was once important matters much less to us.

The word *disciple* comes from *mathetes*, which means "learner." That's what we are, learners. But we are a special kind of learner. I can study French in school without having a special relationship to the French teacher. But I can't study the Christian life as a disciple without having a special relationship to its founder. This is why discipleship as an abstraction slips and slides out of formulas designed to contain it. Life-changing relationships are dynamic, not static. They are alive.

When Jesus steps out of the pages of Matthew, Mark, Luke, and John and walks into my living room, I have to deal with Him, a person. He's not some misty figure in history. Nor is He just a set of teachings found in the Sermon on the Mount. He's alive, and He's dynamically involved in building a relationship with me. I must know who He is and what He wants from me. More than factual information about Him, I must also get acquainted with Him and get some feel for what to expect from Him.

Because He is alive, not dead, and because He is relating to me, I can't put this relationship in a box or expect it to develop according to some formula.

It's the difference between knowing the mathematical formula and knowing the mathematician. Facts and formulas are static. To bind the edge of my round rug, I can compute the circumference using πd on a Tuesday in May. I can still compute that circumference with the same formula on a Friday in October. Knowing the mathematician is not at all the same.

What difference does that make? Does a relationship do something for us that facts in a formula fail to do? Great relationships have several characteristics in common. The first is that we take an interest in what interests our friend. What matters to her suddenly matters very much to us. We discover that we have a curiosity about things our friend likes that we hadn't given any thought to in the past.

Another characteristic of a great relationship is strong affection. We take such delight in our friend that we want to spend as much time as possible with her. Our hearts are knit together in love. That is a bond more powerful than any demands either of us may put on the relationship.

A third characteristic of a great relationship is trust. We go out of our way to be worthy of our friend's trust, and we give trust. This is, of all the characteristics of a great relationship, the most fragile. Trust is slow to build and quick to be shattered. But when it is present, it forms a sturdy bridge over which we can haul anything.

When we get to know Jesus and find Him completely trustworthy, we discover that we can hold to His teachings. When we have accepted that we are loved by Him without any strings attached, it is easier to love others. When what matters to Him matters to us, we won't even notice when other relationships and all that we possess take a secondary place in our lives.

What looked like a bar set impossibly high turns out to be not a bar at all. It is a gateway to joyful service for our Savior and Lord, Jesus Christ.

There is no such thing as discipleship in the abstract. There are only disciples, individual men and women whom Jesus has found and whose lives He is changing. Jesus works with people, not concepts.

This book is not about six principles of discipleship. It's about women whom Jesus encountered. He found them on a well curb, in a temple court, in the marketplace, outside a city gate. They were ordinary people meeting an extraordinary person. They followed Him, and life was never the same for them again.

These are case studies of women in the Gospels who met someone who changed their lives by His interest in them, His unconditional love, His trustworthiness. His love enabled a sinful woman to show great love. His interest prompted a woman of Samaria to bear much fruit. His trustworthiness stimulated Mary of Magdala to give up everything and follow her deliverer.

What looks difficult, even impossible in the abstract becomes spontaneously possible, even easy when we move into a relationship of love and trust with God the Son. This book is for and about women who want to love and serve Jesus Christ, who want to be His disciples.

Questions for personal reflection or group discussion:

1. How do you feel about the characteristics of a disciple as Jesus stated them?
2. Which one do you think would be most difficult for you?
3. In what ways does a relationship change the way you might look at these characteristics?
4. How do you feel about your own originality or uniqueness as a follower of Jesus Christ?

Mary: How to Relate to the Family of Faith

With our four children now in their thirties, Randall and I have gone through the tough transitions of learning to relate to our kids as adults. We can no longer be responsible for them. We don't choose their toys, their diets, their clothes, or their friends. Whatever influence we may have over them now, it cannot be coercive. They may choose to listen to us because they honor us or because we have an expertise they want to learn. But listening to us is their choice, not our right. This calls for an interesting shift in the way we talk to each other and in the expectations we have.

These relationship shifts in the family can create tension for all of us. As parents we know in our heads we need to let go and encourage our children's independence. Doing it consistently is another thing. We feel responsible, and our protective instincts get in the way of what we know in our heads we must do.

During such times we may feel as if we're tiptoeing through a minefield. But the transitions we make as our children mature into adulthood are insignificant compared to the transition made by a woman we meet in the Gospels. Her name is Mary, the mother of our Lord Jesus Christ.

We're familiar with the dramatic story of her terrifying encounter with an angel, Gabriel, in which she agreed to become the mother of the Messiah. We know the story of Jesus' inconvenient birth in a Bethlehem stable. We've heard about the adoring shepherds and their story of a sky full of angels announcing Jesus' birth. We somehow assume that a woman bringing such a special baby into the world would be spared some of the anguish we ordinary parents face.

Yet Mary faced an even tougher transition than you and I face as our children mature. She had to learn to relate in a new way to her son, Jesus, not just as an adult, but as God. Her role as mother had to give way to a new role as disciple or follower of Jesus Christ. The things that happened to shift her to discipleship were so important that all four Gospel writers give us bits and pieces of the story. One particularly painful incident is reported by Matthew, Mark, and Luke. Here is Mark's version:

> Then Jesus entered a house, and again a crowd gathered, so that he and his disciples were not even able to eat. When his family heard about this, they went to take charge of him, for they said, "He is out of his mind." (3:20–21)

It started with the rumors the folks in Nazareth kept hearing about Jesus. Some people were saying He was out of His mind. Others said He did His work through the power of Beelzebub, the prince of demons. Still others simply said He wasn't getting enough rest nor even time to eat. Mary and her sons agreed that Jesus would kill Himself if someone didn't take charge of Him.

They talked it over in the family and decided to bring Him back to Nazareth. They would keep Him out of the public eye for a while and make sure He got enough sleep and ate at the proper times. So they set out for the village where He was teaching.

Their concern for Jesus' health was not misplaced. Needy people seeking His touch on their lives crowded Him wherever He went. Men and women in their desperation and pain pressed Him on every side. He and His disciples tried to retreat from the pushing throngs, but even in a private home they were so mobbed, they were not able to eat. Mark's account resumes in verses 31 through 35:

> Then Jesus' mother and brothers arrived. Standing outside, they sent someone in to call him. A crowd was sitting around him, and they told him, "Your mother and brothers are outside looking for you."
> "Who are my mother and my brothers?" he asked. Then he looked at those seated in a circle around him and said, "Here are my mother and my brothers! Whoever does God's will is my brother and sister and mother."

"Who are my mother and brothers?" What a question to ask! What must Mary have felt in that moment? After all those years of caring for this growing boy, to be rejected in this way? She had risked her reputation to bring Him into the world. She had worked tirelessly during His boyhood to train Him responsibly. Now as she heard Him ask, "Who is my mother?" she was forced to recognize that for Him, the physical ties of family were not as strong as she had thought.

Of all human relationships, few reach deeper than the tie of a mother to her child. When we become mothers, we become partners with God in creation, in bringing a new life into the world. Could any other bond be stronger than that?

Mary was fully human. She must have struggled with the humiliation of this rejection. If we walked slowly back to Nazareth with her after that painful encounter, we might see her close her eyes and shake her head as if to blot out this new reality. It couldn't be true. This special son, the one the angel had said would be great and would be called the Son of the Most High, who would occupy the throne of His father David— surely this son wouldn't turn His back on His own mother!

But what had that old man Simeon said to her that day in the Jerusalem temple where she and Joseph had taken the baby Jesus for His dedication? Hadn't he told her that because of this child a sword would pierce her own soul? Was this what he was talking about? Could anything hurt more than being publicly rejected by her oldest son?

As she walked the dusty path to Nazareth, Mary may have turned over in her mind those exciting early months of her pregnancy spent in the Judean hill country with her cousin Elizabeth. During these three months they were two close friends comparing notes about the infants growing inside their wombs. In hushed voices they combed through their memory of angelic visits. How could it be that God had chosen Mary through whom to keep His promise to Israel?

Then it was time for Mary to return to Nazareth and to deal with the stares and gossip of townsfolk. How difficult it would be to explain to her fiancé, Joseph. What if he refused to believe her story about the angel's visit? But God had convinced Joseph in a dream to risk his own reputation to marry her.

She remembered the heaviness of her pregnancy during that inconvenient trip from Nazareth to Bethlehem. She winced at the memory of the innkeeper's words—"The inn is full. We have no room for anyone else." She felt again the exhaustion of that birth on a pile of straw in a hillside stable. All too soon she and Joseph were bundling up their infant son and making another inconvenient trip, this time southwest to Egypt.

When Joseph had talked of returning to Nazareth after Herod died, she knew she would face townspeople who would never believe her tale of an angel and a virgin birth. She would simply have to grit her teeth and ignore the smirks and rude comments.

But she could do that. After all, she had heard Simeon praising God, "My eyes have seen your salvation, which you have prepared in the sight of all people, a light for revelation to the Gentiles and for glory to your people Israel" (Luke 2:30–32). Mary knew her son was born for greatness. She knew He was sent for the deliverance of Israel. She could ignore the gossips!

Of course, there had been that troubling scene in the temple when Jesus was twelve (Luke 2:41–52). It had felt like a prick of the sword Simeon had predicted would pierce her soul. They had taken Jesus with them on that seventy-mile hike from Nazareth to Jerusalem for the Feast of the Passover. She had felt the excitement of seeing again the City of David, its walls a golden white in the spring sunshine. She had stood in the Court of the Women, awed that God had chosen her people to be a light to the Gentiles. She had thrilled to the pageantry and symbolism of the Passover Feast. Every time she had passed through the temple gates, she had experienced the thrill of being Jewish and being able to worship the God of Israel.

Too soon it had been time to make the long trip back to Nazareth. She relived the panic she had felt that first evening of the trek home when they could not find Jesus among the children in the caravan. She experienced again the pounding heart she'd felt as she and Joseph had bombarded other pilgrims with their frantic questions. Where could Jesus be? Repeating that steep climb, they had retraced their steps to Jerusalem, where they hunted for three long days for their twelve-year-old boy. What relief when they found Him in the temple talking with the teachers of the Law! She remembered the first question out of her mouth: "Son, why have you treated us like this? Your father and I have been anxiously searching for you!"

It was His answer that had pricked her. "Why were you searching for me? Didn't you know that I must be about my Father's business?" What could He have meant by that? Didn't He understand that, as His parents, they had a right to be worried? This son who had given them so much love and joy was, at other times, such a puzzle! They had always taken His obedience for granted. Who was this Father He talked about? When the angel had said He would be called the Son of the Most High, was he telling her that Jesus could never be merely their son?

Then all too soon, the child Jesus was no longer a child. He had left the carpenter's shop in Nazareth and had put on the white robe of a rabbi, a teacher. Now she heard stories trickling back into Nazareth that made the slander she endured during His childhood seem insignificant. People were saying her son was out of His mind! Even her other sons thought it was true.

As Mary trudged down the dusty road to Nazareth from that painful encounter with her firstborn son, she may also have recalled His words to her at that wedding in Cana (John 2:1–11). The wine had run out. When she told Jesus about the bridegroom's embarrassment, He had turned to her, His mother, and had asked, "Woman, what have I to do with you?" That had hurt! She had tried to put it out of her mind at the time. But now came another painful question: "Who is my mother?"

In those moments waiting outside the house where Jesus was teaching, Mary must have felt the full weight of rejection as Jesus answered His own question, "Whoever does God's will is my brother and sister and mother."

Nearing Nazareth, her steps grew heavier as she relived the pain of Jesus' words. If anyone had a claim on Him, surely she did! The difficult path of discipleship for Mary meant laying aside her special relationship to Jesus as His mother and relating to Him in the family of faith through obedience to God. Could Mary the mother become Mary the disciple?

* * *

Simeon had prophesied that a sword would pierce her soul. She felt that sword turn within her again on a black Friday. The long walk from Nazareth to Jerusalem for the Passover feast had been exhausting. When she saw Jesus teaching in the temple, she thought He seemed so old, so tired, so discouraged. Wherever He went, people rushed out to see Him, to hear Him, or to watch Him heal the sick. But always the religious leaders of the nation opposed Him.

As Mary stood at the foot of a Roman cross that black Friday, she thought again of this son who seemed to choose a collision course with the religious authorities. The rumors had never stopped. It seemed that He was always saying something controversial or doing something on a Sabbath that upset the priests and Pharisees. He actually seemed to prefer the Sabbath to heal the sick! Did He have to drive the money changers and swindlers out of the temple courtyard with a whip? Did He have to say such inflammatory things to the Pharisees? If only He had seen the importance of staying on the right side of people in power.

Mary thought again of that day when she and her other sons had gone to take Jesus home. If only He had gone with them then! This terrible moment of crucifixion might have been avoided!

Sometimes crouching against nearby rocks for support, sometimes leaning on the other women from Galilee, she watched helplessly as her firstborn son grew weaker and weaker. What more cruel way to die than this? She forced herself to look at that human body—a body once carried within her own body—now suspended between heaven and earth by two spikes driven through His hands into a crossbeam. She tried to breathe for Him even as she watched Him slowly suffocate.

What had happened to the promise of the angel Gabriel that her son would be "great and would be called the Son of the Most High"? How could everything end this way when the angel had spoken such exalted words to her so many years before?

As she stood there, lost in her grief, she heard Jesus speak to her from the cross. His voice was weak: "Dear woman, here is your son." Then to John He said, "Here is your mother." Not long after that, He cried out, "It is finished!" and her son was gone. Yet in those last moments before His death, Mary was warmed by her son's love wrapped around her against the cold wind and dark skies. In that moment of losing her son Jesus, Mary gained a new family. John the beloved disciple, took her to his house to comfort her and care for her.

"Who is my mother? Whoever does God's will is my brother and sister and mother." Mary had lived with a tension throughout Jesus' earthly ministry, a tension between ties to her physical family and ties to the family of faith. Now, at the foot of the cross, the two roles were brought together into one. Jesus' gift to her in those last moments before His death was to restore her role as mother in a new context.

We meet Mary one more time in the Bible. The story picks up in Acts 1:12–14. Jesus had just ascended into heaven.

> Then [the disciples] returned to Jerusalem from the hill called the Mount of Olives, a Sabbath day's walk from the city. When they arrived, they went upstairs to the room where they were staying. Those present were Peter, John, James and Andrew; Philip and Thomas, Bartholomew and Matthew; James son of Alphaeus and Simon the Zealot, and Judas son of James. They all joined together constantly in prayer, along with the women and *Mary the mother of Jesus*, and with his brothers (emphasis added).

Our last glimpse of Mary is in a prayer meeting with the other followers of Christ. She had made the transition to discipleship. In the process she moved from the fragile ties of a human family to the strong ties of the family of faith.

Unlike Mary, we have no special biological relationship with the Son of God to get in our way. None of us has ever had to travel the rough path Mary had to walk. Even so, we may find ourselves inventing our own ways of relating to Jesus Christ that fall short of God's way.

"Who is my sister? Whoever does God's will is my sister." Nothing less will do. The family of God is a family of faith. Faith means trusting God to do what is best for us as we do what He tells us to do. Our relationship to Jesus Christ begins and moves forward on one basis only: doing God's will. Anything else we substitute for that must be denied.

It is easy for many of us whom God has blessed with families to allow our families to come before our relationship to God. Faced with the anti-family pressures of our culture, we want to turn back the tide of godlessness around us by making a strong family our first priority. Is that wrong? The answer is Yes, when our family becomes our first priority.

Jesus was clear: "If anyone comes to me and does not hate his father and mother, his wife and children, his brothers and sisters—yes, even his own life—he cannot be my disciple" (Luke 14:26).

A strong family is a good goal. But it cannot be our first goal. Commitment to Jesus Christ must come before all other commitments.

An important part of our discipleship as Christian women is to learn how to fuse being a follower of Jesus

Christ with being a neighbor, a teacher, a wife, or a friend. If our focus is on our role as wife and mother instead of our relationship to God, He may need to upset our ideas about priorities. It's tough to discover that what we thought was terribly important doesn't matter to God at all. To help us learn that, God at times turns our lives upside down.

When that happens, we may conclude that everything that has given us significance is gone. But when we look again at Mary on that grim day at the foot of a cross, we know that God is at work even in our most devastating moments of loss. Jesus removed from Mary her role as His mother in order to give motherhood back to her in a new context in the family of God.

Roles change. One woman may lose her role as wife through the death of her husband. Another woman loses her role of wife through divorce. Motherhood can be taken through the death of a child. This kind of tough discipleship pulls us up short. Can we at such times know in a deeper way the God who sees our tears?

The essence of discipleship is to learn to know God, to know Him as completely trustworthy, and on that basis, to do His will. As disciples we grow to trust Him to work all things together for our good as we do His will. When we know God in that way, we can trust Him to "establish the work of our hands" (Psalm 90:17).

He may establish us in familiar roles. He may give us fulfilling new roles. But all of our roles are to be played out in the context of God's work and God's family. It is on that foundation that we build everything else.

As disciples, we learn that all of our human relationships take second place to our relationship to our Creator God and Savior, Jesus Christ. The starting point for each of us as followers of Jesus Christ is to let God be God in our lives. We trust Him and obey Him because He is God.

The good word is that when we do that, God moves into our topsy-turvy world and establishes the work of our hands. He gives us wisdom, a skill for living life wisely. This wisdom may change our values and our priorities, but it also fuses our discipleship to our daily lives in a way that brings contentment, even joy.

Mary survived humiliation. She survived confusion about Jesus and His mission. She survived His death. She lived to see Him raised from death and glorified. She lived to become an integral part of the family of God when she let go of special privilege and took her place as a follower of the Son of God. "Who is my mother? Whoever does God's will is my brother and sister and mother."

Questions for personal reflection or group discussion:

1. Throughout Jesus' earthly ministry Mary lived with a tension between her view of physical family ties and ties to the family of faith. How was that tension resolved for her?
2. In what ways do we as twenty-first-century Christian women also live in tension between our physical families and the family of God?
3. What does it mean to "do God's will"?
4. How does doing God's will affect our priorities?

The Woman at the Well: How to Face Your Self "As Is"

Recently a friend asked me to review for class use a videotape on which I had appeared as a panelist. Without much thought, I popped the cassette into the VCR and pushed the buttons to start the tape. My only thought was to critique the content of the discussion. But suddenly I saw myself on the television screen. I stepped closer. As I stood in the den watching me gesture, hearing me talk, listening to me laugh, I was both curious and apprehensive. I realized, standing there, that I had never seen myself on videotape before. Robert Burns once prayed for the gift "to see ourselves as others see us." For the first time that was happening to me. Good grief! So that's what other people put up with when I'm around!

It struck me that when I look in a mirror, I receive immediate visual feedback so that I can instantly change my facial expression to something more pleasant. But the camera caught me "as is." Two hours of "as is."

The Bible tells us about a woman who met a man who knew her "as is." It appeared that He had no reason to know her, much less reason to bother with her. The man was Jesus. When He encountered this woman, their meeting looked like an accident. It wasn't. But that gets ahead of the story.

Despite the good things He did, Jesus kept upsetting the religious status quo. Again and again He crossed swords with the scribes, the Pharisees, and the teachers of the Law. He irritated them when He drove out of the temple all the unscrupulous merchants who were fleecing the poor pilgrims coming to Jerusalem for the Feast of the Passover. But it wasn't yet time to force the issue with these religious leaders. Instead of continuing His work near the Jewish capital in Judea, He decided to return to Galilee to carry on His ministry.

Our story picks up in John 4:1–6:

> The Pharisees heard that Jesus was gaining and baptizing more disciples than John, although in fact it was not Jesus who baptized, but his disciples. When the Lord learned of this, he left Judea and went back once more to Galilee.
>
> Now he had to go through Samaria. So he came to a town in Samaria called Sychar, near the plot of ground Jacob had given to his son Joseph. Jacob's well was there, and Jesus, tired as he was from the journey, sat down by the well. It was about the sixth hour.

The writer John makes a point of geography that is worth exploring. A glance at a map of Israel in New Testament times shows the province of Galilee in the north, the province of Judea in the south, and the area called Samaria in between. It seems logical that anyone going from Judea to Galilee would have to go through Samaria.

Not necessarily. Most Jews were so unwilling to have any contact with Samaritans that they made a round-about trip to avoid having to walk on Samaritan soil. From Jerusalem they walked seventeen extra miles east to Jericho, crossed the Jordan River, then trekked north through the province of Perea until they could recross the Jordan and enter Galilee. The route was almost twice as long as the direct road through Samaria.

Jews and Samaritans were bitter enemies, much like Jews and Arabs today. Back in 722 B.C. the Assyrian invaders had captured Syria and then the northern ten tribes of the Israelites. Samaria had been the capital of the northern tribes. The Assyrians followed the same pattern on Jewish soil they had used in all their conquests: they rounded up all the people who could keep a sense of national identity alive—the nobles, the scholars, the soldiers, the wealthy—and transported them to other lands, scattering them out across the empire. Then they brought foreigners into the conquered land to settle it and intermarry with the weaker people left behind. This happened to Samaria seven centuries before Jesus was born. Samaritans were a mixed-breed people.

Several centuries later when exiled Jews were allowed to return to Jerusalem to rebuild their temple, the Samaritans offered to help. But the Jews refused to let anyone who was not racially pure help with this sacred task. The rebuffed Samaritans set up a rival temple on Mount Gerizim near Sychar.

So strong was Jewish hatred of Samaritans that a well-known rabbinical ordinance stated, "Let no Israelite eat one mouthful of anything that is a Samaritan's, for if he eat but a mouthful, he is as if he ate swine's flesh." Strong words! In Luke 9:53 we later find Jesus and His disciples on a different journey trying to cross Samaria, only to be turned away from one village. Samaritans hated Jews as much as Jews hated Samaritans. Yet the Bible tells us that Jesus "had to go through Samaria."

It was a tough walk. The path twisted and turned through the mountains of the central ridge. Tired, Jesus sat on the side of Jacob's well to rest while His disciples went into the nearby town of Sychar to buy food. Sitting there under a sweltering noonday sun, He may have noticed the lone woman coming down the hill with a water jug balanced on her shoulder.

We know very little about this nameless woman except that she had been married five times and was presently living with a man who was not her husband. We don't know what had happened to the five men she had married at one time or another. Some or all of them may have died. Some or all of them may have divorced her.

One thing is clear: if any of her marriages dissolved in divorce, she did not initiate the proceedings. Unlike today, a woman in the first century did not have that right. Only a man could end a marriage by divorce. It was part of the Law of Moses under which both Jews and Samaritans lived. Moses had spelled out the law in Deuteronomy 24:1–4:

> If a man marries a woman who becomes displeasing to him because he finds something indecent about her, and he writes her a certificate of divorce, gives it to her and sends her from his house, and if after she leaves his house she becomes the wife of another man, and her second husband dislikes her and writes her a certificate of divorce, gives it to her and sends her from his house, or if he dies, then her first husband, who divorced her, is not allowed to marry her again after she has been defiled. That would be detestable in the eyes of the LORD.

This complicated law prohibited a man from remarrying a woman he had previously divorced. The rabbis had, however, shifted the emphasis from remarriage and used the passage to decide the basis on which a man could divorce his wife. They focused on what it would take for a woman to "become displeasing to her husband."

The rabbinic school of Shammah took a strict view and taught that only some action contrary to the rules of virtue—like adultery—justified divorce. But Shammah's disciple Hillel taught the opposite: "something indecent in her" could mean anything that displeased the husband, like too much salt in the food. So a Jewish man who wanted to divorce his wife could choose to follow the teachings of Rabbi Hillel if that suited him.

Who knows what happened to our nameless woman's five husbands? If she turned out to be a bad cook—or worse, could not bear sons—or any thing else that "displeased" her husband, she could be passed from husband to husband like a bad coin. What must that have meant for her to have experienced loss or rejection five times? The pain of loss experienced once is a pain from which many women never recover. What must it be to know that pain not once, not twice, but five times? The sense of failure. The slap at self-esteem. The panic, wondering what would happen to her next. Being put out of her husband's house with nothing more than a scrap of parchment in her hand that would allow her to marry someone else and try again.

Even worse, a woman in the first century could not compel her husband to give her a certificate of divorce so that she could remarry. This lone woman approaching Jacob's well with a water jug on her shoulder may have struggled with that problem. It was almost impossible for a single woman to survive without the support of a man at that time. If her last husband had refused to give her a certificate of divorce, she may have found herself forced to live with a man she was not free to marry.

Whatever had happened to this woman, Jesus watched her approach the well at noon, the sixth hour, the hottest part of the day. Most women came to the well first thing in the morning or in the evening when it was cooler. Did this woman choose to come for water when she thought no one else would be at the well? Was she attempting to escape the cold stares of townspeople who scorned her? Jesus watched her trudge toward the well, weary with the weight of years of loss or rejection.

As she neared the well, she saw Him sitting there. Who was He? Only women drew water, except for shepherds who watered their sheep. But there were no sheep. This man was clearly no shepherd. He was dressed in the long white robe of a rabbi or teacher.

Even more surprising, He spoke to her: "Will you give me a drink?" To us that simple question is not shocking. But Jesus broke two strong Jewish customs in that moment.

First, a Jewish man did not speak to women in public. If the man were a rabbi or religious teacher, he might not even greet his own wife when passing her on the street. It was a precept of the Jewish moralists that "a man should not salute a woman in a public place, not even his own wife."

Some Pharisees were called "the bruised and bleeding Pharisees" because whenever they saw a woman in public, they shut their eyes. Not surprisingly, they sometimes bumped into walls, injuring themselves. A strange evidence of spirituality! Jesus, however, was not limited by the customs of His day in His approach to women.

The second custom Jesus broke was to drink from a contaminated cup held by a despised Samaritan woman. She was a woman. She was a Samaritan. To make matters worse, she lived with a man to whom she was not married, and that made her unclean. Double jeopardy. The cup was "unclean" twice: because a Samaritan held it and because the woman holding it was unclean.

Any other man at Jacob's well that day would have ignored the Samaritan woman. The barriers of race, religion, sex, character, and social position were too great. But Jesus was different. He had chosen to go to Galilee by way of Samaria. He had chosen this place to rest because a lonely woman needed to hear a word of hope.

"Will you give me a drink?" He asked.

This wary, worldlywise woman countered His question with another question: "You are a Jew and I am a Samaritan woman. How can you ask me for a drink?" (John 4:9).

Her question hung in the air unanswered as Jesus turned His first request inside-out: "If you knew the gift of God and who it is that asks you for a drink, you would have asked him and he would have given you living water" (John 4:10).

What kind of riddle was this? He had asked her for a drink. Then He told her He had "living" water she could ask for. Was this double-talk?

Jesus posed His question to open a conversation. But He also had a different end in view. He wanted to awaken in this woman two things: an awareness of her need and of God's willingness to meet her need. So He told her two things she didn't know. She didn't know "the gift of God," and she didn't know who it was who spoke to her that day.

Standing in the hot sun, bothered by this stranger who broke all the conventions by talking to her, yet intrigued by His offer, she decided to take Him on:

> "Sir," the woman said, "you have nothing to draw with and the well is deep. Where can you get this living water? Are you greater than our father Jacob, who gave us the well and drank from it himself, as did also his sons and his flocks and herds?" (John 4:11–12)

A good series of questions. She could see that Jesus had no way of drawing water from the well. Was He some kind of miracle-worker, greater than the patriarch Jacob, that He could produce living water?

"Living" water was more desirable than other water. It was water from a spring or a fountain, like Perrier. Jacob's well had good water, but it wasn't running or living water. The well was replenished by rain and percolation. It was not fed by an underground spring or stream. It was not "living" water.

Some Bible scholars take this woman to task for interpreting Jesus' words literally. But is this unusual? In John 3 Nicodemus could not understand the new birth, mistaking it for a physical experience. Later in John 4 the disciples mistook Jesus' statement about having food to eat. They interpreted His metaphor as literal food.

"Are you greater than our father Jacob?" the woman asked Jesus. Again He sidestepped her question for the moment. She would get her answer when she had a different perspective and could understand it. Instead He brought her quick mind back to His promise of living water in verses 13 and 14:

> Everyone who drinks this water will be thirsty again, but whoever drinks the water I give him will never thirst. Indeed, the water I give him will become in him a spring of water welling up to eternal life.

She looked at Him sharply. Yes, the first part of what He said was certainly true. Day after day, weary year after weary year, she had carried her water jug from Sychar to the well and back. Anyone who drank that water would be thirsty again. That was clear enough. Wouldn't it be wonderful not to have to come to the well every day? Could this Jewish rabbi deliver on such a promise?

At the heart of Jesus' statement is the fundamental truth that our hearts thirst for something only the eternal God can satisfy. In every one of us lives this nameless longing for what is eternal. Augustine said it well: "Our hearts are restless until they find their rest in Thee, O God." There is a thirst only Jesus Christ can satisfy.

But our Samaritan woman wasn't there yet. She could think only of a supply of water that would relieve her of this daily trip from the village to the well. How could Jesus stimulate a spiritual desire in her mind? To do that, He had to change the subject. Follow their conversation in John 4:15–19:

> The woman said to him, "Sir, give me this water so that I won't get thirsty and have to keep coming here to draw water."

He told her, "Go, call your husband and come back."

"I have no husband," she replied.

Jesus said to her, "You are right when you say you have no husband. The fact is, you have had five husbands, and the man you now have is not your husband. What you have just said is quite true."

"Sir," the woman said, "I can see that you are a prophet."

Go, call your husband.

I have no husband.

Right! You had five, but now you live with a man who is not your husband.

Oops! Caught "as is."

An interesting conversation. Up to this point Jesus had been talking in a word picture about living water that satisfies so that the one drinking it never thirsts again. But the Samaritan woman couldn't connect with what He was saying. Jesus shifted gears so they would not talk past each other. He became absolutely personal and plain. She didn't recognize it yet, but Jesus had just started giving her living water.

Jesus did not judge her. He didn't insult her. He simply verified that she had told the truth. Yet in that statement He tore away her mask. She stood before Him with her embarrassing secret plainly visible. She faced herself as He saw her, "as is." We take that first sip of supernatural living water when we take off our masks and acknowledge ourselves as we really are.

Commentators criticize our Samaritan woman for deliberately changing the subject when Jesus started probing her marital situation. It's possible she was not being evasive. In verse 9 she referred to Jesus as merely a Jew. By verse 12 she wondered if He was a Jew greater than her ancestor Jacob. Now in verses 19 and 20 she has begun to suspect that He could be a prophet. If so, it was appropriate to bring up a question that may well have troubled her:

> Our fathers worshiped on this mountain, but you Jews claim that the place where we must worship is in Jerusalem.

These two people—the Jewish rabbi and the Samaritan woman—stood talking together in the shadow of the two great mountains, Ebal and Gerizim, where Samaritans carried on their worship. Acknowledging her past in the presence of a prophet, she may have faced her need to bring a sin offering and wondered where to bring it. Her spiritual anxiety at having her sin exposed may have pushed her to take her religion seriously.

Jesus made no effort to bring the conversation back to her many husbands or her present relationship. Instead, He took her question seriously and answered her carefully (verses 21–24):

> "Believe me, woman, a time is coming when you will worship the Father neither on this mountain nor in Jerusalem. You Samaritans worship what you do not know; we worship what we do know, for salvation is from the Jews. Yet a time is coming and has now come when the true worshipers will worship the Father in spirit and truth, for they are the kind of worshipers the

Father seeks. God is a spirit, and his worshipers must worship in spirit and in truth."

The Samaritan woman's question was about external religious worship. Jesus wanted her to understand a different kind of worship, an internal worship. In the process, He didn't exactly answer her question about where to worship. Instead, He led her to a place where her question became irrelevant. In her preoccupation with the place of worship, she had overlooked the object of worship, God. When Jesus answered her that spiritual worship of the Father is what matters, He moved her away from holy mountains and temples and rituals.

> The woman said, "I know that Messiah" (called Christ) "is coming. When he comes, he will explain everything to us."
> Then Jesus declared, "I who speak to you am he." (John 4:25–26)

Was this possible? God's Messiah wouldn't waste time talking with a broken woman at a well in Samaria! But could she doubt His word? He had told her things about herself that only a prophet of God could know. He had answered her question about worship seriously. She knew she didn't understand everything He had said, but she did know somehow that she could believe His word. In her encounter with Jesus, she made the journey to faith. We know that from her actions. We pick up the story again at verse 27:

> Just then his disciples returned and were surprised to find him talking with a woman. But

no one asked, "What do you want?" or "Why are you talking with her?"

Then, leaving her water jar, the woman went back to the town and said to the people, "Come, see a man who told me everything I ever did. Could this be the Christ?" They came out of the town and made their way toward him.

She didn't have it all straight. But she had gotten enough to motivate her to share the good news with others. In verse 39 we learn that "many of the Samaritans from that town believed in him because of the woman's testimony." They urged Jesus to stay and teach them. He did so for two more days and "because of his words many more became believers" (verse 41).

How did this woman's life turn out? We don't know. We do know that Jesus did not condemn her. He simply let her know that He knew her, really knew her down deep inside. In knowing her, He did not despise or condemn her. Jesus discipled the woman at Jacob's well by leading her to accept the facts of her life as they were without covering them up.

The beginning of having our thirst quenched is knowing that we are known by God and can still be accepted by Him. Following Jesus means taking a clear-eyed look at the facts of our lives without glossing them over. There's nothing quite like facing the reality of ourselves to help us see our need for God.

More than twenty years ago two friends—Annabelle Sandifer and Jeannette Evans—and I worked together to reach women in Paris, France, with the good news of eternal life through Jesus Christ. We organized luncheons, outreach coffees, Bible studies, women's retreats—anything we could think of to share Christ with women.

To broaden our outreach one year we decided to send Christmas luncheon invitations to the mothers of all the students at the prestigious American School of Paris. Among other luncheon responses, we received a reservation card from a Mrs. Parker. None of us knew who she was.

Half an hour before the luncheon began, while the dining room was still empty, I noticed a dramatically-dressed woman enter the room somewhat cautiously. Garbed in a magnificent suit under a sweeping cape, she had completed the visual drama with an enormous fur hat. A bit daunted by her elegance, I put on my friendliest smile and walked across the room to meet her. Yes, this was Mrs. Parker, but it was clear she had second thoughts about coming to the luncheon. She answered my greeting evasively and left me as soon as she could work her way to a nearby window where she stared at Paris traffic in the street below.

The luncheon seemed to go well. Our speaker that noon was a well-known Christian woman—vivacious, sophisticated, the kind of woman I assumed Mrs. Parker would enjoy. But she looked bored. The speaker ended her talk by saying, "If any of you would like to have me pray for you, give me your name and I'll be glad to do so."

That brought Mrs. Parker to life. "Of all the nerve!" she exploded. "Who does she think she is, offering to pray for me?" With that she gathered up her purse and cape and headed for the door. In the postmortem on that luncheon Annabelle, Jeannette, and I talked about Mrs. Parker and her disruptive departure. We were sure we would never see her again.

The Woman at the Well

We were wrong. A few months later we sponsored a women's retreat south of Paris. Edith Schaeffer of L'Abri in Switzerland agreed to speak. More than two hundred reservations poured in. We were thrilled! Then one day a reservation arrived from Mrs. Parker. What would happen this time? Would she embarrass us again?

The retreat began well. The weather was perfect. Edith Schaeffer thrilled her audience again and again with stories of God's work in the lives of all kinds of men and women. But the three of us kept watching for Mrs. Parker, who had not yet arrived.

She walked in during the afternoon session and found a place in the back of the packed meeting room. I watched her for some positive reaction to the speaker, but her face was impassive. When the session ended, Mrs. Parker appeared to avoid our friendly overtures, choosing to leaf through books on the literature table.

Then she spoke to the quiet woman selling books: "My daughter just became a Christian." Marjorie wasn't sure how to respond. "So is my sister in America," Mrs. Parker went on. "She sends me Christian books." Sensing her need to talk about this, Marjorie offered to drive her back to Paris when the retreat ended.

On the trip back to the city, Mrs. Parker talked about religion, Christianity, churches, and some of her bad experiences with Christians when she was young. Marjorie listened, responded, and prayed.

It is hard to imagine two women more different from each other. Marjorie had come to Paris for physical therapy after being crippled by polio in Central Africa where she served as a missionary. Mrs. Parker lived in the glitziest section of Paris. Two women completely different in style, in values, in goals. Yet between them grew a deep friendship as they talked day after day about what it meant to become a Christian. Two weeks later Mrs. Parker reached out for salvation through Jesus Christ. She joined her daughter and her sisters in the family of God.

One evening at dinner with a French editor and his wife, I mentioned a Mrs. Parker who had recently become a Christian after our women's retreat. Paul leaned forward when I said her name. "Did I hear you say 'Dorian Parker'?" he asked.

"Yes, do you know her?"

"Know her? Everyone in Paris knows her!"

"Then tell me, please, who she is!"

"She is DORIAN, often called the most beautiful woman in the world."

Revlon's first Fire and Ice Girl in the early 50s, she was one of the most photographed women in the world. A premiere model in Paris, she later opened the largest modeling agency in Europe. She married five times and gave birth to five children, but not always children of the men to whom she was married at the time.

Dorian. After enormous success, her life had begun to unravel. Back taxes owed to the French government would soon close down her business. In the cut-throat competition of international modeling, her business partner betrayed her. Her lover, a Spanish count and the father of her younger son, had died in a racing accident. Her son was on drugs and failing in school. Life was not beautiful.

After three decades of living without much thought for the people she had walked over, she faced herself and didn't like what she saw. She needed help. She needed God.

The Woman at the Well

When I first met Dorian, I saw a woman still glamorous in her fifties, a woman who had held the world on her palm and had swung it like a bauble at her wrist. She could be intimidating to other women and still attractive to men. Who could have guessed her inner thirst? Jesus knew and He met her at the well of her life.

When John wrote his account of Jesus' life and ministry, he observed that Jesus knew what is in each of us (John 2:25). He then recorded two stories, one about a Pharisee named Nicodemus (chapter 3), and one about the Samaritan woman (chapter 4). No two people could have been less alike than they. He was a Pharisee, she a woman living in sin. He was a religious leader, she an outcast. He was a Jew, she a Samaritan. He was at the top of the social ladder, while she was at the bottom. Nicodemus visited Jesus at night; Jesus arranged to encounter the woman at midday. Jesus confronted religious Nicodemus with his spiritual need to be born again. He approached this immoral woman with her thirst, a thirst He could fill. Jesus knew what was in Nicodemus and He knew what was in the woman from Samaria.

As with Nicodemus, the Samaritan woman, or Dorian, Jesus Christ meets us where we are. He seeks us and opens a conversation with us. He is, in Francis Thompson's words, the "Hound of Heaven" who pursues us with relentless love. He does so because He sees our need. He knows that our hearts thirst for something only the eternal God can satisfy. He sees the nameless, unsatisfied longing, the vague discontent, the lack, the frustration even before we admit it's there. We are never far from the longing for the eternal that God has put in our souls. It is a thirst only Jesus Christ can satisfy.

Our deepest thirst can never be satisfied until we know God, who is water to parched ground. We can't know God until we see ourselves and see our sin. Yet we may spend a lifetime covering up what we are. We have forgotten, or perhaps we never knew, that we cannot get anywhere with God until we recognize our sin. When we meet Jesus Christ, we discover that He knows us. We can't hide, grab for a mask, or play "Let's Pretend." He knows us deep down inside where we keep our secret file. He has read everything in that file. He knows us. Even more surprising, in spite of knowing us to our core, He loves us.

When we understand that, Jesus can begin giving us living water. He begins quenching our thirst by letting us know that He knows us but we are still accepted by God. That is life-changing, life-sustaining living water.

A first-century much-married woman. A twentieth-century much-married woman. Both let Jesus show them what they had been and what they could become when they were forgiven and wrapped in the warm love of God. Through their witness others came to the Savior. Dorian and the woman at the well. Both drank deeply of the living water and then started telling others, "Come and see!"

Questions for personal reflection or group discussion:

Augustine wrote, "Our hearts are restless until they find their rest in Thee, O God."

1. Have you found that you are never safe from the longing for eternity that God has put in your soul? If so, how have you experienced that longing?

2. What do you have to know in order to have that longing satisfied?

3. Jesus moved the Samaritan woman from a preoccupation with external religion to an inner conviction that He was God's Messiah and the Savior of the world. You, too, must make that journey. What have been some of the signposts along the way as you have traveled that road?

4. What connection do you see between being a member of the family of God and being a messenger to others to bring them into God's family?

Mary and Martha: How to Live Successfully in Two Worlds

When I entered fifth grade, I began studying what was then called "domestic science." By the time I reached high school, the name had changed to "home economics." I understand college course catalogs now label it "human ecology." By any name it was the same: a semester of cooking, a semester of sewing, a semester of cooking, a semester of sewing. You may have found yourself in a similar track.

I'm not sure which I hated most—the cooking or the sewing. At age ten I could not separate eggs neatly or make decent flat-felled seams. I remember mostly that I dreaded the hours spent in the domestic science rooms.

We learned to sew using treadle machines. No electric wizards then. When I stopped recently at a fabric store for a pattern, I glanced at the array of modern sewing machines on display—wonderful electronic computerized miracle workers! While I stood there admiring technology in the service of seamstresses, I also noticed one thing that has hardly changed since my first introduction to domestic science fifty years ago. On the front of the sewing machine just above the needle is a dial that adjusts the tension on the thread as the machine sews.

For a strong, firm seam a thread from the spool above and another thread from the bobbin below must interlock smoothly and tightly in the fabric. An experienced seamstress checks the thread tension and makes minute adjustments in setting that dial because she understands how important it is that the tension be regulated properly.

At times as I sew, I accidentally bump that dial. I hear the click-click that tells me I've messed up the delicate balance of upper and lower threads. I know that no seams will be strong and usable until I get the tension adjusted again. Everything else has to stop until I'm satisfied that the threads are interlocking properly.

As I read through Luke 10 recently, I thought about the tension dial on my sewing machine. Luke writes about a dinner party held in a home in Bethany in verses 38–42 (NKJV):

> Now it happened as they went that Jesus entered a certain village; and a certain woman named Martha welcomed him into her house. And she had a sister called Mary, who also sat at Jesus' feet and heard his word. But Martha was distracted with much serving, and she approached him and said, "Lord, do you not care that my sister has left me to serve alone? Therefore, tell her to help me."
>
> And Jesus answered and said to her, "Martha, Martha, you are worried and troubled about many things. But one thing is needed, and Mary has chosen that good part, which will not be taken away from her."

The scene: a hot day at the end of the rainy season as summer was beginning. A whitewashed village on a hillside just two miles east of Jerusalem. The home of Martha who was possibly a well-to-do widow who had taken in her younger sister Mary and younger brother Lazarus.

She welcomes Jesus and His followers to her home in Bethany. She hurries to arrange a comfortable seat for Jesus and then to bring a cool drink to each of her guests. She nods to Mary who fills the basin near the door with water, then takes a towel and begins to wash each guest's feet. Jesus' followers seat themselves around the large room, chatting quietly about events of recent days. Villagers begin to crowd the doorway, anxious to come in and listen to the great Rabbi, Jesus. This is not His first visit to Bethany. The townsfolk have heard some of His surprising stories before. Perhaps he will tell them more. A few edge in and sit down outside the ring of disciples. Martha and Mary also take their places at Jesus' feet. We know that from Luke 10:39—Martha had a sister called Mary who also sat at Jesus' feet and heard His word. Apparently they both took the posture of learners or disciples, sitting at Jesus' feet.

I don't know how long Martha sat there listening to the Lord Jesus. But I have a feeling that if she was anything like me, she sat there that day with a divided mind. After all, here were thirteen men who would be hungry and needed to be fed. What was on hand to feed them? What would it take to get everything ready? Would she need to slip out and run to a few shops for grain or fruit?

I identify with Martha. I know exactly what she was doing as she sat there. First, she made a mental inventory of everything in the pantry. After that, she planned the menu, making sure she didn't overlook anything. Then she made a list in her head of all the tasks that would have to be done. When she had thought everything through, she glanced around the room surreptitiously to see the best route through the crowd to get from where she was sitting into the kitchen. When she had plotted her exit, she could sit there no longer. She had to get busy! After all, she was the hostess. It was her responsibility to meet the needs of her guests. No one would think less of Lazarus or Mary if the meal were not adequate. The blame would land squarely on her. No time to sit and listen to Jesus now. Perhaps after all the work was done.

Once in the kitchen she felt that flush of excitement that comes to many of us when we are about to do something special for someone we really care about. We want everything to be perfect—well, at least as nearly perfect as possible. Our love energizes us. We are exhilarated by the opportunity to show our love for someone special.

Can you see Martha, now in the familiar territory of her kitchen, turning into a whirlwind of activity? First, start the beans and lentils cooking with onions and garlic. Then dress the lamb for roasting. Grind the grain and mix the bread for baking. Then prepare the figs and pomegranates. Get water to mix with the wine. Set the table. Stir the beans and lentils. Turn the lamb on the spit. Start baking the bread.

Glancing out the window at the position of the sun in the sky, Martha suddenly realized it would soon be mealtime and she was far from finished. She may have felt what I feel when I've been carried along on the crest of my enthusiasm only to realize I'm running out of time and I can't finish everything I planned to do. When that happens, I get angry—angry with myself and angry with anyone else who might have made a difference in accomplishing my plans.

I suspect that is what happened to Martha. Suddenly the plans and the work that had started out as pure joy turned sour. Luke tells us in verse 40 that she was distracted by all the preparations she was making. The harder she worked, the more worked up she became.

It was Mary's fault. If Mary had been there to help her, it would have been different.

We all know that feeling, don't we? It's bad enough having everything to do. It's even worse when someone we think should be helping us pull the load lets us down. Our irritation about the unfairness of it all builds to the bursting point.

That's what happened to Martha. She explodes in verse 40: "Lord, do you not care that my sister has left me to serve alone? Therefore tell her to help me."

Interesting, isn't it, that Martha spoke her irritation to Jesus, not to Mary. Perhaps she had already tried unsuccessfully to catch Mary's eye and signal her to get up and help. Or she may have nudged Mary who shook off her nudge and went on listening to Jesus. We all have ways we use to get a message across. We clear our throat. We drum our fingers on the table top. We make attention-getting motions. It irritates us even more when the other person ignores us!

Whatever had already happened, Martha spoke directly to Jesus, accusing Him of not caring about her. She was sure that, if He really cared, He would tell Mary to get up and help her.

I'm intrigued by the way Martha linked Jesus' care for her to His willingness to tell Mary to get busy. Martha thought she knew just how Jesus should demonstrate His care—by lightening her load.

That is exactly what we see Him doing, though not in the way she expected. In His response we learn much about our discipleship as Christian women:

> Martha, Martha, . . . you are worried and upset about many things, but only one thing is needed. Mary has chosen what is better, and it will not be taken away from her (Luke 10:41).

The problem did not lie in the work Martha was doing. It was her attitude of fretting and worry that created the bad situation. Jesus knew that Martha put too much stress on things that didn't matter. Martha's problem was one of balance, of holding life in the proper tension. Take a closer look at what Jesus said and did not say to this overburdened woman.

First, Jesus did not rebuke her for making preparations for Him and His disciples. If she as the hostess in the home had decided to skip any food preparation, her guests would have gone hungry. What was going on in that Bethany kitchen was important.

Do you recall what Jesus had said to Satan when tempted in the wilderness at the outset of His public ministry? In Matthew 4:4 we read, "Man does not live by bread alone." Jesus did not say, "People don't live by bread." We do live by bread. We have bodies that must be fed. Jesus knew that and fed people—as many as five thousand at one time.

But Jesus also knew that people are more than bodies. We do not live by bread alone. To feed our spirits is at least as important as feeding our bodies. Martha's problem was not that she was preparing food for her guests to eat. That was necessary, and in her role as hostess, it was her place to see that it was done. But she gave it too much importance. Instead of settling for a simple supper, she tried to impress with an elaborate meal. Jesus in essence told her that one dish would have been enough.

We all have responsibilities we carry out every day of our lives. We go to the office. We cook. We grade papers. We clean the house. We do the laundry. We do these things, and we want to do them well. Dorothy Sayers reminds us that no crooked table legs came out of the carpenter shop in Nazareth. God is not honored by shoddy work or the neglect of our necessary duties in life.

But we must be sure that the necessary doesn't get out of proportion and distort our lives. We can easily confuse means and ends. Without thinking, we can turn what is a means to living for God into an end in itself. When we take something that is not too important and make it primary in our lives, what is otherwise harmless can become a stumbling block for us.

One of the things Jesus saw that afternoon two thousand years ago was that Martha was looking down on what Mary had chosen to do. Martha imposed her value system—possibly a sparkling house and certainly a sumptuous meal—on Mary. If bustling around was "necessary" for Martha, it must also be necessary for Mary.

Note that Jesus did not tell Martha to do what Mary was doing. At the same time, He pointed out that Mary had chosen the good part. In saying this, Jesus made a little play on words that does not come through in English translations. In essence He said, "Martha, you are preparing many dishes for us to eat, but Mary has prepared the one dish you can't fix in your kitchen."

While food was necessary, something much simpler would have been better, allowing Martha to continue sitting with Mary and learning from Christ.

Do you think Jesus was being a bit hard on Martha? After all, she was doing all this work to please Him! Yet do you think He was pleased with her request that He tell Mary to get up and help her? Do you think Mary was pleased to be humiliated in that way? Do you think the disciples and neighbors were pleased to have the Teacher interrupted in that way? And what about Martha herself? Do you think she was pleased with herself? We know when we have spoiled things for ourselves and others around us. And spoil things Martha did!

As you picture this scene in your mind, what image of Martha comes into your head? Elisabeth Moltmann-Wendel remarked that whenever she thinks of Martha, she remembers a picture from a children's Bible. In it Mary is sitting at Jesus' feet listening and Martha is in the background, leaning against the kitchen door with an evil, mistrustful look on her face.

When we think about these two sisters, we tend to imagine Mary with an aura of holiness around her, and we associate Martha with olive oil and fish.

When someone says, "She's a Martha-type," we know just what that means. Someone who is practical, competent, down-to-earth. Marthas are certainly useful and necessary. The church would be in a tough spot if we were all Marys. But when it comes to painting a model or an ideal, it's Mary all the way. That puts us in a bind of sorts, if we think about it. Martha's work is necessary—in the church and in the home. But Mary gets the halo.

Martha, called the patron saint of housewives and cooks, comes in for quite a bit of bashing. Martin Luther wrote, "Martha, your work must be punished and counted as naught . . . I will have no work but the work of Mary."

Stiff words! So I feel a bit sheepish about being a Martha. But Martin Luther was wrong. Martha's work must not be punished and counted as naught. Martha's attitude needed correcting. Martha's perspective needed changing. But Martha's work is good and necessary. The reality is that as followers of Jesus Christ, we need to cultivate both the Martha and the Mary in each of us.

Earlier in Luke 10 we find the story of a lawyer who tried to trap Jesus by asking Him what he had to do to inherit eternal life. Jesus turned the question back on the lawyer by asking him simply, "What is written in the law? What is your reading of it?" The lawyer responded with that great statement taken from Deuteronomy 6:5 and Leviticus 19:18—we are to love the Lord our God with all our heart, with all our soul, with all our strength, and with all our mind, and our neighbor as ourselves.

The lawyer got the answer absolutely right. Jesus agreed, saying, "You have answered correctly. Do this and you will live."

The lawyer could have left it at that, but he didn't. He pressed Jesus with another question: "And just who is my neighbor?" To answer that, Jesus told one of those wonderful stories that take us by surprise.

The story was about a man traveling from Jerusalem down to Jericho on a dusty mountain road. Some thieves attacked him, stripped him naked, beat him up, and left him half dead. First, a priest came by. He might have just finished his week of service rotation in Jerusalem and was on his way home for another year. He saw this poor man, but went out of his way to avoid any contact with him. Then a Levite came along. Levites in first-century Israel were a kind of lower-order priest who sang at the time of the sacrifice and who served as a doorkeeper and servant to the higher-order priests. The Levite, like the priest, glanced at the injured man and passed by on the other side of the road.

The third person who came along was a Samaritan, despised by the Jews. You have to know how much Jews detested Samaritans to have any idea how shocking this story was that Jesus would say a Samaritan came along. This despised foreigner saw the man, and, instead of doing what the religious Jews had done, he stopped and dressed and bandaged the poor man's wounds, put the man on his donkey, and took him to an inn where he cared for him. He even paid the innkeeper to continue caring for the man while he went on his way.

What was the punch line? When Jesus finished the story, He asked the lawyer, "Who do you think was a neighbor to the injured man?" Of course, the lawyer had to say, "The one who showed mercy to him." And Jesus answered, "Go and do likewise."

Wasn't that just what Martha had done? Hadn't she inconvenienced herself to treat Jesus and His disciples kindly? Wasn't she meeting someone else's need? Absolutely! Wasn't she being a good Samaritan while Mary ignored the physical needs of their guests as the two religious Jews had ignored the man who was beaten and robbed?

Take a second look at the answer for which Jesus commended that first-century lawyer: we are to love the Lord our God with [from] all our heart, with all our soul, with all our strength, and with all our mind, and our neighbor as ourselves.

Note the order of the two loves: God first, then neighbor. Not the other way around. It is not a question of contrasting the activist life to the contemplative life. It's a matter of priorities. We put listening to and learning the Word of God before service. That equips and inspires us for our service for God to others.

What Jesus wanted that day was not Martha's lentils and lamb, but Martha herself. The one dish she could not prepare in her kitchen was her relationship to God. She could prepare that dish only by remaining at Jesus' feet and letting Him provide the food for her soul.

Martha wanted Jesus to lighten her load that day. He did exactly that, but not the way she thought it should be done. He knew that our relationship with God does not develop in the midst of fretting busyness. The one thing needful is to hear God speak to us. Mary chose to put time into that primary relationship and not to be distracted by trivia.

"Martha must be a Mary," wrote one commentator, "and the true Mary must also be a Martha; both are sisters." That brings me back to my sewing machine tension dial. If the tension on the top thread is too loose, the underside of the fabric will be snarled with excess thread. The seam has no strength. It pulls apart hopelessly the moment pressure is applied to it. The only thing a seamstress can do is to pull out all the threads, adjust the tension, and start over.

We also have no usable seam if the threads are not feeding from both the top spool and the underneath bobbin. We could try to sew all day with only the top spool on the machine and nothing in the bobbin holder. We would not have a single seam. The Martha thread and the Mary thread must both be properly feeding and interlocking if we are to have any seam at all. The balance between the two has to be finely adjusted if the resulting seam is to be strong and usable.

We live in this world. This means we concern ourselves with food and clothes and homes and family and jobs and studies. But we also live in the world of the spirit. We concern ourselves with our relationship to God. That was Martha's real problem. She was sewing with no thread in the bobbin.

To get our service right, we get our priorities right. We let Jesus minister to us before we go out to minister for Him. That is God's order: we first love the Lord our God with all our heart, soul, strength, and mind, and then we are prepared to go out and love our neighbor as ourselves. When we turn that upside down, we may end up feeling overworked and unappreciated. When we keep our priorities in line with God's priorities, we will find that God enables us to do what needs to be done with joy and satisfaction.

Questions for personal reflection or group discussion:

1. When you think of Mary and Martha, with whom do you naturally identify?
2. What steps could you take to gain a better balance between the priorities of Mary and the priorities of Martha in your life?
3. How does worry affect a woman's relationship to God?
4. What have you learned from Mary and Martha that will affect your discipleship in the future?

Martha and Mary: How to Nourish Hope in Times of Loss

When my husband finished his studies at Denver Seminary in 1956, we moved to his first pastorate in a small town in central Wyoming. As we got acquainted with the leaders of the church, we came to appreciate one older couple in particular. Gene, a retired carpenter, arrived at the church every morning to help build an addition to the church education wing. Mae stopped by almost as often. We admired the tireless commitment to Jesus Christ and to His church they both lived in front of us daily.

About six months after we arrived, a phone call brought the news that Don, Gene's and Mae's only son, had just been crushed to death in a local open-pit mine accident. We hurried across town to be with our friends as they groped through their shock and disbelief. It would be an excruciating time for them as they moved through their grief. But we were sure they would make it. They had all the Christian resources to support them during this crisis. Other friends came in, and we were confident that an entire community would surround them, their daughter-in-law, and two grandsons with love and concern.

A few days after the funeral Gene returned to his volunteer work on the church building. But on Sundays he came to church alone. When we dropped by their house, we sensed that Gene was finding strength to cope with his grief, but it was different for Mae.

When we asked about this, we learned that from the time word of the accident came, Mae turned her back on God. How could she believe in a God who would deny them their only child and deny their grandsons a father? God could not possibly be loving and kind and, at the same time, deal them such a blow. Whenever we visited her, we listened to her case against God. It was clear that the facts of her faith and the facts of her life didn't mesh. The faith that we thought would sustain her seemed to get in her way.

Mae reminded me of two other women who sent for Jesus when their brother was seriously ill. But Jesus didn't arrive in time to help them. When He finally showed up, both women said to Him, "Lord, if you had been here, our brother wouldn't have died!" These sisters had enough faith to believe that if Jesus had come, He could have healed their brother. But it looked as if Jesus had let them down.

The story is found in John 11. The first six verses tell us this:

> Now a man named Lazarus was sick. He was from Bethany, the village of Mary and her sister Martha. This Mary, whose brother Lazarus now lay sick, was the same one who poured perfume on the Lord and wiped his feet with her hair. So the sisters sent word to Jesus, "Lord, the one you love is sick." When he heard this, Jesus said, "This sickness will not end in death. No, it is for God's glory so that God's Son may be glorified through it." Jesus loved Martha and her sister and Lazarus.

Yet when he heard that Lazarus was sick, he stayed where he was two more days.

That's the setting. Lazarus was sick. His two sisters, Mary and Martha, turned at once to their friend Jesus, hoping He would come quickly and heal their brother before it was too late.

Knowing that Jesus loved this trio, we would expect Him to set out immediately for Bethany to do what He could to spare them anxiety and grief. Yet we see Jesus not responding in the way the two sisters hoped. Instead of leaving at once for Bethany, He stayed where He was for two more days.

An important principle in life is that love permits pain. We don't want it that way. We want to believe that if God truly loves us, He will not allow anything painful to invade our lives. But this is not so. God's love does not guarantee us a shelter from difficult experiences that are necessary for our spiritual growth. Love and delay are compatible.

If Jesus had rushed off to Bethany as soon as He received word of Lazarus' illness, Mary and Martha would not have been suspended between hope and despair, hope that the one who could help their brother would arrive in time, despair that He would come too late. They would have been spared the anguish of watching Lazarus sink into death. They would have avoided the agony of those last moments before they closed Lazarus' eyes and prepared his body for burial. They would have forestalled the desolation of bereavement. But Jesus didn't come.

He knew that it was time for Mary, Martha, and His disciples to learn what they could not learn if He intervened too quickly. John 11 tells us how completely in control of the situation Jesus was. He knew just what He was doing. He knew that the spiritual growth of Martha and Mary and His band of disciples traveling with Him depended on the right timing. How do we know that? Read John 11:7–16:

> Then Jesus said to his disciples, "Let us go back to Judea."
> "But Rabbi," they said, "a short while ago the Jews tried to stone you, and yet you are going back there?"
> Jesus answered, "Are there not twelve hours of daylight? A man who walks by day will not stumble, for he sees by this world's light. It is when he walks by night that he stumbles, for he has no light." After he had said this, he went on to tell them, "Our friend Lazarus has fallen asleep; but I am going there to wake him up."
> His disciples replied, "Lord, if he sleeps, he will get better." Jesus had been speaking of his death, but his disciples thought he meant natural sleep.
> So then he told them plainly, "Lazarus is dead, and for your sake I am glad I was not there, so that you may believe. But let us go to him."
> Then Thomas (called Didymus) said to the rest of the disciples, "Let us also go, that we may die with him."

Divine timing. Jesus knew that Mary and Martha would never know Him as the Resurrection and the Life had Lazarus not died. David would not have known God as his Rock and his Fortress had he not been hunted by

Saul in the mountains of Engedi. The Israelites would not have known God as their Deliverer had they not been slaves in Egypt. Our painful experiences can reveal God to us in new ways. Jesus knew precisely what He was doing.

On His arrival, Jesus found that Lazarus had been in the tomb for four days. Many Jews had come from Jerusalem to Bethany to comfort Martha and Mary in the loss of their brother. Sympathy for them was the first of all duties. Nothing else was more important than expressing sorrow with the bereaved.

In the hot climate of Israel the deceased had to be buried immediately after death. Women anointed the body with the finest spices and ointments, then wrapped it in a linen garment with the hands and feet swathed in bandage-like wrappings and the head enclosed in a towel. Everyone who could possibly come would join the procession from the house to the tomb. Curiously, women walked first because, according to the teachers of the day, it was a woman by her sin in the Garden of Eden who was responsible for death coming into the world.

At the tomb friends made memorial speeches. Then the mourners formed two long lines between which the family members walked. As long as the dead body remained in the house, the family was forbidden to prepare food there, to eat meat or drink wine, or to study. When the body was carried out, all the furniture was turned upside-down and the mourners sat on the ground or on low stools. On returning from the tomb, they ate a meal of bread, hard-boiled eggs, and lentils, symbolizing life, which was always rolling toward death.

Deep mourning lasted seven days, during which no one could anoint himself, put on shoes, engage in study or business, or even wash. Thirty days of lighter mourning followed the week of heavy mourning.

In the middle of this period of deep mourning, Martha heard that Jesus was entering the village. Violating the conventions of the East, she went out to meet Him while Mary stayed in the house. The gospel writer records the remarkable conversation Martha and Jesus had in John 11:21–27:

> "Lord," Martha said to Jesus, "if you had been here, my brother would not have died. But I know that even now God will give you whatever you ask."
>
> Jesus said to her, "Your brother will rise again."
>
> Martha answered, "I know he will rise again in the resurrection at the last day."
>
> Jesus said to her, "I am the resurrection and the life. He who believes in me will live, even though he dies; and whoever lives and believes in me will never die. Do you believe this?"
>
> "Yes, Lord," she told him, "I believe that you are the Christ, the Son of God, who was to come into the world."

"Lord, if you had been here, my brother would not have died." In that statement Martha gave voice to her doubt that Jesus had unlimited power. Had He been there, this would not have happened. He had to be present to heal her brother. Yet her general confidence in Jesus shines through: "But I know that even now God will give you whatever you ask."

Jesus answered her by turning her mind to the promise of the resurrection: "Your brother will rise again." Martha seemed impatient as she shot back, "Yes, Lord, I know he will rise again in the resurrection at the last day."

She knew the truth. She had the doctrine down right. In fact, she had a stronger spiritual base than the Sadducees who denied the resurrection. In her statement she bore witness to the strong teaching of her nation's faith. But she didn't find much comfort in the future tense. In that moment she needed something more immediate than an event as far off as the resurrection at the Last Day. The doctrine was not particularly consoling in her time of sorrow.

Jesus saw that and turned her idea of resurrection as a future event into a present reality: "I am the resurrection and the life." What must Martha have felt in that dramatic moment! "I am the resurrection and the life!" With those startling words Jesus brought Martha's thoughts from a dim future hope to a present fact. He gave her faith its true object, Himself. Confidence in Jesus Christ, the God-Man who is the resurrection and the life, could replace her vague hope in a future event.

How do we get that confidence? Jesus told us how in verse 25: "He who believes in me will live, even though he dies; and whoever lives and believes in me will never die."

When we believe in Jesus Christ, we gain a quality of life that is larger than death. Death becomes not the end of life, but the door into a larger life. People call our world "the land of the living." We might better call it "the land of the dying." We begin to die the moment we are born, and our lives are an inexorable move toward death. But those who have believed in Jesus Christ know that when death comes, we do not pass out of the land of the living but into the land of the living. We are not on our way to death. We are on our way to life. That's what it means to be born again. That's what it means to have eternal life. That's what it means to believe in Jesus Christ.

How did Jesus end His statement to Martha? He asked, "Do you believe this?" With that question He brought her to the question of personal faith. The faith that leads to eternal life can never be a faith we have inherited from our grandparents or that we acquire from being around the pastor. It is a personal commitment each one of us must make.

To Jesus' question Martha gave a remarkable answer (verse 27): "Yes, Lord, I believe that you are the Christ, the Son of God, who was to come into the world." Compare that to Peter's great confession (Matthew 16:16). Jesus had asked him, "Who do you say I am?" Peter had responded, "You are the Christ, the Son of the living God." Jesus responded that upon that confession, that truth, the church would be built.

Martha understood the same truth. Where had she learned it? Had she sat at Jesus' feet? Had she listened to Him teach the crowds? Clearly this woman, though her faith was imperfect, grasped the central truth on which it could grow: Jesus is the one sent by God.

It is the same for us today. It is on the truth Martha spoke that day in Bethany two thousand years ago that you and I come to the One who is the resurrection and the life. We cannot begin to grow until we see Jesus for who He is and we come to Him as we are.

The story moves on. Martha returned to the house and, taking Mary aside, told her that the Teacher had arrived and asked for her. Mary got up quickly and went to meet Jesus. She, in turn, spoke the same words Martha had used: "Lord, if you had been here, my brother would not have died." The same words Martha had used, but with one omission. Martha had gone on to say, "But I know that even now God will give you whatever you ask." Martha, for all her shortcomings, spoke of her faith. Mary, in contrast, was overwhelmed by her grief. She had sat at Jesus' feet and learned from Him. But now in His presence she was wrung out with her all-consuming sorrow.

When we read the other Mary-Martha story in Luke 10, it appeared that Mary was the "spiritual" one and Martha was the "unspiritual" one. Now as we look at these same two women, we discover that practical Martha had understood enough to give a magnificent confession of faith in Jesus Christ. Mary, on the other hand, was too engulfed in her loss to do more than say, "Jesus, if you had been here, my brother would not have died."

Note how Jesus adjusted to each one's need. With Martha, even in a time of deep mourning, He spoke deep theological truth. With Mary He sympathized. He met her where she was so that He could take her to a different level of faith. Thus it is with each of us. God starts with us where we are. But He doesn't leave us there. He moves us to a deeper level of faith.

The stage was now set. Four days had passed since Lazarus died. The usual Palestinian tomb was a cave with shelves cut in the rock on three sides. At the opening of the tomb a groove was made in the ground and a great wheel-shaped stone was set in the groove so it could be rolled across the entrance to the cave. For the Jews it was important that the entrance be well sealed. They believed that the spirits of the departed hovered around the tombs for four days, seeking entrance again into the body of the departed one. But after four days they left because by then the body would be so decayed they could no longer recognize it.

The mourners had followed Mary and now gathered in front of the cave. The oriental point of view was that the more unrestrained the mourning, the more honor they paid to the dead. These who had come to comfort Mary and Martha were not quietly weeping with heads averted. Instead, they honored Lazarus with unrestrained wailing, with hysterical shrieking.

Jesus stood in the midst of the crowd of mourners. In both verses 33 and 38 John described Him by using a Greek word that is not accurately translated in many Bibles. Jesus was more than "deeply moved." He shuddered with indignation.

Indignation at what? Jesus stood there that day as the Lord of Life, the one who had just told Martha that He was the resurrection and the life. There He was face to face with all the effects of the Fall: death, human misery, broken hearts. He had come into the world to deliver us from death and condemnation. He knew that as He confronted and conquered death that day, the final conquest could come in only one way. He, too, would have to pass through death. He would have to taste its bitterness. He would have to die.

He shuddered—shuddered at the awfulness of death. He shuddered at the consequences of sin. He shuddered at the pain of alienation. He shuddered with indignation that any of this had to happen. And then He acted. He spoke four times.

Speaking to the mourners, He simply said, "Take away the stone" (John 11:39). Jesus could have told the stone to roll away without human help, but He didn't. Those who stood there that day were given that task. God works with an economy of divine power. He requires us to do what we can do. He tests us by involving us in His miracles. "Take away the stone."

Had the Jews standing there heard correctly? Take away the stone? Surely Jesus couldn't be serious! Martha echoed their thoughts when she protested, "But, Lord! By this time there is a bad odor, for he has been there four days!" Martha just missed the point of that conversation out on the roadside. Jesus had to remind her, "Did I not tell you that if you believed, you would see the glory of God?" (verse 40). Jesus worked to raise Martha's faith to a higher level so that she could look beyond the earthly, the practical, and the mundane to see spiritual reality. "Take away the stone."

The second time Jesus spoke, it was to God: "Father, I thank you that you have heard me. I knew that you always hear me, but I said this for the benefit of the people standing here that they may believe that you sent me." Martha had said she believed that. But did the others? Did Mary? Did the disciples? Jesus laid His divine claim on the line. He did it to lead people to faith.

The third time Jesus spoke, He addressed Lazarus: "Lazarus, come out!" (verse 43). The dead man stumbled out, his hands and feet wrapped with strips of linen and a towel around his face. The crowd fell back, awestruck. Were their senses playing tricks on their minds? They had seen a dead corpse carried into that tomb four days earlier. It could not be true that Lazarus was alive again!

Jesus had not prayed, "Father, raise him from death!" Nor had He said, "In the name of the Father, come out." He had told Martha that He was the resurrection and the life. He acted on His own authority. He was the Lord of life. And Lazarus came out.

The fourth time Jesus spoke, it was again to the astonished audience: "Take off the grave clothes and let him go" (verse 44). The gasping bystanders needed to touch Lazarus and see for themselves that He was not a ghost.

Two things happened. First, many of the Jews who had come to visit Mary put their faith in Jesus (verse 45). That was the immediate result. Second, word of this incredible miracle soon reached the religious leaders in Jerusalem. They saw Jesus as a threat to their power. They met to seal His fate with a sentence of death.

A sentence of death? Yes, for Him. But a sentence of life for all of us who believe. He is the resurrection and the life. The one who believes in Him will live, even though that person dies. Whoever lives and believes in Him will never die. Do you believe this?

The old storytellers in many lands tell of a fabulous bird, sacred to the sun, called the phoenix. This huge bird, covered with an iridescent rainbow of gorgeous feathers, had no equal on earth. Not only was no other bird so beautiful, but none other sang so sweetly nor lived so long. The storytellers could not agree on the age of the phoenix. Some said the bird lived for five hundred years. Others said its life was more than twelve thousand years long.

When those years ended the phoenix made itself a nest of twigs from spice trees, set its nest on fire, and, with the nest, was consumed. Nothing remained except a scattering of ashes on the earth. But then, the storytellers said, a breeze caught those ashes and somehow from them there arose another phoenix, a new firebird even more splendid than the one that had died. He would spread his wings, they said, and he would fly up to the sun.

The storytellers spun this myth in the fond hope that somehow it could be true. They spoke to something deep within each of us, the longing that out of the destructive tragedies of life, something better, more magnificent might come. What the storytellers could only imagine contains a truth of which Jesus Christ is the reality. Just as the more glorious phoenix can rise only from the ashes of its dead self and ruined nest, so great faith rises only from our dashed hopes and ruined dreams.

"If God wants you to trust Him," wrote Donald Gray Barnhouse, "He puts you in a place of difficulty. If He wants you to trust Him greatly, He puts you in a place of impossibility. For when a thing is impossible, then we who are so prone to move things by the force of our own being can say, 'Lord, it has to be you. I am utterly, absolutely nothing.' "

Lazarus lived only to die again. A second time the sisters went to the tomb with the corpse of their beloved brother. This time there was no resurrection. But Jesus had taken Martha's theology and had given it vitality: "He who believes in me will live, even though he dies; and whoever lives and believes in me will never die." If you believe in a God of resurrection, you can face the cemetery and know that even out of death can come life. It is, in the words attributed to St. Francis of Assisi, in dying that we live.

But not all funerals lead to life. When Mae lost her only son, she lost sight of God and His power and love. She could not see that the phoenix rises from the ashes of its own death. She missed the reality that life invades death. She forgot—or never knew—that Jesus Christ passed through death to conquer it for all time and eternity.

As we experience the pain of loss, we can miss the phoenix. Yet Jesus speaks the same words to us that He spoke to Martha two thousand years ago on the road into Bethany: "I am the resurrection and the life." After death comes resurrection. We can trust God's perfect timing. We can trust His love. We can come through our difficult experiences stronger in faith and hope as we learn that God is there for us in our loss, in our sorrow. What we let Christ do in our situation makes the difference.

Questions for personal reflection or group discussion:

1. When you think of Martha and Mary, what do you think were stumbling blocks to faith for them?
2. Can you identify some stumbling blocks to faith in your life? If so, what are they?
3. How can knowing who Jesus is make a difference in your faith?
4. How can you experience immediate benefits (that is, power or strength) from your faith?

The Canaanite Woman: How to Pursue Faith in Life's Crises

Most of us who are parents have experienced those moments of inner panic that come when one of our children must be rushed unconscious to a hospital after an accident or when their temperature shoots to 105 degrees in the middle of the night. Though my children are now adults, I still get a knot in my stomach when I remember how helpless and desperate I felt each time that happened. In those moments we pray, not just in our heads but from somewhere in our guts, knowing that all the resources for saving our child lie outside ourselves.

If we get to a doctor in time, we may learn that an antibiotic or a hospital stay will be enough to return our child to health. Or the specialists may tell us that this priceless little child will live out her life with a disability. That can be a sentence of death-in-life that may send us on an endless search for a different diagnosis or a miracle cure.

Mark tells us of a desperate mother:

> As soon as she heard about [Jesus], a woman whose little daughter was possessed by an evil spirit came and fell at his feet. The woman was a Greek, born in Syrian Phoenicia. (7:25)

A demon-possessed daughter. What must that have meant for this frantic mother? Clinicians examining demon possession from New Testament times to our present day have found three characteristics almost always present in the demon-possessed person.

First, the facial features are distorted, sometimes so much that the person is no longer recognizable. Along with this, a demon-possessed person will in some cases contort his body or become physically agitated. Second, the voice changes, often deepening to the point that a woman's voice sounds like a man's. Third, the person displays a different personality. A normal person may become coarse and filthy. A gentle person may become aggressive and harsh. A refined person may use only gutter language.

Case histories underline the extraordinary strength of such people. In documented cases it has taken three or four adults to hold down a demon-possessed child.

What terror this mother must have felt as she watched her little girl become someone unrecognizable to her. To see the sparkle in her eyes displaced by a glittering hardness. To see her smile twist into a sinister grimace. To hear a voice that was not her little girl's voice. To expect the familiar voice and hear deep bass tones and strange pronunciations. To watch a personality emerge that is alien and repulsive. Where had her little girl gone? What had happened to her daughter who could no longer be held and loved? What could be done to bring back the gentle child who had disappeared inside the body of this monster?

What had gone wrong? What could she have done to keep this from happening to her little girl? How had she failed as a mother? How could she appease the gods for her failure and thus free her daughter from this cursed demon?

What must it have been to live each day in fear, not knowing what it would bring? Would her child embarrass her? Attack her? Turn viciously on children in the neighborhood? Tormenting herself day and night, this desperate mother must have reached out for any possible remedy that could release her daughter from this bondage.

We don't know how the woman heard about Jesus. Nor do we know what she heard. What had someone told her that made her so sure He could help her? We know only that she had heard something that drove her to come to Him for help.

As our story opens, Jesus had been ministering in Galilee, the Jewish province in northern Israel, beyond Samaria. For reasons not explained to us in the text, Jesus chose to withdraw from Jewish territory to a neighboring country on the Mediterranean coast:

> Jesus left that place [near the Sea of Galilee] and went to the vicinity of Tyre. He entered a house and did not want anyone to know it; yet he could not keep his presence secret. (Mark 7:24)

Even up in Galilee, several days' journey by foot from the Jewish capitol of Jerusalem, Jesus could not get away from the religious leaders who hounded Him wherever He went. Mark 7 opens with some Pharisees and teachers of the Law coming up from Jerusalem and attempting to trap Jesus into speaking against the Law of Moses. After a debate about what was ritually clean or unclean, Jesus turned away from the religious leaders and addressed the large crowd that followed Him wherever He went: "Listen to me, everyone, and understand this. Nothing outside a man can make him 'unclean' by going into him.

Rather it is what comes out of a man that makes him unclean" (7:14).

This was a sore point with the religious leaders throughout Jesus' earthly ministry. They had spent their lives keeping all the minutiae of the Law. They lived in dread of any contamination from the outside that would make them ritually unclean. When this young rabbi let His followers eat without obeying all the rituals of washing, it threatened all they believed. It challenged the profession they had given their lives to following. It could destroy their supporters' confidence in this legalistic way of life. In short, if Jesus continued to say these things, He could put them out of business.

It's not clear whether Jesus left the region around the Sea of Galilee because the confrontation with the religious leaders was leading prematurely to the cross He knew lay ahead. Or He may simply have needed a break from the constant crowds that dogged Him night and day. We find Him taking refuge near the city of Tyre, hoping that no one would know He was there. But as Mark tells us, in no time word about Him got out. And a Greek woman, born in Syrian Phoenicia, found out about Him and came to Him for help.

Matthew 15:21–25 begins the story this way:

> Leaving that place, Jesus withdrew to the region of Tyre and Sidon. A Canaanite woman from that vicinity came to him, crying out, "Lord, Son of David, have mercy on me! My daughter is suffering terribly from demon-possession."
>
> Jesus did not answer a word. So his disciples came to him and urged him, "Send her away, for she keeps crying out after us."

> He answered, "I was sent only to the lost sheep of Israel." The woman came and knelt before him. "Lord, help me!" she said.

All Mark told us is that the woman begged Jesus to drive the demon out of her daughter. But Matthew paints a picture of our Lord Jesus Christ that shocks us. The first time the woman approached Him, He ignored her. The text says, "Jesus did not answer a word."

We don't like to think of Jesus being unresponsive to someone in need. We prefer a Savior who is always there for us, ready to hear our prayer. Yet it is clear in the text that Jesus simply ignored this distraught woman. Whatever she felt at that moment, she didn't give up.

We know that because the disciples were annoyed with her. She must have been so persistent, so unwilling to leave that they could stand her no longer. They appealed to Jesus to send her away because she kept pestering them.

It wasn't that they were unaccustomed to crowds. They had just come from Galilee where mobs of people thronged them wherever they turned. They had been running interference for Jesus for months now. They were used to doing it. But something about this woman got to them. They begged Jesus to send her away because she was driving them crazy.

In verse 24 Jesus answered the disciples in a way that seemed to have nothing to do with their request. He said simply, "I was sent only to the lost sheep of Israel." The woman, still standing there, must have heard His remark. She would have found cold comfort in it. Did He mean that only Israelites—Jews—could expect any help from Him?

She had already acknowledged that He was a Jew. In Matthew 15:22 we heard her address Him as "Lord, Son of David." We don't know from this how much she knew about the religion of the Jews, but she knew about the great king David and she understood that Jesus was in David's line. Did she know—had she heard—that here was the Messiah of the Jews? We don't know. But her way of addressing Jesus tells us that she knew something about who He was that made her persist in the face of silence, and then exclusion.

Nothing deterred her. In verse 25 we read, "The woman came and knelt before him. 'Lord, help me!' she said."

Then came a third kind of refusal. We find it in Mark 7:27: " 'First let the children eat all they want,' he told her, 'for it is not right to take the children's bread and toss it to their dogs.' "

Do Jesus' words seem even more harsh? No matter how we interpret this, Jesus appears to insult this foreign woman. Jesus called Gentiles "dogs" in the same way that people today may use pejorative names for people of other nationalities. To call someone a "dog" in first-century Israel was insulting.

In the Middle East in Jesus' time a dog was never allowed indoors. Dogs were despised as filthy creatures. They roamed around, uncared for and half wild. A dog prowled through the streets searching for food. In temperament these wild dogs were not much different from wolves. Adult Middle Easterners would not associate with dogs.

In essence Jesus told this woman that the Jews needed to be fed first. What rightfully belonged to them should not be given away to others until their needs were met. But this bright, witty woman was not put off by Jesus' statement: "Yes, Lord," she replied, "but even the dogs under the table eat the children's crumbs" (Mark 7:28). She heard Him use a word for "dogs" that really meant "puppies." That was all she needed to hear.

In Middle Eastern families with children, little dogs—puppies—were allowed in the house as playthings for the children. Their place during mealtime was under the table. They caught the crumbs. And probably they also caught bits of food slipped under the table by sympathetic children.

She responded, "Yes, Lord, what you say is true. But even the puppies under the table eat the children's crumbs." Imagine Jesus with a twinkle in His eye and a playful tone in His voice. Something He did or said gave this woman hope and the courage to respond as she did.

Had Jesus said what He did in a harsh voice, she may have answered Him with bitterness. But His voice must have belied His words. She entered into the spirit of the test and responded to His words brilliantly: "Yes, the children must be fed. No one questions that. But puppies are still able to get the crumbs. The Jews have a full portion in you. They have your presence. They have your word. They sit at your feet. Surely they won't grudge me what I ask. Casting the demon out of my daughter is no more for you than dropping a crumb to a puppy. No one will be deprived if you do this for me. Lord, you have so much that even while the children are fed, the dogs may get the crumbs without depriving the children. There is enough for your children and still something for me."

How did Jesus answer her? Matthew tells us:

Then Jesus answered, "Woman, you have great faith! Your request is granted." And her daughter was healed from that very hour (15:28).

The faith of this woman is stunning. She had very little going for her. There she stood, a Greek woman born in Syrian Phoenicia, a Canaanite. She probably had a religious heritage very different from the Jews. The Canaanite religion was polytheistic. That is, the people worshiped many gods. In earlier times followers of that religion offered human sacrifices. Jezebel, wife of the Old Testament king Ahab, came from the same region of Tyre. She forced the worship of the pagan god Baal on the Israelites. Canaanite religion was radically different from the Jewish worship of only one God, Jehovah. This Canaanite woman knew very little about true religion, and much of what she knew was wrong.

In spite of her lack of training in the Jewish religion, in spite of the fact that she could not have heard a great deal about Jesus, in spite of the fact that she may never have seen Him before this encounter, she believed that He could help her.

Within Judaism Jesus had met with resistance and unbelief on every side. But outside Israel, He met a pagan woman whose faith staggered Him. Her faith was greater than His closest followers had shown. "Woman, you have great faith!"

As He said that, did Jesus remember having just rebuked Peter with the words, "You of little faith—why did you doubt"? In the chapter immediately preceding the encounter with this Canaanite woman, Matthew recorded the incident of Jesus walking on the sea (Matthew 14:22–34). There we learn that the Savior had sent the disciples ahead to cross the lake while He dismissed the crowds and went up into the hills to pray.

A strong wind had come up, and the disciples were not able to make much headway rowing their fishing boat across the sea of Galilee that night. In the middle of the night as they fought against the storm, they saw Jesus walking on the water. They were terrified. Jesus tried to dispel their fear by identifying Himself and by telling them to take courage and not be afraid.

Then Peter—bold, brave, brash Peter—shouted out across the waves, "Lord, if it's you, tell me to come to you on the water." Jesus invited him to come, and Peter got out of the boat and started across the water to Jesus. Then he saw the wind, lost confidence, and started to sink into the water. He yelled out, "Lord, save me!" Jesus immediately reached out His hand and caught him. Verse 31 records Jesus' remark to Peter: "You of little faith—why did you doubt?"

Peter, the Jew, a man brought up in the synagogue, one who had already traveled all over Galilee and down to Judea with Jesus. Peter, someone who had heard Jesus teach and preach, had seen Him heal the sick, cast out demons, and raise the dead back to life. Peter, who had every reason to have strong faith, to him Jesus said, "Peter, you of little faith—why did you doubt?"

To the Canaanite woman—a pagan woman without the right religious teaching, who had never seen Jesus before, who knew next to nothing about God's promises to the Jews through the prophets—to this Canaanite woman Jesus said, "Woman, you have great faith!" Jesus found faith where He did not expect it.

This contrast turns things upside down. We assume that the person with the greatest knowledge of the Bible will be the strongest Christian, full of faith in times of trouble. We don't expect much at all from someone who hasn't been to church or Sunday school. But here we see faith strong and persistent in a woman with next to no spiritual training or background. In contrast, we see the great apostle, the one who served as foreman or leader of the twelve disciples, the great preacher at Pentecost, the one to whom Jesus delivered the commission, "Feed my sheep"—to Peter came the rebuke, "Why did you doubt?" God will overlook ignorance, but He will not overlook unbelief.

Little faith. Great faith. Peter was influenced by His surroundings. He did well as long as he ignored the wind and the waves and just kept moving toward Jesus. But his circumstances distracted him.

The woman, on the other hand, would not let anything turn her from her goal. She brushed off the disciples, she ignored Jesus' silence and His remark about being sent only to the people of Israel. She simply refused to let her circumstances sidetrack her from her goal.

Little faith. Peter was in precisely the same amount of danger of drowning from the moment he got out of the boat until he crawled back in with Jesus' help. While Peter thought he was in a lot of danger out there on the lake, he was actually in no danger at all. Jesus was there. Weak faith, little faith, swings like a pendulum between great confidence and great fear. One moment Peter was walking on the water. The next moment he was going to drown. When Peter threw himself into the sea and started walking toward the Savior, he proved that Jesus was worth trusting. But his trust evaporated when he focused on his circumstances.

We may think, "Yes, I'm more like Peter than I am like the Canaanite woman. My faith isn't much. It swings like a pendulum. One moment I'm walking on water. The next moment I'm neck-deep in water and headed down."

Take heart. A little bit of faith is still faith. A drop of water is water every bit as much as a reservoir of water. A spark is as much fire as a blaze. Little faith is still faith.

Even better, little faith can become great faith. The Peter we meet in his later letters could write:

> In this you greatly rejoice, though now for a little while you may have had to suffer grief in all kinds of trials. These have come so that your faith—of greater worth than gold, which perishes even though refined by fire—may be proved genuine and may result in praise, glory and honor when Jesus Christ is revealed. (1 Peter 1:6–7)

Jesus found this genuine faith in a woman who pleaded for her child. She wouldn't let go. She wouldn't give up. She hung on even when Jesus ignored her and spoke coolly to her. She simply wouldn't take "no" for an answer. Jesus was her only hope for her child. She saw light in the darkness. She hung on as if Jesus had given her a promise instead of a rebuff. Spurgeon observed that great faith can see the sun at midnight. Great faith can reap harvests in mid-winter. Great faith can find rivers in high places. Great faith is not dependent on sunlight. It sees what is invisible by any other light. Great faith hangs on to God.

Jesus delighted in this woman's vibrant faith. He looked at her faith the way a jeweler looks at a rare but unpolished stone. He tested her as a master jeweler buffets and grinds the impurities away from the face of the gem. By His silence and His rebuff He polished her until her faith sparkled. Jesus used her affliction to make her faith shine like a rare jewel.

This woman's crisis—a demon-possessed little daughter—brought her to Jesus Christ. Without that crisis, she might have lived and died and never have seen the Savior at all.

Crises can be God's device to move us to new ways of thinking about Him and to new levels of confidence in Him. Although we prefer good health, sickness can be good if it leads us to God. We prefer security, but difficulties serve us well when they bring us to Christ.

A nameless Canaanite woman, a foreigner, reminds us that in our crisis experiences, we can hang on and trust God because He is the only one who is trustworthy.

Questions for personal reflection or group discussion:

1. Why do you think the Canaanite woman had "great faith"? Where did it come from?
2. What was Peter's problem that Jesus rebuked him for having "little faith"?
3. How can you show that you are a woman of faith?
4. What will be some of the results in your life if you, too, have "great faith"?

The Hemorrhaging Woman: How to Find Jesus in Your Pain

When my friend Joann met her future husband and they lived out a storybook courtship, she anticipated that their Christian marriage would be "happily ever after." A decade later, the marriage exploded in her face. Her husband left her for another woman, and she began the long, painful task of bringing up two young boys alone. Financial problems dogged her. The frustrations of being both mother and father, homemaker and wage-earner drove her into depression and sapped all of her energy. Loneliness became her constant companion.

One of her greatest disappointments was the lack of support she felt from the family of God. The past twelve years have been marked by an unending struggle to pay the bills, rear her two sons (now teenagers) to Christian manhood, and rebuild the self-esteem that had been pulverized by the divorce.

Most of us have friends, like my friend Joann, who stagger under seemingly unbearable burdens, but who still hope that somehow Jesus Christ can make a difference in their lives. If we walk with Jesus through the Gospels, we see Him surrounded by such people. Matthew 9 opens with a group of men who were beside themselves to know what to do about a paralyzed friend. They had heard rumors about the young rabbi called Jesus. Could He do something for their friend? They hoisted the man up on his mat and brought him to Jesus. Later in Matthew 9 a ruler of the synagogue pleaded with Jesus to do something about his little daughter who had just died. As Jesus left the ruler's house, two blind men followed Him, calling out, "Have mercy on us, Son of David!" As they left Jesus' presence, a demon-possessed man, unable to talk, was brought to Jesus. In a single chapter Matthew shows us the desperate needs of very different people who had one thing in common: they hoped that, in the midst of crushing despair, Jesus could make a difference in their lives.

Matthew spills over with the compassion of Jesus for suffering people. It ends with these words:

> Jesus went through all the towns and villages, teaching in their synagogues, preaching the good news of the kingdom and healing every disease and sickness. When he saw the crowds, he had compassion on them, because they were harassed and helpless, like sheep without a shepherd. Then he said to His disciples, "The harvest is plentiful, but the workers are few. Ask the Lord of the harvest, therefore, to send out workers into his harvest field" (9:35–38).

In the middle of chapter 9 we encounter another desperate person, a woman who had hemorrhaged for twelve long years. Her story reaches us not only through Matthew's gospel, but through Mark's and Luke's as well. We begin exploring this woman's suffering in Mark 5:24:

> So Jesus went with [Jairus, the ruler of the synagogue.]

The Hemorrhaging Woman

A large crowd followed and pressed around him. And a woman was there who had been subject to bleeding for twelve years. She had suffered a great deal under the care of many doctors and had spent all she had, yet instead of getting better she grew worse.

Twelve years! While we aren't positive what this bleeding was, it is usually assumed that it was a continuous menstrual period—for twelve long years. Even in today's world with modern medicine to help us, that would be exhausting and debilitating. As for any modern woman today, for her it would have meant being sapped of energy. It meant constant suffering and weakness. It may have meant depression. But in the time of Jesus, it was much, much worse.

To begin with, her bleeding made her a social outcast. The nature of her ailment in Israel was particularly degrading. From a Jewish perspective a woman could not suffer from any more terrible and humiliating disease than constant hemorrhaging. Women with flows of blood were ritually unclean, literally untouchable.

The Law laid this down in Leviticus 15:25–27:

When a woman has a discharge of blood for many days at a time other than her monthly period or has a discharge that continues beyond her period, she will be unclean as long as she has the discharge, just as in the days of her period. Any bed she lies on while her discharge continues will be unclean, as is her bed during her monthly period, and anything she sits on will be unclean, as during her period. Whoever touches them will be unclean; he must wash his clothes and bathe with water, and he will be unclean till evening.

Leviticus 15 concludes with these words spoken by God to Moses and Aaron: "You must keep the Israelites separate from things that make them unclean."

Can you imagine the implications of being "unclean" for twelve years? Most commentators believe that her husband would have divorced her. Others suggest that she would have been obliged to leave him. In any event, she could not maintain a normal relationship. She would be cut off from all good Jews, both male and female. Even to come in contact with a chair she had sat on or a bed she had lain on was to contaminate oneself. Such a person would have to wash his clothes and bathe with water—and still be considered unclean until evening.

That was one consequence for this first-century woman in Israel. She was isolated from all community life, avoided, excluded. She could not go to the temple nor to the synagogue. She was shut off from the corporate worship of God. And no one could touch her, brush against her in a crowd, or come in contact with anything she had touched. She infected everything.

How could she shop in the street stalls for fruits or vegetables? She could touch nothing. If she brushed up against the shopkeeper, he was defiled. How could she walk about town without contacting anyone? Imagine the terrible exclusion and isolation she lived with for twelve long years! Unclean. Unclean.

Furthermore, in her day a woman with continuous bleeding was suspect. People assumed she was being punished by God for some secret sin. This tradition went well beyond the Law of Moses. She was probably excommunicated, divorced, ostracized, all on the basis of a false notion of her illness. It is unimaginable to be cut off from everything and everyone important to you— your family, your home, your church, your friends. Would you torment yourself, asking why this had happened to you? For what unknown sin was God punishing you? Can you picture yourself spending twelve years like that? What weary desolation she must have felt!

The second consequence we read in Mark 5:26:

> She had suffered a great deal under the care of many doctors and had spent all she had, yet instead of getting better she grew worse.

The Talmud sets out no fewer than eleven different cures for bleeding. Some were tonics and astringents. Others were superstitious notions. For example, one remedy was to carry the ashes of an ostrich egg in a linen bag in the summer and in a cotton bag in the winter. I don't know how available ostrich eggs were in Israel at that time, but I am sure this woman found one, cremated it, and carried the ashes as the Talmud prescribed.

Another "cure" was to carry around a barleycorn that had been found in the dung or feces of a white she-ass. Can you imagine trying to find such a thing? It would be one thing to find a white female donkey. It would be something else to locate a barleycorn in the excrement of that beast.

It is probable that this poor woman had tried all eleven cures in the Talmud and had seen other doctors who prescribed equally bizarre, often painful, possibly dangerous remedies. She tried everything and had gone to every available doctor, Mark tells us, but was worse instead of better.

We meet her in that huge crowd of people pressing around Jesus. Probably she should not have been there. What if someone bumped into her and became infected with her uncleanness? She must have been desperate for a cure—anything to leave behind this life of isolation and humiliation.

Mark continues the story in chapter 5:27:

> When she heard about Jesus, she came up behind him in the crowd and touched his cloak, because she thought, "If I just touch his clothes, I will be healed." Immediately her bleeding stopped and she felt in her body that she was freed from her suffering.

A miracle! Twelve long years of continuous bleeding, and in that moment when she touched Jesus' cloak she knew she was healed.

Some commentators quibble about the fact that this woman's faith was tainted with superstition. She thought that just touching Jesus' clothes would effect the healing. Whether there was an element of magic in her faith is not especially important. What matters is that she had enough faith to believe that Jesus could help her. Somehow she had confidence that the slightest contact with Him would heal her.

She heard that Jesus was in town. A flicker of hope stirred in her mind. Perhaps He could help her. No one else had. Could she find Him? She crouched against a wall, trying to make herself as inconspicuous as possible so no one would recognize her and order her away. Would Jesus pass this way? Was there a chance?

The Hemorrhaging Woman

The sound of an approaching crowd reached her. See both hope and fear in her eyes. Anxiously she pressed against a doorway, hoping against all her fears that Jesus would come her way. Perhaps she talked to herself: "If I can only touch His clothes. Do I dare? I'll contaminate the Teacher if I do. It will make Him unclean. But I've heard that He touched lepers. They were unclean, like me, and He touched them and healed them. But maybe because I'm a woman, He wouldn't want to heal me. If He's a good Jew, He prays every morning, thanking God that He wasn't made a woman. Then, too, I've spent all I have on doctors and I don't have anything left to pay Him with. On the other hand, I've heard that He takes pity on the poor." She struggled to hang on to hope as waves of despair rolled over her.

In the midst of her turmoil, the crowd pushed and shoved around the corner. There in the midst of the pressing mob was the Teacher, Jesus, the one who might help her. Desperation and hope propelled her forward, away from the shelter of the wall and doorway. So many people! How could she possibly get through such a thick mass of people? So weak. So tired. So frail. Carefully, as unobtrusively as possible, she worked her way through the throng, afraid every moment someone who knew her would order her back. Fear pulled her back. Determination pushed her on.

Finally, coming up behind Jesus, she reached out and touched the blue and white tassel on the hem of His robe. Every good Jewish man wore four white tassels bound in blue thread on the four corners of His robe—one in front, one on each side and one in back. This was called the hem of the garment. She reached out tentatively, then with desperate determination, grasped that tassel. The word Mark uses in the Greek means "clutch." She didn't just brush her hand against the tassel. She clutched it. The Law said she should not touch, but in her desperation, she not only touched, she clutched the tassel. And in that moment all the weakness and sickness that had plagued her every day for twelve long years was gone. Into her body flowed an indescribable surge of health.

In that moment Jesus ignored her superstition and focused on her faith. Follow the story in Mark 5, beginning with verse 30:

> At once Jesus realized that power had gone out from him. He turned around in the crowd and asked, "Who touched my clothes?"
>
> "You see the people crowding against you," his disciples answered, "and yet you ask, 'Who touched me?' "
>
> But Jesus kept looking around to see who had done it. Then the woman, knowing what had happened to her, came and fell at his feet and, trembling with fear, told him the whole truth. He said to her, "Daughter, your faith has healed you. Go in peace and be freed from your suffering."

Luke 8:45–48 tells essentially the same story but adds a few details Mark omitted:

> "Who touched me?" Jesus asked.
>
> When they all denied it, Peter said, "Master, the people are crowding and pressing against you."
>
> But Jesus said, "Someone touched me; I know that power has gone out from me."

The Hemorrhaging Woman

Then the woman, seeing that she could not go unnoticed, came trembling and fell at his feet. In the presence of all the people, she told why she had touched him and how she had been instantly healed. Then he said to her, "Daughter, your faith has healed you. Go in peace."

"Who touched me?" Jesus asked. You can understand why Peter and the other disciples were puzzled. No doubt a lot of people were touching the Master. But this was different. Jesus knew He had been touched in faith.

Do you think He really didn't know who had touched Him? It seems clear that He wanted to lift this woman's faith to a higher level. She had believed in the magical power of His clothes. He wanted her to know that she had exercised faith in Him and that her faith, not the hem of His robe, had healed her. And He wanted to do that in front of the crowd. Up to that moment she had been an outcast. Now she was set in front of that mob as an example of faith.

What would you have felt had you been in her place that day? In an instant she was healed. She could tell. She knew it had happened. But now as she crept away in the crowd, she heard Him ask, "Who touched me?" Would He find out that she had done it? Would He punish her for making Him unclean?

Finally, sure that she would be discovered, she came trembling with fear. After she told her story of twelve years of illness and isolation, then of her touch and healing, Jesus called her, "Daughter." This is the only place in the New Testament where Jesus called a woman "daughter."

Relationship! After twelve years of being cut off from all relationships, here is one who puts Himself in relationship to her. Whatever cringing unworthiness or inferiority she felt after twelve years of isolation from everyone else, in that moment He affirmed her as a person and called her into relationship with Himself.

For twelve years this woman had been lost in the crowds of life. She had become all but invisible except when others feared she would contaminate them. But when Jesus reached out to her, she could not remain lost in the crowd.

Do you ever feel lost in the crowd? Do you sometimes feel invisible, unwanted? When we reach out to Jesus in faith—perhaps with only a little bit of faith—it is enough. He will find us, lift us up, and call us "Daughter" as He puts us into relationship with Himself. Even more, once He puts us into that relationship to Himself, we have all of God's love and all of God's power at work on our behalf. It's not a question that one person uses up more of God's love and power and leaves less for other people. Not at all. God's love and power are infinite. There is enough for all of us.

Augustine said, in reading this story, "flesh presses, but faith touches." Jesus can always tell the difference. He knew which was simply the jostling of the crowd and which was the touch of faith. He could tell the difference in Israel two thousand years ago. He can tell the difference today. He knows the touch of need and responds to us.

Did you notice what did not happen in this story? We did not see the woman begging and pleading to be healed. She simply reached out in faith and touched the tassel of His robe—and she was healed. Jesus did not make her go through any kind of ritual. It was enough that she believed. The moment she took hold, healing came.

Jesus' public ministry lasted only a short three years. He had much to do and teach. But He always had time for individuals who needed Him. He saw Zacchaeus in the sycamore tree. He saw blind Bartimaeus at the gate to Jericho. He even saw the thief on an adjacent cross. He took time for a woman who had been bleeding for twelve long years. He asked nothing more of her than that she should believe He had the power to do for her what she could not do for herself.

It is the same for us today. Jesus asks only that we believe that He has the power to do for us what we cannot do for ourselves. It's the only way we can be in relationship to Him. Our faith may be imperfect. It may be weak. But when we come with whatever faith we have, He reaches out to us with healing. And we, too, will hear His word, "Go in peace."

The Greek text actually says, "Go into peace." Isn't that splendid? Move out of restlessness and into peace. Leave turmoil behind and move into peace. What a magnificent place to live—in peace. That was Jesus' legacy to His disciples just before His crucifixion: "Peace I leave with you; my peace I give you. I do not give to you as the world gives. Do not let your hearts be troubled and do not be afraid" (John 14:27).

That promise given two thousand years ago to a band of followers in an upper room at that last supper before Jesus died is a promise that comes down the centuries to you and me. Go into peace. It is Jesus' gift to each of us. It comes to us as we reach out in faith and touch Him. He knows the touch of faith. He always responds.

Questions for personal reflection or group discussion:

1. What do you think it takes to come to Jesus in your time of need?
2. Jesus ignored the woman's superstitiousness and responded to her faith. Can you count on Jesus to do the same for you? Explain.
3. The woman thought she was lost in the crowd, but Jesus singled her out. What does that mean for you today?
4. Jesus did not merely heal the woman of her hemorrhage. What else did He do for her? How does that apply to you today?

Two Widows: How to Give and Receive Graciously

A friend recently changed jobs and moved into a new office. He invited me to stop in the next time I was in the neighborhood. When I walked into his office, I was impressed. On the wall behind his desk are several framed photographs—one of my friend with Billy Graham, another signed to my friend by Garrison Keillor, a third autographed to him by a United States senator. I had no idea my friend had acquaintances in high places!

Suppose we were invited into the office of Jesus Christ. Whose pictures would we find on the wall behind His desk? Would we find a picture of Zacchaeus, the rich but despised tax collector? Or of a nameless sinful woman who lavished her love and thanks on Jesus by washing His feet with her tears and anointing them with perfumed oil? Perhaps. But we might also find the picture of two widows—one to whom Jesus showed grace, and the other who showed Him thanks.

Widows. What does that mean to us today? Even in modern Western societies, a widow seldom has an easy time of it. In most cases, when her husband dies, a widow's financial base is severely cut. If she is over sixty-five, she is eligible for some Social Security benefits. She can get basic medical care through

Medicare. She can receive food stamps if she needs them. There are a few structures in place to help the single elderly who are poor. It's not a lot, but it can make the difference between life and death.

If a widow today is under sixty-five, she can count on little help except food stamps. She probably works to support herself. In most cases, she likely doesn't earn enough to do more than meet her basic bills. Women, on the average, earn only two-thirds as much salary as men earn for the same level of work. Worse, most older women do not have the skills to work at anything other than entry-level jobs. Unless a widow's husband has left her with good insurance policies and with the house mortgage paid off, a nice savings account or a good investment program, her standard of living has probably dropped significantly since she became a widow. That's one of the facts of widowhood today. She may spend her final years in genteel poverty.

In Jesus' day a woman was, for the most part, even worse off. As a rule, she was in a position of total dependence on a man—her father, husband, son, brother, or brother-in-law. When a woman's husband died, she had only a few options. If she had a son, he took over the management of his father's estate and she could stay on in the household. If she was childless, she usually returned to her father's house—if he was still alive. Perhaps things could be arranged so that she would have the opportunity to marry again.

Another option was to ask that the Hebrew law of levirate marriage be applied. You may remember the conversation Jesus had with some Sadducees back in Mark 12:18–23, a passage that makes clear what levirate marriage was about:

Then the Saducees, who say there is no resurrection, came to him with a question. "Teacher," they said, "Moses wrote for us that if a man's brother dies and leaves a wife but no children, the man must marry the widow and have children for his brother. Now there were seven brothers. The first one married and died without leaving any children. The second one married the widow, but he also died, leaving no child. It was the same with the third. In fact, none of the seven left any children. Last of all, the woman died too. At the resurrection whose wife will she be, since the seven were married to her?"

Interesting question! It gives us a good idea how levirate marriage worked in Jesus' time. A widow was at the mercy of the brothers of her dead husband. If there were no brothers, or if the brothers decided not to perform their duty to her, she could be completely without economic security, not to mention emotional support or social acceptance.

What was the purpose of levirate marriage? Breeding. The whole idea was to ensure that she bore a son in the name of her dead husband. If she were beyond child-bearing age, it was unlikely that anyone would bother with her. A widow without a son to care for her in her old age was completely without resources.

Jesus met such a woman at a city gate when He intercepted a funeral procession. Her story begins in Luke 7:11–12:

Soon afterward, Jesus went to a town called Nain, and his disciples and a large crowd went

281

along with him. As he approached the town gate, a dead person was being carried out—the only son of his mother, and she was a widow. And a large crowd from the town was with her.

Jesus, surrounded by His disciples and a large crowd of people, approached the town of Nain at the moment a funeral procession came out the gate. They could hear the mourners before the procession came into view. Some of the townsfolk sang a lamentation. Others cried out, "Alas! Alas!" Still others moaned and beat their breasts. The noisy procession pushed through the town gate and moved toward the burial site.

Then Jesus spotted the four men carrying the corpse on a stretcher. It wasn't hard to tell, despite the cacophony of wailers, who was the bereaved. A lone woman, weeping, stumbled along, overcome by her grief.

Can you imagine a sadder funeral—that of the only son of a widow? Here was a mother left alone with her family line cut off. Her husband had died some time earlier. Now her only son was also gone. She had lost the two most significant people in her life. Even more, she may have lost her means for survival as well.

The text tells us that Jesus felt compassion for her. His heart went out to her. Then He added action to His compassion. Luke tells us:

When the Lord saw her, his heart went out to her and he said, "Don't cry."
Then he went up and touched the coffin, and those carrying it stood still. He said, "Young man, I say to you, get up." The dead man sat up and

began to talk, and Jesus gave him back to his mother.

They were all filled with awe and praised God. "A great prophet has appeared among us," they said. "God has come to help his people." This news about Jesus spread throughout Judea and the surrounding country (7:13–17).

Jesus' first action touches us with His compassion, but it seemed like a futile thing to do. How could He tell her, "Don't cry"? The woman had just lost her only son! Was He insensitive to her loss? Or was He able to turn her grief into joy? Only His second action could make sense of His first action.

Once again Jesus violated rabbinic practices by voluntarily touching what was ritually unclean. He reached out and laid His hand on the stretcher. The mourners stopped their wailing in mid-sentence. The crowd fell back. Who was this rabbi who dared to touch the bier of the dead?

Did the Lord need to do that in order to work a miracle? Not necessarily. When Jesus stood in front of Lazarus' tomb, He merely commanded the dead man to come out. He could bring people back to life with only a word. But here at Nain's gate in front of a huge crowd, Jesus did the unthinkable. He made Himself ritually unclean by reaching out and touching the contaminating bier. In that action He underlined once again that it is not what happens on the outside that sullies us, but what goes on in our hearts.

Then Jesus spoke: "Young man, I say to you, get up!" Townspeople and mourners looked at each other. The man must be mad! Couldn't He see that the person was dead? Every eye was riveted on the stretcher. People gasped as the young man sat up. They were even more astonished when he began to talk. Was this possible? Who ever heard of the dead coming back to life? Yet they had seen it with their own eyes.

Had you been standing by Nain's town gate that day, what would you have felt? Amazed? Scared? Speechless? Possibly all of these.

The Bible tells us that Jesus gave the young man back to his mother. The stunned pall bearers lowered the stretcher. Jesus may have reached out His hand to the youth and helped him step out onto the road. Her face still streaked with tears, the widow rushed to embrace her now-living son.

Jesus did this amazing miracle for one reason: His heart went out to this poor bereaved widow who had just lost her future, her only son.

Faith wasn't part of the package. Jesus had no conversation with the woman about believing in Him, about having to have faith in order to see God's miracle. Jesus knew that when a person is struggling under a heavy burden of grief, it is not the time for a theology lesson. It is a time for compassion. Jesus did what He could because His heart was touched with the woman's misery.

It is a great thing to know that Jesus is touched by our sadness and reaches out to comfort us, without our having to merit or earn anything. We may easily get the impression that the Christian life is some kind of trade-off: if we have a certain amount of faith, we can expect a certain amount of return from God. More faith—more things from God. A kind of pious bargaining. But that's where we get it all wrong.

What Jesus did for that widow at Nain's gate two thousand years ago was to give her His gift of sheer grace. She had done absolutely nothing to deserve that miracle. Yet Jesus reached out to her in her sorrow and gave her son back to her. He gave her back her future. He does the same for us today. By grace and nothing else He gives us a future and a hope.

* * *

How do we respond to God's grace when we have received it? Jesus made sure that His disciples did not miss one important way of responding to God. The time is many months later. The scene is the temple courtyard in Jerusalem.

Worshipers at the temple first entered the outer court, called the Court of the Gentiles. Jews then passed through the Gate Beautiful into the Court of the Women. Only Jewish men could enter the innermost court, the Court of Israel.

In the Court of the Women—accessible to all Jews—stood thirteen collection boxes. They were called the "trumpets" because they were shaped like the bell of that instrument. Each of these thirteen collection containers had a different purpose. One was for gifts to buy oil, another for corn, another for wine, and so forth, items needed for the daily sacrifices and for the general maintenance of the temple.

We don't know much about how Jesus worshiped or what He did when He went to church. But one thing is certain: He was interested in the offering. Mark tells us how Jesus spent some of His time in the temple:

> Jesus sat down opposite the place where the offerings were put and watched the crowd putting their money into the temple treasury. Many rich people threw in large amounts. (Mark 12:41)

We may think that God's interest in what we do stops with how often we pray or read the Bible. Not so. Jesus is keenly interested in what we give to God's work as well. When we go to church, He is as aware of what we put in the offering plate as He is of the songs we sing and the prayers we pray.

When He preached the Sermon on the Mount, Jesus made clear that where we put our treasure tells people where our hearts are (Matthew 6:21). The attitude we have about money tests the reality we profess. What we give or hold back demonstrates what our priorities are. No wonder Jesus was interested in the offering that day in the temple courtyard.

As He sat there, what did He see? Mark wrote that many rich people threw in large amounts of money. From Matthew 6:2 we can even imagine donors approaching the collection boxes preceded by hired musicians blaring on trumpets to call attention to the gift. In the midst of these wealthy donors, Mark tells us, "A poor widow came and put in two very small copper coins, worth only a fraction of a penny" (Mark 12:42).

Seeing this, Jesus did and said something strange. He called His disciples over, pointed to the widow and said,

> I tell you the truth, this poor widow has put more into the treasury than all the others. They all gave out of their wealth; but she, out of her

Two Widows

poverty, put in everything—all she had to live on. (Mark 12:43–44)

That may sound a bit ridiculous to us. Of course, she hadn't put in more! In fact, it was impossible to put in anything at all and at the same time put in less. According to the system in her day, one could not give less than "two mites," the two small copper coins.

Jesus was not talking about actual amounts of money. He was talking about proportions. What matters to God is what we give in proportion to what we keep. It is easy to think that because I can't give as much as I'd like, I shouldn't bother giving my little bit to God. That is exactly the kind of thinking Jesus wanted to counteract.

Whatever we are able to give to God—whether it is money, time, or energy—is measured not by how much, but by how much in proportion to what we are able to give. As Jesus explained to His disciples, "She, out of her poverty, put in everything—all she had to live on." The poor widow that day had to choose between having something to eat or giving to God. She couldn't give half to God and keep half for a bit of bread. It was a question of giving all to God or keeping it for herself. She chose to give all to God. It was her wholehearted devotion that grabbed Jesus' attention that day.

She might have come to the temple courtyard that day wondering if she should make such a personal sacrifice. After all, what little she had to give would hardly buy a bit of lamp oil for the temple sacrifice. Intimidated by the magnitude of others' gifts, she might have hung back, watching as wealthy Jews, with trumpets blaring, poured their money into the collection boxes. Did it really matter to God whether or not she contributed two tiny copper coins?

Even worse, everyone knew that the teachers of the Law, the people who maintained the temple system, were corrupt. Then as now, widows were particularly vulnerable targets of unscrupulous religious leaders who sometimes took advantage of them. While sitting in the temple courtyard that day, Jesus had just warned His listeners:

> Watch out for the teachers of the law. They like to walk around in flowing robes and be greeted in the marketplaces, and have the most important seats in the synagogues and the places of honor at banquets. They devour widows' houses and for a show make lengthy prayers. Such men will be punished most severely. (Mark 12:38)

What does it mean that religious leaders "devour widows' houses"? The Pharisees, we learn from the historian Josephus, prided themselves on being exact teachers of the Law. In Judaism a teacher of the Law could not take any pay for teaching others. He was supposed to have a trade or a profession by which to support himself, and he was required to teach without pay.

Many Pharisees, however, managed to persuade ordinary people—often widows—that the most significant thing they could do was to support a Pharisee in the manner to which he would like to become accustomed. It appears that women were particularly susceptible to this proposition. Many widows were known to have spent all they had to support a teacher of the Law. Pharisees took advantage of these women. They often extorted great sums of money for advising them, or they diverted entire estates away from the owners for their own use.

Jesus had seen this and recognized what could easily happen to such women. Sitting in the temple courtyard, He had just warned about teachers of the Law who devour widows' houses when His attention was arrested by a poor widow approaching the offering boxes. Now as she paused, clutching the two tiny copper coins—all she had—did she think about the corrupt leaders who would spend these coins carelessly? Should she deny herself necessary food when she could do so little and when her gift might be diverted to crooked people?

As she extended her hand and dropped the two coins into one of the trumpets, she knew that, in spite of it all, she was giving to God. It was more important to her to show gratitude to God than to have food. She came to worship God with what she had, with what she could give. Her devotion to God was from her heart. She gave all she had.

In pointing out this poor widow in the temple courtyard, Jesus teaches us that God judges what we give by the quality of our giving, not by its quantity. The person He held up as a model of generosity is someone who gave less than a cent. What made it worth more than the vast wealth of others is that it was all that she had.

During our years in a central Wyoming pastorate, we frequently hired a short, stout grandmother to babysit our four children. To do this for us, Mrs. Knapp had to drive an unpredictable, old car into town some distance from the mesa where she and her husband lived in a tiny house. At one point they were able to have running water installed in the house, but they could never afford to put in a bathroom. Had I been Mrs. Knapp, I'm sure I would have saved all the babysitting money and butter-and-egg money for a real, inside bathroom.

What often brought me up short was that Mrs. Knapp babysat, not for a bathroom, but to have something to give to God each Sunday. As I dropped a tithe check into the offering plate each Sunday, I knew Mrs. Knapp was dropping in much, much more. Most of us gave out of our abundance. She, out of her poverty, put in all that she had. Jesus never missed seeing her gift.

Often weary, never sure her car would run, burdened for her husband, Mrs. Knapp always showed up at our house with a smile. She was earning something to give to God. And she was enriched by that.

When you and I give, we are doing something God-like. And when we give, we put meaning and purpose into all our getting. It is, as Jesus said, "more blessed to give than to receive" (Acts 20:35).

I stood in my friend's office admiring the pictures on his wall. And I thought of the pictures Jesus might have on His wall. Surely Mrs. Knapp's picture will be there, next to that of the widow in the temple courtyard.

By grace Jesus gave one widow her future. By grace Jesus Christ gives each of us a future and a hope. As we come to understand that, we begin to see why, like the widow in the temple courtyard, we can give to Jesus all that we have. Two tiny coins? We can part with them. Whatever we have, we can give to God freely and fully, not because we bargain with Him, but because we have received freely of His grace.

> We give Thee but Thine own,
> Whate'er that gift may be,
> All that we have is Thine alone,
> A trust, O Lord, from Thee.

Two Widows

Grace and giving. God's grace goes out to the helpless, and it is often from the helpless that the greatest praise comes to God. The more we understand God's grace, the more freely we give to God.

Questions for personal reflection or group discussion:

1. As you think about Jesus' compassion for the widow of Nain, what promise does that incident hold out to you as a follower of Jesus today?
2. How do you feel about receiving grace from the hand of God without being able to pay Him back?
3. What do you think Jesus meant when He said that the widow had put more into the temple treasury than all the rich people who had tossed in large amounts? How does that apply to what we can give God today?
4. Have you had experiences that show that God cares for helpless women today just as He cared for them two thousand years ago? If so, describe your experiences.

A *Sinful Woman*: How to Cultivate an Attitude of Gratitude

Gratitude can be a slippery thing to express. Some people have a way with words and sound wonderfully grateful even when they're not. The words, tone of voice, and gestures are all exactly right. But something puts us off: we detect the insincerity and we doubt that we are hearing genuine appreciation. Other people want desperately to express their gratitude but never seem to find the right words to communicate what they feel. They stumble over their tongue and then fall silent, afraid that if they say anything, it will come out wrong. Then there are the folks who never understand their indebtedness to a family member or a friend and make no effort to say thanks. Most of us have a hard time dealing with someone who takes another's kindnesses for granted.

The gospel writers recorded stories about Jesus' encounters with pairs of people who could not be more different in their attitude toward gratitude. We find one such pair in Luke 7. Simon is a punctilious Pharisee, the nameless woman a "sinner." He was outwardly civil but had no warmth. She broke conventions to express her love. He responded to the gift of forgiveness with a cool "Oh." She lavished her Lord with her gratitude.

Luke starts the story this way:

> One of the Pharisees invited Jesus to have dinner with him, so he went to the Pharisee's house and reclined at the table. When a woman who had lived a sinful life in that town learned that Jesus was eating at the Pharisee's house, she brought an alabaster jar of perfume, and as she stood behind him weeping, she began to wet his feet with her tears. Then she wiped them with her hair, kissed them and poured perfume on them. (7:36–38)

The scene is laid in Galilee. Jesus had just healed a centurion's servant who had been close to death. A day later He intercepted a funeral procession at Nain's city gate and restored a dead son to his widowed mother. The rumors flying across the countryside about this astonishing young rabbi from Nazareth seemed to become more unbelievable every day. A Pharisee named Simon knew it was time to arrange a meeting with Him.

If he gave a dinner party and included Jesus in the guest list, Simon could avoid having to mingle with townsfolk in the marketplace. It would also give Him an up-close opportunity to study this potentially-dangerous new teacher. The last time Jesus had preached in their synagogue and marketplace, some of the worst people in town had shown up. The gossip was that some of those people got "converted." In fact, the word was that a town prostitute had gotten the idea from the rabbi's preaching that even she could be forgiven by God and could be given a new beginning. Simon was sure that righteousness couldn't be bought with a mere prayer.

Jesus and His disciples arrived and the meal started. Then, unexpected and uninvited, a woman came in and stood behind Jesus weeping, wetting His feet with her tears, wiping His feet with her hair, then pouring perfume on them.

For most of us today that scene doesn't jibe with anything in our experience of modern houses, modern tables, modern chairs, or modern customs. Did people just wander into houses uninvited while people ate?

In first-century Israel meals were often almost public. Spectators could crowd around as the guests dined. It was not unusual that an uninvited person should show up during the dinner party.

From Leonardo DaVinci's famous painting of the Last Supper we may have the impression that Jesus and His disciples sat on stools with their legs under the table, as we do today. That was not the case. Guests reclined on couches set like wheel spokes around the table. They leaned on their left side and reached for food with their right hand, the top part of their bodies toward the table and their feet stretched out behind them. Sandals had been removed at the door. It was easy enough for this woman to enter the house, stand behind Jesus and weep, only to have her tears fall on His extended feet.

Luke tells us that she was a woman who had led a sinful life. The words used to describe her are sometimes translated "prostitute" elsewhere in the New Testament. If not truly a prostitute, she may have been an abandoned woman. One commentator suggests that she may have passed her life in crime. Whatever she had done to merit her peculiar label, she was known in the community as a sinful woman. The startling thing was that such a woman would make her way to the house of Simon, a Pharisee, of all people.

Pharisees had a reputation for avoiding anything or anyone who might contaminate them. The word

Pharisee itself means "separation." During the four-hundred-year period between the end of the Old Testament and the beginning of the New Testament a group of men formed an order, called the Pharisees, committed to keeping the Jewish people from mixing with the idolatrous people around them. In the process they became satisfied with a religion that focused on externals like ritual washings and precise offerings. Certainly a sinful woman would not be welcome in their presence. It was unheard-of that a sinner should venture into the house of a Pharisee. What gave this woman the courage to appear in the house of Simon that day?

She dared come to Simon's house for only one reason: she had heard that Jesus was there. From the story Jesus later told Simon, it is certain that the woman had already received forgiveness for her many sins. She had possibly heard Jesus teach or preach and had become conscience-stricken because of her sinful life. Now that she knew where to find Him again, she had come.

She may have entered the door with some hesitation, but once she spotted where Jesus was reclining at the table, she passed quickly behind the other guests to His place. Tears blinded her as she bent over the feet of the Teacher. This was the one who had told her about God's forgiveness. This one had given her all she needed to start life again. Overcome by her gratitude, she could not hold back her tears. They spilled over the Teacher's feet. Reaching up and loosening her hair, she used it to begin wiping the Teacher's feet.

That act of unbinding her hair seems inconsequential to us today, but first-century Jewish women would never allow anyone outside their families to see them with loosened hair. Yet, oblivious to public opinion, this woman did the unthinkable: she let down her hair and used it to towel Jesus' feet dry.

Suspended around her neck on a cord was a perfume flask made of alabaster. These flasks were considered so much a part of a Jewish woman's dress that wearing them even on the Sabbath was not forbidden. To use the perfumed oil, the wearer broke off the long, thin neck of the flask and poured out the contents. As this woman dried her tears from Jesus' feet, she reached for the flask, snapped off the neck, and slowly anointed those feet with the perfumed oil. Suddenly the room was filled with the exquisite fragrance. If others had paid no attention to the woman to that point, they could ignore her actions no longer.

Love. Grateful love. Unconscious of the stares, the hisses, the rude comments, this woman poured out her love with that perfumed oil. She lavished that love on the one who had freed her to begin life anew.

> When the Pharisee who had invited him saw this, he said to himself, "If this man were a prophet, he would know who is touching him and what kind of woman she is—that she is a sinner."
>
> Jesus answered him, "Simon, I have something to tell you."
>
> "Tell me, teacher," he said. (Luke 7:39–40)

Because Jesus had not drawn back from this woman and ordered her away, Simon inferred that the Teacher could not know her character. The Jews believed that being able to discern spirits was an important mark of the Messiah, the great prophet. When Jesus let the woman touch Him, Simon saw this as evidence that Jesus could not possibly be the Messiah. On the one hand, if Jesus didn't know what kind of woman she was, it proved that He was no prophet. On the other hand, if He did know what kind of woman she was and still let her touch Him, it would prove that He was not holy. Simon was sure that the Messiah would never deliberately choose to let a sinful woman make Him ritually unclean. Either way, it was clear that Jesus could not be the Christ of God.

Did Simon catch the irony of that moment? "If this man were a prophet, he would know." Immediately Jesus picked up on Simon's thought and responded to it: "Simon, I have something to tell you." Simon's answer was polite but cool: "Teacher, say it."

What followed was one of Jesus' marvelous little stories we call parables:

> Two men owed money to a certain moneylender. One owed him five hundred denarii, and the other fifty. Neither of them had the money to pay him back, so he canceled the debts of both. (Luke 7:41–42)

It was as if Jesus said to Simon, "It's true that one debtor owed ten times as much as the other, but both were debtors. Don't forget that, Simon. You may look down your nose at this woman because she has a reputation as a sinner. You surely don't think that you are not a sinner!" Of course, Simon would have answered that he was also a sinner, but not like that woman.

Some time later in His ministry, Jesus told another story about a Pharisee and a tax collector who both went up to the temple to pray. The Pharisee stood up and said, "God, I thank you that I am not like other men—

robbers, evildoers, adulterers—or even like this tax collector. I fast twice a week and give a tenth of all I get" (Luke 18:11–12). This Pharisee had no sense that he owed God anything. He may, if challenged, have acknowledged a small "five-denarii debt" to God. But to be placed in the same category of debtor like the tax collector or like a sinful woman? Never.

Drawing Simon into the story, Jesus then asked, "Now which of [these two debtors] will love the creditor more?" With grudging indifference Simon answered, "I suppose the one who had the bigger debt canceled." "You have judged correctly," Jesus affirmed.

Both debtors had nothing with which to pay their debt. Yet both were forgiven freely. Simon needed to see that although this woman had been a notorious sinner, she was forgiven. Her tribute of love proved her gratitude for God's forgiveness.

Turning toward the woman but still talking to Simon, Jesus asked:

Do you see this woman? I came into your house. You did not give me any water for my feet, but she wet my feet with her tears and wiped them with her hair. You did not give me a kiss, but this woman, from the time I entered, has not stopped kissing my feet. You did not put oil on my head, but she has poured perfume on my feet. (Luke 7:44–46)

"Do you see this woman, Simon?" Simon thought Jesus didn't see what sort of woman she was. Jesus knew that it was Simon who was blind. He could not see her as a forgiven woman. He could see her only as the sinful woman she had been. So Jesus set her in contrast to His host: "Simon, let me help you see her."

Jesus began by saying, "You didn't give me any water for my feet, but she wet my feet with her tears and wiped them with her hair." Simon bit his lip. It was true that he had deliberately ignored all the usual rites of hospitality toward his guest.

Jesus hadn't complained about Simon's cold welcome. But He had noticed it. Now He linked it to Simon's lack of gratitude for God's forgiveness. "Simon, didn't you just tell me that the person who has been forgiven a huge debt will feel great love for the one who forgave? This woman had a great debt. But it was forgiven. Now look at her gratitude! Look at her love! What does your treatment of me say about your gratitude?"

"Simon, you did not give me a kiss, but this woman, from the time I entered, has not stopped kissing my feet." The host normally greeted each guest with a kiss on the cheek. This woman, making up for Simon's deliberate coldness to his guest, gave the unusual sign of deep reverence for an honored teacher: she kissed his feet.

"Simon, you did not put oil on my head, but she has poured perfume on my feet." Once again Simon had ignored his duty as host by not anointing his guest with oil. Once again a grateful, forgiven woman did what the calculating Pharisee chose not to do.

In pouring perfumed oil on Jesus' feet, this woman performed a rite most often performed by men. Prophets anointed kings. Hosts anointed guests to refresh them. The disciples anointed the sick with oil as a cure. Women anointed only dead bodies for burial. This forgiven woman anointed Jesus, not on His head as Simon should

A Sinful Woman

have done, but on His feet—the body part assigned to slaves.

Jesus' last word to Simon before addressing the woman was, "He who has been forgiven little loves little." "Simon, do you get the point? You think you see so well, yet you see nothing clearly. You are religious—a Pharisee—and you draw back from this sinful woman. You thank God that you are not as this woman. You can hardly imagine entering heaven side by side with someone like her. But it is she who has experienced forgiveness. You haven't begun to understand forgiveness because you haven't begun to understand your need. I know you have been forgiven little because you show so little love."

Turning to the woman, Jesus said, "Your sins are forgiven." The perfect tense of the verb in Greek makes it clear that her forgiveness was not the result of her love. It was the other way around. She had already been forgiven. Here, in front of Simon and others crowding that dining room, Jesus publicly declared her to be a forgiven woman. Whatever she had been was past.

That forgiveness became the springboard for her lavish love. It is the same for us today. "We love [God] because he first loved us" (1 John 4:19). God starts the process by loving us unconditionally and forgiving us because of Jesus' sacrifice for our sins. The more we come to understand that forgiveness, the more we will love. Forgiveness is the cause. Love is the effect. Forgiveness is the reason and love is the result. Forgiveness is the root and love is the fruit.

Could Simon possibly understand what that sinful woman did that day at his dinner table? Did Simon give any thought to his own lovelessness? We love in proportion to our consciousness of having been forgiven. If we have no sense of debt to Christ, we will love little.

Jesus' last word to the woman was, "Your faith has saved you; go in peace." It was not her love that saved her. It was her faith. Because she was accepted by God, she could go in peace. She would probably never be accepted socially by Simon and his crowd. Others in the town might continue to look down on her. But they knew nothing of the grace of God. She could go in peace because her future was secure. She belonged to God.

In Luke's account our nameless woman was also wordless. The writer, in fact, gives us a conversation almost exclusively between Simon and Jesus about this woman. Only at the end does Jesus speak directly to her. Nothing is recorded that she might have said in response. Yet her deed spoke more eloquently than a thousand words.

At issue is not whether we can find beautiful words to frame our appreciation, but whether we feel the gratitude that impels us to find a way to express it. Do we understand, to borrow David's words, that God has brought us up out of a horrible pit, out of the miry clay, and has set our feet upon a rock and established our steps (Psalm 40:2)? Or do we feel closer to Simon, quite sure that God must be happy that such nice people as we have enlisted in His cause? As Jesus put it to Simon, "The one who has been forgiven little loves little."

When we see our sin and see God's grace at work in our lives, we will find a way to say thank you. It may be eloquently expressed in words. Or it may be even more eloquently framed without words as we give the best we have to the one who has saved us.

A Sinful Woman

Questions for personal reflection or group discussion:

1. What was wrong with Simon's attitude toward the sinful woman?
2. What was wrong with Simon's understanding of righteousness?
3. What do you think Jesus wanted Simon to learn from the parable about two debtors?
4. What do you believe it takes to be forgiven by God?

The Woman Taken in Adultery:
How to Respond to the God
of the Second Chance

When my office phone rang one day, I was surprised to hear the voice of a dear friend several thousand miles away: "Alice, I'm so embarrassed and humiliated, I don't know what to do. I've made a fool of myself over a man in our church. Here I am, a married woman, and I fell in love with this guy I've been working with in evangelism. It seems as if everyone in town knows how idiotic I've been. It has ruined my testimony at the church and it has mortified my husband. What should I do? Is there any way I can ever hold my head up again? Can God forgive me and give me another chance?"

I held the phone in my hand, and in that long moment between the time she spoke and I responded, I wondered how I should answer her. This was no academic question about forgiveness. It was the stuff of real life. When we've made a mess of things or have wasted our opportunities, can we start over again?

As I held the phone, I thought of another woman who had made a mess of her life. It nearly caused her death. Then Jesus came along.

* * *

Jesus was marching toward crucifixion on a Roman cross. No matter what He did, the Jewish religious leaders determined to get Him at any cost. The "Get Jesus" committee was out in full force. If we glance back at John 7:1, we see that "Jesus went around in Galilee, purposely staying away from Judea because the Jews there were waiting to take his life."

It was autumn, the time of the annual Feast of the Tabernacles, one of the three principal Jewish festivals. Urged by his brothers to go with them down to Jerusalem for the feast, Jesus declined. But after they had left for Judea, He secretly made the trip to the capitol city for the feast.

In the midst of the festive revelry, it seemed that everyone was gossiping about the same subject: Jesus. Who was He? Some said He was a good man. Others thought He was a deceiver. Pilgrims, townsfolk, and priests alike asked the question, "Who is this man?" The seventh chapter of John rustles with mutterings, accusations, and conjectures about Him.

Again and again Jesus slipped through the fingers of the angry religious leaders. As the curtain goes up on chapter 8, Jesus was once more teaching in the temple courtyard. Those who hated Him most were making another attempt to trap Him. They had failed again and again, but this time it appeared that they had Jesus right where they wanted Him—caught on the horns of a dilemma. Follow the story in John 8, beginning with verse 2:

> At dawn [Jesus] appeared again in the temple courts, where all the people gathered around him, and he sat down to teach them. The teachers of

the law and the Pharisees brought in a woman caught in adultery. They made her stand before the group and said to Jesus, "Teacher, this woman was caught in the act of adultery. In the Law, Moses commanded us to stone such women. Now what do you say?" They were using this question as a trap, in order to have a basis for accusing him.

This "Get Jesus" committee had remembered the ancient Law of Moses in which anyone caught in the act of adultery should be put to death. That law had apparently not been enforced for generations. But the teachers of the Law and the Pharisees saw in that law the possibility of trapping the irritating rabbi from Nazareth.

To spring the trap they would need to catch someone in the midst of an adulterous act. In the Mardi Gras atmosphere of the festival that would not be difficult. The city streets were cluttered with hundreds of tiny booths, flimsy shelters of branches and leaves, constructed to last only the eight feast days. They had only to loiter on one of these streets and listen for the telltale sounds of lovemaking. Married people more likely made love in the privacy of their own homes. Finding a culprit should be simple.

They quickly rounded up a woman caught in the act. You may ask why they brought only the woman. Where was her male partner? The law stipulated that both should be stoned to death.

The context makes it clear that these religious leaders did not do this because they hated adultery. Nor did they do it because they loved godliness and wanted to uphold the Law. They simply hated Jesus. One guilty person would do quite nicely. They didn't need the man as well.

What was the snare in verse 6 that these leaders set for Jesus? If Jesus said that the woman should be stoned, two things would happen. First, they could denounce Him to the Romans as one who usurped the prerogatives of the Roman government, the right to put criminals to death. Second, He would lose the love and devotion of the great mass of ordinary people who knew that His teachings included the need to show mercy.

On the other hand, if Jesus answered that she should not be stoned, they could say that He taught people to break the Law of Moses. Then He could be accused before the Sanhedrin as a false Messiah. Everyone knew that the Messiah must maintain or restore the sovereignty of the Law.

That was the dilemma they set before Jesus that day in the temple: infringe on the rights of the Roman government or deny the authority of the Mosaic Law. In their cunning they thought that, any way He moved, they had Him in checkmate.

There in the shadow of Herod's magnificent temple the drama began to unfold. Seated, perhaps in the Court of the Women, Jesus taught the crowds. Suddenly the sound of His voice was drowned out by scuffling feet and angry voices coming through the massive brass doors from the Court of the Gentiles. Approaching men jostled into the courtyard, dragging someone along. The crowd parted enough so that the scowling men could thrust a woman forward. People who had been listening intently to the Teacher now shifted restlessly, wondering what would happen next. They knew by the robes and headpieces that the intruders were Pharisees and teachers of the Law. And while some stared at the woman curiously, others looked away to avoid her shame as she stood there, disheveled, humiliated.

Then the religious leaders spoke: "Teacher, this woman was caught in the act of adultery. In the law, Moses commanded us to stone such women. Now what do you say?" Jesus didn't take them on in a debate. Instead, Jesus bent down and started to write on the ground with His finger.

No one moved. The terror-stricken woman looked into His face. What would the Teacher say? Would He condemn her to death? The tension grew as He said nothing. A few Pharisees glanced at one another with a glint of victory in their eyes. They had Him this time! He would know He was defeated.

Instead of speaking, He knelt on the ground. What did that mean? They repeated the question, "What do you have to say about this woman?" His finger traced Aramaic letters in the dust. They crowded closer to read what He wrote. By now the woman, still trembling, turned slightly to stare at the moving finger as the teachers of the Law pressed Him for an answer. At that Jesus stood up and made one comment: "If anyone of you is without sin, let him be the first to throw a stone at her." And with that He stooped down again and continued writing in the sand on the pavement of the temple courtyard.

What He wrote is not recorded. Yet the word John used gives us a clue. The normal word in Greek meaning "to write" is *graphein*, but the word used here is *katagraphein*. That word can mean "to write down a record against someone." It may be that Jesus was confronting the teachers of the Law and the Pharisees with a record of their own sins.

"All right! Stone her! But let the man who is without sin be the first to cast a stone! You want your pound of flesh. You insist on keeping the Law scrupulously. Do what you think you must do. But only if you are blameless."

The word for "without sin" can also mean "without a sinful desire." Jesus was raising the bar. These legalistic religious leaders thought they had to jump only so high. Jesus said, "No, you have to jump this high. Not only your deeds count. Your thoughts and your desires count as well. Yes, you may stone her, but only if you never wanted to do the same thing yourselves." If they were going to be legalistic, they had to apply the same law to their own hearts.

Jesus moved the question from the legal domain—the Law of Moses—where the Pharisees had put it, to the moral ground of their own sinful desires. They operated on the basis of justice. Jesus operated on the basis of grace.

In Deuteronomy 17:6–7 Moses spelled out the procedure for stoning someone to death. There we read:

> On the testimony of two or three witnesses a man shall be put to death, but no one shall be put to death on the testimony of only one witness. The hands of the witnesses must be the first in putting him to death, and then the hands of all the people.

The death penalty was carried out by having one of the witnesses throw the accused from a scaffold, after which the other witness would throw the first stone or roll down a large boulder that would crush the accused to death. In doing this, the witnesses would feel the responsibility they bore in giving evidence. Any accuser in a capital offense had to serve as executioner. Jesus in essence said, "You profess to honor the Law of Moses. I remind you that this same Law requires the witnesses to be the executioners. Do you have clear consciences concerning the seventh commandment?"

Jesus knew the hearts of His opponents. He did not say that the woman had not sinned. Nor did He say that her sin should be shrugged off. She had sinned—against her husband and against God's law. But in the presence of her accusers, He did not mention her sin. He referred only to theirs. He reminded her accusers that they had no right to bring a charge against her. Their unchastity was notorious. Their own motives and lives were far from pure.

In that moment Jesus defended women for all time. In one sentence He laid down a single standard for faithfulness in marriage that applied to both men and women.

Verse 9 reveals what the scribes and Pharisees were really after. It was not to vindicate the purity of God's law. They simply wanted to get Jesus. If the Pharisees had been sincere in their indignation about this woman and her sin, they would have taken her to the officially constituted judge. But it was not her adultery they were against. It was Jesus. Seeing that their plan had failed, they took the only course remaining to them. They withdrew. In doing that, they silently admitted what had really brought them to the temple court that day.

What decided the matter was not that the woman hadn't sinned. She had. Jesus' point was that the motives of the witnesses were corrupt. Those who were to throw the first stone were technically qualified to do so, but they were not morally qualified. As Jesus sprang the trap on them that they had set for Him, conscience was at work. These men were wicked and hardened. Yet they felt something inside themselves they could not ignore. Supposed to be moral examples to the people, they knew their own hearts. Sheepishly, one by one, they slunk away.

Astonishment must have spread across the woman's face as Jesus straightened up and asked her,

> "Woman, where are they? Has no one condemned you?"
>
> "No one, sir," she said.
>
> "Then neither do I condemn you," Jesus declared. "Go now and leave your life of sin." (John 8:10–11)

Was it possible that her accusers had left? Could it be that her ordeal was over? Had she heard this Teacher correctly? Was He really saying that He did not condemn her? Was she free, really free to return home and start life over?

Some people, reading this account, have concluded that Jesus was soft on adultery. Others have accused Him of making a detour around the Law. Neither is true. We know from Deuteronomy 17 that no one could be accused or condemned except by the testimony of two witnesses. No one stayed to accuse her. With no accusers, the Law could say nothing.

Jesus neither condoned her adultery nor condemned her. He gave her another chance.

He did not treat the woman as if her sin didn't matter. Far from it. He did not say to her, "Your sins are forgiven." She had not repented nor had she asked for forgiveness. In saying, "I am not going to condemn you now—go and sin no more," He gave her a chance to repent and believe.

What she had done did matter. Broken laws and broken hearts always matter. But Jesus knew that every one of us has a future as well as a past. He offered this woman a second chance.

Jesus did not say to her, "It's okay. Go on doing what you've been doing." No. He said, "Stop what you've been doing. Go and sin no more!" He pointed her in a direction she might not have realized was possible.

Many times we continue to do things we don't feel good about because we don't know we have any alternatives. God says to us, "You have alternatives." Jesus gave her a choice that day. She could go back to her old life or she could reach out for a new life of purity under God's law.

The meaning of repentance is "to forsake sin." It means to change our mind in order to change our life. Repentance isn't just feeling sorry or saying we're sorry or wishing or hoping that we won't do something bad again. The life of repentance is action. Until we turn from what is wrong, we haven't repented.

Turning from the woman, Jesus addressed the crowd: "I am the light of the world. Whoever follows me will never walk in darkness, but will have the light of life." Did the woman hear His words? He called her out of darkness to live in the light. He had exposed sin in the religious leaders. He did not gloss over sin in this woman's past. He called her to walk in the light.

From the biblical record in John 8, this woman's story is unfinished. Jesus Christ, standing in that temple courtyard two thousand years ago, gave her a second chance. The Bible doesn't tell us what she did with that opportunity.

A more important question is what we do with the second chance, the third chance, the tenth chance, the hundredth chance that God gives us to trust Him, to follow Him, to serve Him. The story of our lives isn't over.

We may look back on a secret sorrow or on a blatant sin and think there is no second chance. That's not so. God reaches out to us with another chance.

Yet if we have spent more time listening to modern-day "teachers of the Law and Pharisees" than we have to Jesus Christ, we may find that hard to believe.

We all know religious people who live by the Law, who criticize and condemn us. They stand over us, watching for every mistake. They may descend on every misstep we take with savage punishment. Such people use authority to destroy others, not to redeem them, heal them, or cure them. They may be blind to the fact that "there, but for the grace of God, go I."

If you grew up with people like that, you may think that God doesn't give second chances or third chances to people who sin. Jesus has a different word for you: "I do not condemn you. Go now and leave your life of sin."

That is what matters. Not what is past but what lies ahead. Every day God gives us another chance, a new opportunity to follow Him, to serve Him, to love Him, to carry out His will for our lives.

I held the phone in my hand and thought of this woman who had mishandled life as my friend had mishandled hers. What did I know from Jesus' actions that would answer my friend's question: when you've made a mess of things, can you start over again? After a long moment, I spoke, "I can promise you this. There is forgiveness, full and complete, from the Christ of the second chance. Can you start over again? God's answer is 'YES, YES, a thousand times YES.' "

Questions for personal reflection or group discussion:

1. What do you imagine God thinks and feels about you if you have made a mess of your life?
2. Do you think some sins are harder than others for God to forgive? If so, what are examples of "big ones"?
3. How do you feel about God giving people a second chance when they've committed a grievous sin?
4. What do you think "grace" means?

Mary of Bethany: How to Make Jesus Your Priority

In *Beloved*, Toni Morrison's Pulitzer Prize-winning novel about Civil War-era Black slave women, Grandmother Baby Suggs decided to celebrate her daughter-in-law's escape from slavery. She invited friends and neighbors for dinner. In the end, ninety people came and feasted on turkey, catfish, and fresh berry pies far into the night. As the house rocked with laughter, someone raised the question, "Where does she get it all, Baby Suggs? Why is she and hers always the center of things? How come she always knows exactly what to do and when?"

As guests passed the question from one to another,

it made them furious. They swallowed baking soda the morning after to calm the stomach violence caused by the bounty, the reckless generosity on display at house #124. Whispered to each other in the yards about fat rats, doom and uncalled-for pride. The scent of this disapproval lay heavy in the air.

Baby Suggs, hoeing her garden the next day, tried to understand what was happening. "Then she knew. Her friends and neighbors were angry at her because she had overstepped, given too much, offended them by excess."

317

In the years that followed, she, her daughter-in-law, and her grandchildren faced one tragedy after another without the support of their friends and neighbors.

Baby Suggs' experience of rejection for her bounty reminded me of another woman who gave her best in one lavish gesture. She, too, was misunderstood and condemned. The woman is Mary, the younger sister of Martha and Lazarus. John tells her story this way:

> Six days before the Passover, Jesus arrived at Bethany, where Lazarus lived, whom Jesus had raised from the dead. Here a dinner was given in Jesus' honor. Martha served, while Lazarus was among those reclining at the table with him. Then Mary took about a pint of pure nard, an expensive perfume; she poured it on Jesus' feet and wiped his feet with her hair. And the house was filled with the fragrance of the perfume. (12:1–3)

Of no other person in the Gospels is it written that "wherever the gospel is preached throughout the world, what she has done will also be told, in memory of her" (Mark 14:9). What was so remarkable about Mary's act that Jesus would make such a statement? Her story merits a closer look.

Word had reached friends of Jesus in Bethany that He was returning to Jerusalem to celebrate the Passover. Simon, a leper whom Jesus had most likely healed, hosted a dinner party for the Lord. Martha—another good friend—served, and Lazarus, her brother, reclined at the table with Jesus and the other guests.

When Simon decided to organize a feast to honor Jesus, he took a great risk. In the verses immediately preceding Mary's story, John tells us that from the moment Jesus had brought Lazarus back to life, the chief priests and the Pharisees "plotted to take [Jesus'] life." The threat to His life was so real that

> Jesus no longer moved about publicly among the Jews. Instead he withdrew to a region near the desert, to a village called Ephraim, where he stayed with his disciples. . . . But the chief priensts and Pharisees had given orders that if anyone found out where Jesus was, he should report it so that they might arrest him. (John 11:54, 57)

Not only did Simon take a risk inviting Jesus; he added to the danger by including Lazarus in the guest list as well. John reported that "the chief priests made plans to kill Lazarus as well, for on account of him many of the Jews were going over to Jesus and putting their faith in him" (John 12:10–11). Simon's gratitude to Jesus gave him courage to do what could get him into serious trouble with the religious leaders.

The dinner party was underway. In the midst of the festivities, Mary took an alabaster flask of very expensive oil of spikenard, broke the flask, and poured out the contents, first on Jesus' head, then on His feet.

One day, as I stood in line at the check-out counter of a second-hand thrift store, I noticed a full two-ounce bottle of cologne on a nearby shelf. With nothing better to do while waiting my turn, I pulled off the cap and sniffed the fragrance. It was enchanting! I had never heard of the Swiss perfumerie, but the price was right ($1.41!), so I added it to my other purchases. During the next year I used the cologne freely. Then the bottle was empty.

Some close French friends, planning a trip to America last year, wrote and asked what they could bring over for us. I dashed off a letter asking for another bottle of this exquisite but unknown perfume. To my delight, they brought me a bottle as a gift. To my astonishment, I learned that the two ounces of cologne I had used carelessly cost $75. Had I known its true value, I would have used it more cautiously.

Mary did not pick up her alabaster flask of oil of spikenard at a second-hand thrift shop for $1.41. She knew the value of her gift as she twisted off the top of the flask and began anointing Jesus.

One pound of oil of nard. Nard, squeezed from a plant grown in India, was the most expensive perfume in the world. Mark makes a point of telling us that Mary's nard was "pure"—not nard plus something else, and not an imitation. This was not cologne or eau de toilette. It wasn't a cheap copy-cat version of nard. No "If you like Giorgio, you'll *love* Primo!" It was the real thing, exquisite and extraordinarily expensive. And she had a "pound" of it, twelve ounces in today's measurements. One and a half cups. Do you know what she did with it?

Twisting the neck on the alabaster jar, Mary felt the thin, pastel stone give way. The delicious fragrance of the nard rushed up to her, and she smiled with delight. She lifted the vase up and tilted it slightly so that the perfume drizzled onto Jesus' head. It was a Jewish custom to anoint the head for feast days, and Jesus had come for the Passover Feast.

What Mary did was generous and she could have stopped there. But she didn't. Next, John tells us, she poured the fragrant oil on Jesus' feet. Just as if it were common water. She poured out so much nard that as it ran down His ankles and between His toes, she was obliged to loosen her hair and use it to towel off the excess.

Mary had sat at Jesus' feet (Luke 10:38–42) and had known His comfort and then His miracle when Lazarus, her brother, had died (John 11:28–44). Now, out of her gratitude and love, she responded to Jesus with the best she could give. She had already given Him her heart. Now she poured out the most costly gift she could offer to the one who had done so much for her.

The fragrance filled the room. No one present could ignore what she had done. She may not have heard the guests' gasps of surprise, but she could not miss the voice of Judas Iscariot as his cutting question sliced into her consciousness. "Why this waste of perfume? It could have been sold for more than a year's wages and the money given to the poor."

The sting of criticism. It's a lash we've all felt. What seemed like such a good idea to us looks stupid or thoughtless or selfish to someone else. The reaction takes us by surprise when that happens. We draw back from the cutting words. We expect people inhaling the fragrance to be pleased by it. Instead we are attacked. We ask questions we can't easily answer: Why are they frowning instead of smiling? Why is there more criticism than praise? What prompted this indignation in the place of approval?

Judas, with narrowed eyes, spat out his scornful criticism of this woman. He saw nothing good in Mary's act. At best it was extravagant. At worst it was evil. Think of the hungry who could have been fed. Think of the naked who could have been clothed.

What Judas said was accurate. The perfume could have been sold and the money given to the poor. The alabaster flask had contained pure nard, worth more than a year's wages. (Calculating Judas knew the exact worth of her gift.) A year's wages would meet the needs of a destitute family for twelve months or more. A year's wages could finance a soup kitchen and feed many people. A year's wages could provide shelter for street children. Had Mary made a grievous mistake in pouring out her twelve ounces of nard in one lavish gesture of love for Jesus Christ? She must have wondered if she would have been wiser to do as Judas suggested. It hadn't even crossed her mind! Had she missed the point of Jesus' life and ministry to such a degree that she had wasted an opportunity to help the poor? She burned with embarrassment as she thought of Judas's condemnation.

As Mary stood there that day, empty flask in hand, staring in an agony of self-doubt at her accuser, she heard another voice respond to Judas.

> "Leave her alone," said Jesus. "Why are you bothering her? She has done a beautiful thing to me. The poor you will always have with you, and you can help them any time you want. But you will not always have me. She did what she could. She poured perfume on my body beforehand to prepare for my burial. I tell you the truth, wherever the gospel is preached throughout the world, what she has done will also be told, in memory of her." (Mark 14:6–9)

What is the purpose of perfume, if not to be used to bring fragrance into someone's life? Is it merely a commodity to be sold to one buyer and then another, always changing hands in exchange for money, never being used? What gives it its value? Jesus told Judas that Mary had used the perfume in the right way: she had anointed His body beforehand for His burial.

Judas had heard Jesus' predictions of His impending arrest and crucifixion. He may have already concluded that Jesus was a loser. Only a few days later he would go to the chief priests and betray his Master for thirty pieces of silver. Judas placed Jesus' value at a handful of silver coins and complained that Mary set His value above a year's wages.

Judas sounded so sensible! By his criticism he placed himself on the side of the hurting and oppressed. But Jesus wasn't taken in by Judas's "concern for the poor." "If you really are concerned about the poor," He replied, "you'll always find opportunities to be liberal toward them. But Mary is doing something practical, too. In a few days when I am put to death, she won't have an opportunity to anoint my dead body. She's doing that now." Simon's dinner party was the scene of Jesus' funeral anointing.

When Jesus called Mary's deed "a beautiful thing," was He merely being chivalrous? Did she deserve such high praise? In Bethlehem a thousand years earlier as Samuel inspected each of Jesse's sons to see which one he should anoint as the next king of Israel, he was sure Eliab would be God's choice. But the Lord said to Samuel,

"Do not consider his appearance or his height, for I have rejected him. The LORD does not look at the things man looks at. Man look at the outward appearance, but the LORD looks at the heart." (1 Samuel 16:7)

As Jesus reclined at Simon's table that day, He looked beyond Mary's deed to Mary's heart. He had also looked beyond Judas's words to Judas's heart. Judas's criticism was ugly because it came from an ugly motive. Mary's deed was beautiful because it came out of her love for Jesus Christ. The worth or worthlessness of any gift depends on our motive. What we give to Jesus Christ for self-serving reasons will come to nothing. But what we give to Him out of love will never be forgotten.

Nothing, absolutely nothing that we do out of love and loyalty to Jesus Christ fails to be beautiful, no matter how silly or wasteful it may seem to others. God judges our deeds by the motives that prompt them. The smallest work done by the weakest woman will not be overlooked by God. In God's book of everlasting remembrance not a single kind word or deed, not a cup of cold water given in His name will be omitted.

Far from being wasteful and wicked, Mary had done a beautiful thing. She had given her very best. Jesus said to her in essence, "Mary, your deed is so beautiful, I will never forget it or allow the world to forget it. Hand in hand you will walk across the centuries with me. Wherever My story is told, yours will be told also."

Jesus gave great praise to women who were great givers. When the poverty-stricken widow approached the offering boxes in the temple with only two tiny mites between her and starvation, with reckless abandon she gave all that she had to God. He remarked to His disciples sitting nearby, "This poor widow has put more into the treasury than all the others. They all gave out of their wealth; but she, out of her poverty, put in everything— all she had to live on" (Mark 12:43–44). It was not a question of how much she gave but of how fully she gave.

324

Mary of Bethany

When Mary poured more than a year's wages on Jesus' head and feet in one great gesture of love, Jesus approved of her gift. It is interesting that Jesus never had a word of praise for prudent, conservative giving, but He showed great enthusiasm for those who gave with abandon.

The honor roll of women who gave with abandon has continued down the centuries. Amy Carmichael turned her back on a secure and happy life in England to rescue young girls from temple prostitution in India. Mary Slessor left Scotland to plant churches and start schools in Nigerian jungles where no other European dared go. Three medical doctors—Maybel Bruce, Mary Wilder, and Ann Irish—gave up comfort and security in America to start a medical center for Muslim women in the hottest, driest, most draining part of Pakistan. Each of these women poured out the perfume of their lives in abandoned giving to Jesus Christ.

Mary's gift looked extravagant and wasteful. Judas said it did no good. But Judas had no scales for weighing what God values. To him the most priceless things seemed worthless. But Jesus put a different value on her gift. As she poured out her perfume with abandon on Him, He would soon pour out His life with abandon for her.

Bob Jones, Jr., captured this truth when he wrote,

A broken vase of priceless worth rich fragrance shed
In ointment poured in worship on Thy head.
A lovely thing all shattered thus—"What waste,"
    they thought,
But Mary's deed of love Thy blessing brought.
A broken form upon the cross and souls set free.
Thy anguish there has paid the penalty

Sin's awful price in riven flesh and pain and
  blood—
Redemption's cost, the broken Lamb of God.

We who serve the lavish God of heaven ask, "How
can I repay the LORD for all his goodness to me?" (Psalm
116:12). We know that one of His blessings is to allow us
in worship to pour out the best we have for Him.

Questions for personal reflection or group discussion:

1. Think of one experience in your life in which you
   gave Jesus Christ a sacrificial gift of your time, of
   your energy, or of your money. Describe that event.
2. As you think about that event, what did you get out
   of it? Misunderstanding? Appreciation? Criticism?
   Praise?
3. If you had it to do over, would you do it again?
   Explain.
4. Why do you think our motives are so important to
   God? Why shouldn't the deed be enough regardless of
   our motives?

Mary Magdalene: How to Walk by Faith and Not by Sight

In *Women's Ways of Knowing,* an important study of the way women think about themselves and about life, Mary Belenke and her fellow researchers identified five ways women know things. One of them is called "received knowledge." We all know things because someone told them to us. Most of us have a large fund of received knowledge, a stash of facts and opinions we didn't think up on our own but we accept. We "know" how to use a washing machine and grow houseplants, and where to buy the freshest vegetables or find the best book bargains. We may also have learned to name some of the constellations and all the books of the Bible. We've spent our lives acquiring this kind of knowledge.

Surprisingly, many women limit what they "know" to what they have received from someone else. They look to an authority outside themselves for instruction in every area of life. An interior decorator tells them which home furnishings to buy. A hair stylist decides how they should wear their hair. A personal shopper chooses their clothes after a color analyst has given them a swatch chart of colors to wear. These women know a great deal and know that they know a lot. But they trust only what comes from outside themselves as "real" knowledge.

Sometimes such a woman faces a crisis. Perhaps an authority falls from grace or disappoints her. Or two equal authorities disagree. Whom can she believe? At that point a woman may move to a different way of thinking about herself and about her world.

These studies about the way women think intrigue me. In most cases, it takes some kind of crisis, a confrontation, a disappointment, or a disaster to move a woman from unquestioning reliance on outside human authorities to a different way of thinking and knowing. She has to make room for new learning.

We seldom move from one comfortable level of learning and knowing to another unless we are forced in some way to move. I benefited most from teachers who made me think instead of letting me parrot the textbook or my lecture notes.

We don't do ourselves a favor if we insist on staying at one learning level when we need to move to another one. We often don't like the circumstances that push us to change. We'd prefer to be left alone in our comfortable tranquility. But that is not the path to growth.

Nor is it the path to true discipleship. If we are to grow as Christian women in our understanding of God, we have to expect the tough circumstances that confront and disappoint us. It takes grim life experiences to build muscle into our souls.

The process of following Jesus as His disciples is the process of making room for new ways of looking at life and at ourselves. In this book we have watched Jesus move His mother, Mary, to a different way of seeing her relationship to her Son. We have seen Him move Martha to a different way of viewing her service to God. We have listened in as Jesus gave a Samaritan woman her first drink of living water as she saw herself with masks stripped away. We have observed Him guiding two sisters to a different way of thinking about death.

Jesus was a master teacher. We might have expected Him to use only one method for getting His message across, but He taught different people in different ways. We might have thought He would choose only the most promising pupils for His class. Instead, He included men and women other teachers would have ignored. One choice pupil of the Master Teacher was Mary Magdalene. She possibly spent more time with Jesus than any other woman in the gospels.

Mary of Magdala found that her discipleship as a follower of Jesus Christ was a constant learning process. She had already learned much as one who traveled with Jesus. But in one of the final scenes in the Gospels, she was once again back in school, learning something new about being a disciple.

Though she is mentioned by name fourteen times in the gospels, we actually know only four things about Mary Magdalene. The first two we see in Luke 8:1–3:

> Jesus traveled about from one town and village to another, proclaiming the good news of the kingdom of God. The Twelve were with him, and also some women who had been cured of evil spirits and diseases: Mary (called Magdalene) from whom seven demons had come out; Joanna the wife of Cuza, the manager of Herod's household; Susanna; and many others. These women were helping to support them out of their own means.

The first fact we know about Mary of Magdala is that Jesus cast seven devils out of her. We don't know when or where. Both Mark and Luke give us the fact, but neither gives us the story. We do know from her name that Mary came from Magdala, a town about three miles from Capernaum on the northwest shore of the Sea of Galilee. It was the territory that Jesus continually criss-crossed in His itinerant ministry in Galilee. At some point they met and the miracle of her deliverance took place.

Delivered from being possessed by seven devils. What must that have meant for this woman? We do not know how long or in what way she was tormented by demon-possession. But we do know that any possessed person was an outcast from normal society. Some afflicted people were more animal than human, living in caves, roving around the countryside terrifying people with their distorted faces and wild eyes. Created by God, they were being destroyed by Satan. What it meant for Mary to be possessed by seven demons we cannot guess. But for her, deliverance must have been a life-changing liberation. Her bound spirit was set free. Her cramped limbs relaxed. Her contorted face became serene.

The second thing we know about Mary is that she traveled all over Galilee and down into Judea with Jesus and the Twelve. If you suffered from a terrible affliction for years and then found a doctor who could release you from your suffering, you would probably want to stay as close to that doctor as possible. Mary Magdalene became a permanent itinerant with Jesus' band of followers.

Most of us probably assumed that Jesus and His disciples traveled around strictly as a male group: the Savior and the twelve men whose names we may have memorized in Sunday school. There are a number of reasons we might assume that.

For one, during the first century in Israel, some rabbis taught that good religious men did not speak to women in public. A Pharisee would not speak even to his own mother if he met her on the street. The careful segregation of men and women in that culture would make anyone traveling with both male and female followers too counter-culture to be listened to.

Furthermore, the Law declared that a woman during her menstrual period was ritually unclean. Everything she touched was defiled. At such a time she needed to be tucked away where she could not contaminate anyone else. How could Jesus and the Twelve risk contamination by these women traveling with them?

Public opinion about a mixed band of followers traveling around with Jesus might have raised moral questions. When we think about Jesus and His disciples in the Gospels, the people involved are the men we've come to know—Peter, James, and John, Andrew, Nathanael, Bartholomew, Judas, and the others. How could this group of women travel as members of Jesus' band without raising eyebrows?

The gospel writers don't answer that question for us. What we do know is that while Jesus' enemies accused Him of Sabbath-breaking, of drinking too much wine, and of associating too closely with tax collectors and other disreputable types, at no time did they ever raise a question about sexual immorality. We must assume that these men and women traveled together in a way that avoided scandal.

First named among the women in that band was Mary Magdalene. We know nothing more about her background. Some commentators believe she came from a wealthy family and was thus able to help support Jesus and His other followers. That may or may not have been the case.

You may have heard of the musical stage show called "Jesus Christ Superstar." In it Mary Magdalene was portrayed as a woman who practiced the "oldest profession on earth," prostitution. Yet in the Scripture we find no basis for that idea.

This myth about Mary Magdalene started in the sixth century when a pope named Gregory linked her with the sinful woman who anointed Jesus' feet with expensive perfumed oil. Ever since, throughout the past fourteen centuries artists have portrayed Mary Magdalene as a voluptuous hooker. Churches have named homes for rescued prostitutes as Magdalene houses. Despite the myth, Mary Magdalene was not a prostitute. Furthermore, we have no evidence that demon possession led to immorality in anyone's life. Demon possession doesn't produce sin.

The first two facts we know about Mary are that Jesus cast seven demons out of her and that she was a permanent part of the group that traveled with Him. The third thing the Bible tells us about Mary is that on a bad Friday called Good Friday she stayed at the cross long after the disciples had fled. From Mark we learn that "some women were watching from a distance. Among them were Mary Magdalene, Mary the mother of James the younger and of Joses, and Salome. In Galilee these women had followed Him and cared for his needs. Many other women who had come up with him to Jerusalem were also there" (Mark 15:40–41).

After three agonizing hours, Jesus died. Joseph of Arimathea, along with Nicodemus, came to take the body of Jesus off the cross and place it in a tomb. Matthew tells us that "Joseph took the body, wrapped it in a clean linen cloth, and placed it in his own new tomb that he had cut out of the rock. He rolled a big stone in front of the entrance to the tomb and went away. Mary Magdalene and the other Mary were sitting across from the tomb" (Matthew 27:59–61).

All four gospel writers take pains to tell us that Mary and the other women not only stayed through the awful hours of crucifixion but made sure they knew where Jesus had been buried so they could come after the Sabbath and finish anointing the body. When we look at Mary Magdalene and the others, we see women who were completely committed to Jesus Christ even in the midst of their bitter grief.

It comes as no surprise that we find these same women, with Mary Magdalene apparently leading them, up before dawn on Sunday morning, hurrying to the garden tomb. Here were women carrying out their normal role in Jewish society, preparing a dead body for proper burial. As they went, they fretted about a very real problem they faced: who would roll away the large stone at the entrance to the tomb?

They knew the size of the stone. They had watched as Joseph and Nicodemus hastily laid Jesus' body in the tomb and rolled the heavy cartwheel across the opening. They also knew that the stone was sealed by the Roman government. That seal could not be broken. Yet they were determined to do the right thing for Jesus. They had cared for His needs for three years as He traveled around Galilee and back and forth to Judea. They had taken His physical well-being as their responsibility. So in His death they could not shrink from giving Him a correct burial. Despite the obstacles—a huge stone and a Roman seal—they seized the first opportunity to come to the tomb.

When they arrived, what did they find? Mark tells us that "they saw that the stone, which was very large, had been rolled away" (Mark 16:4). In that moment began Mary's next lesson in discipleship. She had set out that morning with one set of expectations and quickly found them turned upside down. John reports the incident this way:

> Early on the first day of the week, while it was still dark, Mary Magdalene went to the tomb and saw that the stone had been removed from the entrance. So she came running to Simon Peter and the other disciple, the one Jesus loved, and said, "They have taken the Lord out of the tomb, and we don't know where they have put him!"
>
> So Peter and the other disciple started for the tomb. Both were running, but the other disciple outran Peter and reached the tomb first. He bent over and looked in at the strips of linen lying there but did not go in. Then Simon Peter, who was behind him, arrived and went into the tomb. He saw the strips of linen lying there, as well as the burial cloth that had been around Jesus' head. The cloth was folded up by itself, separate from the linen. Finally the other disciple, who had reached the tomb first, also went inside. He saw and believed. (They still did not understand from Scripture that Jesus had to rise from the dead.)
>
> Then the disciples went back to their homes, but Mary stood outside the tomb crying. As she wept, she bent over to look into the tomb and saw two angels in white, seated where Jesus'

body had been, one at the head and the other at the foot. (20:1–11)

Mary, seeing the stone rolled away, made an assumption. She concluded that Jesus' body had been taken away and laid elsewhere. In that moment she could not think of Jesus as anything but dead. She had watched Him die. She had seen Him placed in this tomb.

Running to Peter and John, she followed them back to the tomb but stood outside weeping. This was the final blow. Enormous emotional tension had built up over the preceding weeks. Standing there she may have remembered that last trip from Galilee to Judea, that seventy-mile walk to Jerusalem. Among other things had been Jesus' ominous prediction of His coming death. But overshadowing that had been the thrill of Jesus' triumphal entry into Jerusalem. She had heard the adulation of the crowds crying out, "Hosanna to the Son of David! Blessed is he who comes in the name of the Lord! Hosanna in the highest!"

She had stood in the Court of the Women and watched as Jesus entered the temple and overturned the tables of the money-changers. She swelled with pride as He drove out evil men who were fleecing the poor pilgrims coming to the Holy City to celebrate the Passover. She held her breath, seeing the fury of the chief priests and Pharisees as Jesus taught for the last time in the temple courtyard.

She may have watched at the house of Simon the Leper as Mary of Bethany anointed Jesus. If so, she heard Him again predict His own death. She may have been present at Jesus' trial. We know she was there as He was led away to execution. She was there as the nails were driven into His hands and feet. She was there when the spear split open His side. She was there as the sky darkened at midday and a strong earthquake broke open rocks and graves. She had stood with the other women at the foot of the cross watching the one who had delivered her from seven demons now seemingly unable to deliver Himself. She watched Him die.

The highs and lows of that week all flowed together. She felt again the sting of contradiction as she remembered hearing crowds chant "Hosanna" one day and "Away with him! Crucify him!" only a few days later. Mary who had experienced that emotional roller-coaster now stood at the tomb, wrung out, devastated by the thought that, even in death, Jesus was violated. His body had been taken. Her wrenching sobs expressed all the dashed hopes and desperation she felt.

> Mary stood outside the tomb crying. As she wept, she bent over to look into the tomb and saw two angels in white, seated where Jesus' body had been, one at the head and the other at the foot.
>
> They aked her, "Woman, why are you crying?"
>
> "They have taken my Lord away," she said, "and I don't know where they have put him." At this, she turned around and saw Jesus standing there, but she did not realize that it was Jesus. (John 20:10–14)

When Mary and the other women had arrived at the tomb earlier that morning, she had sped off to find Peter and John. Meanwhile the others entered the tomb and met the angels who said:

Mary Magdalene

"Why do you look for the living among the dead? He is not here; he has risen! Remember how he told to you, while he was still with you in Galilee: 'The Son of Man must be delivered into the hands of sinful men, be crucified and on the third day be raised again?' " (Luke 24:5–8)

But now the weeping Mary, who had missed those words the first time, did not wait for those words of hope when she saw the angels. Blinded by her grief, she turned away from them. As she turned, she saw a man standing nearby. He spoke exactly the same words she had just heard from the angels in John 20:15–18:

"Woman . . . why are you crying? Who is it you are looking for?"
Thinking he was the gardener, she said, "Sir, if you have carried him away, tell me where you have put him, and I will get him."
Jesus said to her, "Mary."
She turned toward him and cried out in Aramaic, "Rabboni!" (which means Teacher).
Jesus said, "Do not hold on to me, for I have not yet returned to the Father. Go instead to my brothers and tell them, 'I am returning to my Father and your Father, to my God and your God.' "
Mary Magdalene went to the disciples with the news: "I have seen the Lord!" And she told them that he had said these things to her.

What did it take to move Mary from desolation to exultation, and to galvanize her for witness? Only one thing. Jesus spoke her name in a voice she knew, and it was enough.

The Good Shepherd called the name of this weeping sheep, Mary, and she knew His voice. Suddenly everything that had been all wrong was now all right. The one who had been dead was now alive. The one who had delivered her from seven demons was once again with her. In her ecstatic joy she flung her arms around Him. Jesus gently disengaged her clinging hold on His body and gave her a task: Go and tell my brothers. In a split second this disciple had moved from abject sorrow to euphoria: the Teacher is alive! Now she had work to do.

The fourth thing we know about Mary Magdalene is that she was sent by Jesus as the first witness to the resurrection. He commissioned her to tell His brothers the good news. She became, as Augustine called her, "an apostle to the apostles."

Mary's mental horizon had been fixed in the past. Her thoughts had been riveted on a dead body. Only the living Christ Himself could move her out of her focus on the past into the future. In the future she was to go and tell.

Mary Magdalene was not the only follower of Jesus who needed a changed focus. In the same chapter John recounts Jesus' encounter with another of His followers:

> Now Thomas (called Didymus), one of the Twelve, was not with the disciples when Jesus came [on Easter evening]. So the other disciples told him, "We have seen the Lord!"
>
> But he said to them, "Unless I see the nail marks in his hands and put my finger where the nails were, and put my hand into his side, I will not believe it."

A week later his disciples were in the house again, and Thomas was with them. Though the doors were locked, Jesus came and stood among them and said, "Peace be with you!"

Then he said to Thomas, "Put your finger here; see my hands. Reach out your hand and put it into my side. Stop doubting and believe."

Thomas said to him, "My Lord and my God!"

Then Jesus told him, "Because you have seen me, you have believed; blessed are those who have not seen and yet have believed." (John 20:24–29)

In both cases Jesus made a special appearance to one of His followers—to Mary in the garden and to Thomas in the upper room with the locked door. Both Mary and Thomas had thought Jesus was dead. They were preoccupied with the Jesus of the past. Only the physical presence of Jesus would convince them otherwise.

These who had set their minds on what they could see or touch had to learn to worship and love by faith. They could not cling to Jesus' physical presence. They had to learn to relate to the Savior in a different way.

Mary knew Jesus' voice when He spoke her name. To her Jesus gave a commission: go and tell. To Thomas, who had refused to believe the testimony of the other disciples, He gave a gentle rebuke: you have believed because you have seen me. Blessed are those who have not seen and yet have believed.

When I was a child, my parents took me to church almost every time the doors were open. Our church had a strong evangelistic outreach. Every service closed with a public invitation to non-Christians to come to Christ.

Each summer the church sponsored six weeks of tent meetings at which various evangelists preached every night. Over the years our family never missed a service. It was not surprising that at the age of eight I went forward in a tent meeting to ask Jesus to come into my life.

What was supposed to be a source of great peace, however, was for me a source of great torment. During the next ten years I was wretched. I was sure God had not heard my prayers and made me a part of His family. In listening to all the visiting preachers at our church, I had gotten the idea that I'd feel cleansed from sin if God had truly forgiven me. I didn't have any earth-shaking, shivery experiences like the ones the evangelists described as part of other people's conversions. For me that meant I was not yet a Christian.

As a child and then as a teenager, I agonized and prayed. I wanted the experience that would confirm for me that God had, indeed, forgiven me and made me His child. I didn't understand that there are "diff'rent strokes for diff'rent folks."

To some people come experiences like Mary's in the garden or like Thomas's in the upper room. To others of us comes the word Jesus spoke to Thomas: Blessed are they who have not seen anything spectacular and yet have believed. I began to understand this only dimly after my first year in college. Later experiences as a pastor's wife and as a missionary helped me see more clearly that God deals with each of us as individuals. He calls each of His sheep by name. He knows exactly what we need as we walk with Him.

That is what our discipleship is about. It means learning to believe whether or not we have tangible evidence to go on. It means learning to trust our sovereign, loving God to do what is best for us, whether He does it with some dramatic experience or with silence.

How has God worked in your life? What have you learned about Him that makes a difference in your life? Where have you moved in your understanding of who God is and what He is doing in and through you? Your answers to such questions will tell you the shape of your discipleship.

Women as well as men were disciples of the Savior in Israel two thousand years ago. They followed Him, listened to Him, learned from Him, ministered to Him. We don't have Jesus' physical presence among us to see and touch and help as they did. We have been asked to "walk by faith and not by sight." But our discipleship can be just as real as theirs. We have the Bible to guide us and the fellowship of other Christians to sustain us and correct us.

In school we moved along from learning addition to subtraction to the multiplication tables, then on to fractions, percentages, equations, and theorems. We learned them so we can now balance a checkbook, work in a bank, or become an astrophysicist. All of that learning was to good purpose.

Jesus, the Master Teacher, guides each of us in different ways to learn what we need to know. No two of us have the same life experience. He takes us where we are and works with us there, but always to the same purpose. He wants to move us from ignorance of God to acquaintance to a deep relationship as His daughters. He moves us from no faith to faith to an unshakable confidence in the living God. He teaches us to see tough times as God's way of moving us to new ways of thinking about ourselves and our purpose in life. We walk with God each day as learners so that we can distinguish good from evil. We go on to maturity.

Questions for personal reflection or group discussion:

1. Mary Magdalene saw Jesus and heard Him call her name before she recognized Him. How can you recognize the living Christ today?
2. What does it mean to "walk by faith and not by sight"?
3. As you look at yourself as a learner in the hands of the Master Teacher, Jesus Christ, what experiences has He used to encourage you and teach you to keep on following Him?
4. What goals would you like to set for your discipleship as a Christian woman in the twenty-first century?

Note to the Reader

The publisher invites you to share your response to the message of this book by writing Discovery House Publishers, Box 3566, Grand Rapids, MI 49501, USA. For information about other Discovery House books, music, or videos, contact us at the same address or call 1-800-653-8333. Find us on the Internet at http://www.dhp.org/ or send e-mail to books@dhp.org.